The Quran With Tafsir Ibn Kathir Part 20 of 30: An Naml 056 To Al Ankabut 045

The Quran With Tafsir Ibn Kathir
Part 20 of 30:
An Naml 056 To Al Ankabut 045

With
Arabic Script, Transliteration of Arabic, Meaning in English and Ibn Kathir's Abridged Tafsir (Explanation)

Muhammad Saed Abdul-Rahman

BSc, DipHE

© Muhammad Saed Abdul-Rahman, 2012
ISBN 978-1-86179-885-5

All Rights reserved

British Library Cataloguing in Publication Data. A Catalogue record for this book is available from the British Library

Designed, Typeset and produced by:
MSA Publication Limited, 4 Bello Close, Herne Hill,
London SE24 9BW
United Kingdom

Cover design: Houriyah Abdul-Rahman

TABLE OF CONTENTS

TABLE OF CONTENTS V

PRELUDE XI
    OPENING SERMAN XI
    OUR MISSION XII
    BIOGRAPHY OF HAFIZ IBN KATHIR (701 H - 774 H) XII
        Ibn Kathir's Teachers xii
        Ibn Kathir's Students xiii
        Ibn Kathir's Books xiii
        Ibn Kathir's Death xiv

PREFACE 15
    ABOUT THIS BOOK 15
    PERFORMING PROSTRATION WHILE READING THE QUR'AN 15

PART 20 FULL ARABIC TEXT 1

CHAPTER (SURAH) 27: AN-NAML (THE ANT, THE ANTS), VERSES 056–093 12

    Surah: 27 Ayah: 54, Ayah: 55 (end of Part 19; used here to give the fullness the following tafsir), Ayah: 56 (start of Part 20), Ayah: 57 & Ayah: 58 12
        Tafsir Ibn Kathir 13
            Lut and His People 13
    Surah: 27 Ayah: 59 & Ayah: 60 14
        Tafsir Ibn Kathir 14
            The Command to praise Allah and send Blessings on His Messengers 14
    Surah: 27 Ayah: 61 16
        Tafsir Ibn Kathir 16
    Surah: 27 Ayah: 62 17
        Tafsir Ibn Kathir 17
            The Story of a Mujahid who fought for the sake of Allah 18
    Surah: 27 Ayah: 63 19
        Tafsir Ibn Kathir 20
    Surah: 27 Ayah: 64 20
        Tafsir Ibn Kathir 20
    Surah: 27 Ayah: 65 & Ayah: 66 21
        Tafsir Ibn Kathir 21
            The One Who knows the Unseen is Allah 21
    Surah: 27 Ayah: 67, Ayah: 68, Ayah: 69 & Ayah: 70 22
        Tafsir Ibn Kathir 23
            Scepticism about the Resurrection and Its Refutation 23
    Surah: 27 Ayah: 71, Ayah: 72, Ayah: 73, Ayah: 74 & Ayah: 75 24
        Tafsir Ibn Kathir 24

Surah: 27 Ayah: 76, Ayah: 77, Ayah: 78, Ayah: 79, Ayah: 80 & Ayah: 81 25
    Tafsir Ibn Kathir 27
        The Qur'an tells the Story of the Differences among the Children of Israel, and Allah judges between Them 27
        The Command to put One's Trust in Allah and to convey the Message 27
Surah: 27 Ayah: 82 27
    Tafsir Ibn Kathir 28
        The Emergence of the Beast of the Earth 28
        Another Hadith 29
        Another Hadith 29
        Another Hadith 29
        Another Hadith 30
Surah: 27 Ayah: 83, Ayah: 84, Ayah: 85 & Ayah: 86 31
    Tafsir Ibn Kathir 32
        Gathering the Wrongdoers on the Day of Resurrection 32
Surah: 27 Ayah: 87, Ayah: 88, Ayah: 89 & Ayah: 90 33
    Tafsir Ibn Kathir 34
        The Terrors of the Day of Resurrection, the Rewards for Good Deeds and the Punishments for Evil Deeds 34
Surah: 27 Ayah: 91, Ayah: 92 & Ayah: 93 37
    Tafsir Ibn Kathir 38
        The Command to worship Allah and to call People with the Qur'an 38

INTRODUCTION TO CHAPTER (SURAH) 28: AL-QASAS (THE STORY, STORIES) 39
  IBN KATHIR'S INTRODUCTION 39

CHAPTER (SURAH) 28: AL-QASAS (THE STORY, STORIES), VERSES 001–088 40
Surah: 28 Ayah: 1, Ayah: 2, Ayah: 3, Ayah: 4, Ayah: 5 & Ayah: 6 40
    Tafsir Ibn Kathir 41
        The Story of Musa and Fir`awn, and what Allah intended for Their Peoples 41
Surah: 28 Ayah: 7, Ayah: 8 & Ayah: 9 42
    Tafsir Ibn Kathir 43
        How Musa's Mother was inspired and shown what to do 43
        Musa, peace be upon him, in the House of Fir`awn 43
Surah: 28 Ayah: 10, Ayah: 11, Ayah: 12 & Ayah: 13 44
    Tafsir Ibn Kathir 45
        The intense Grief of Musa's Mother, and how He was returned to Her 45
Surah: 28 Ayah: 14, Ayah: 15, Ayah: 16 & Ayah: 17 47
    Tafsir Ibn Kathir 48
        How Musa killed a Coptic Man 48
Surah: 28 Ayah: 18 & Ayah: 19 48
    Tafsir Ibn Kathir 49
        How the Secret of this Killing became known 49
Surah: 28 Ayah: 20 50

Table of Contents

vii

    Tafsir Ibn Kathir 50
Surah: 28 Ayah: 21, Ayah: 22, Ayah: 23 & Ayah: 24 50
    Tafsir Ibn Kathir 51
        Musa, peace be upon him, in Madyan, and how He watered the Flocks of the Two Women 51
Surah: 28 Ayah: 25, Ayah: 26, Ayah: 27 & Ayah: 28 52
    Tafsir Ibn Kathir 53
        Musa, the Father of the Two Women, and His Marriage to One of Them 53
Surah: 28 Ayah: 29, Ayah: 30, Ayah: 31 & Ayah: 32 55
    Tafsir Ibn Kathir 56
        Musa's Return to Egypt and how he was honored with the Mission and Miracles on the Way 56
Surah: 28 Ayah: 33, Ayah: 34 & Ayah: 35 58
    Tafsir Ibn Kathir 59
        How Musa asked for the Support of His Brother and was granted that by Allah 59
Surah: 28 Ayah: 36 & Ayah: 37 60
    Tafsir Ibn Kathir 61
        Musa before Fir`awn and His People 61
Surah: 28 Ayah: 38, Ayah: 39, Ayah: 40, Ayah: 41 & Ayah: 42 61
    Tafsir Ibn Kathir 62
        The Arrogance of Fir`awn and His ultimate Destiny 62
Surah: 28 Ayah: 43 64
    Tafsir Ibn Kathir 64
        The Blessings which Allah bestowed upon Musa 64
Surah: 28 Ayah: 44, Ayah: 45, Ayah: 46 & Ayah: 47 65
    Tafsir Ibn Kathir 66
        Proof of the Prophethood of Muhammad 66
Surah: 28 Ayah: 48, Ayah: 49, Ayah: 50 & Ayah: 51 68
    Tafsir Ibn Kathir 69
        The stubborn Response of the Disbelievers 69
        The Rebellious do not believe in Miracles 69
        False Accusation that Musa and Harun (peace be upon them both) practiced Magic 70
        The Response to this False Accusation 70
Surah: 28 Ayah: 52, Ayah: 53, Ayah: 54 & Ayah: 55 71
    Tafsir Ibn Kathir 72
        The Believers among the People of the Book 72
Surah: 28 Ayah: 56 & Ayah: 57 74
    Tafsir Ibn Kathir 74
        Allah guides Whom He wills 74
        The Excuses made by the People of Makkah for not believing, and the Refutation of Their Excuses 75
Surah: 28 Ayah: 58 & Ayah: 59 76
    Tafsir Ibn Kathir 76
        The Destruction of Towns, which are not destroyed until Evidence is established against Them 76

Surah: 28 Ayah: 60 & Ayah: 61 77
    Tafsir Ibn Kathir 78
        This World is transient and the One Whose concern is this World is not equal to the One Whose concern is the Hereafter... 78
Surah: 28 Ayah: 62, Ayah: 63, Ayah: 64, Ayah: 65, Ayah: 66 & Ayah: 67 79
    Tafsir Ibn Kathir 80
        The Idolators and Their Partners and the Emnity between Them in the Hereafter 80
Surah: 28 Ayah: 68, Ayah: 69 & Ayah: 70 82
    Tafsir Ibn Kathir 82
        Allah Alone is the One Who has the Power of Creation, Knowledge and Choice............. 82
Surah: 28 Ayah: 71, Ayah: 72 & Ayah: 73 83
    Tafsir Ibn Kathir 84
        Night and Day are among the Blessings of Allah and are Signs of Tawhid 84
Surah: 28 Ayah: 74 & Ayah: 75 85
    Tafsir Ibn Kathir 85
        Rebuking the Idolators 85
Surah: 28 Ayah: 76 & Ayah: 77 86
    Tafsir Ibn Kathir 86
        Qarun and His People's exhortation 86
Surah: 28 Ayah: 78 87
    Tafsir Ibn Kathir 88
        Allah informs us how Qarun responded to the exhortations of his people when they sought to guide him to what is good. 88
Surah: 28 Ayah: 79 & Ayah: 80 88
    Tafsir Ibn Kathir 89
        How Qarun went forth in His Finery, and His People's Comments 89
Surah: 28 Ayah: 81 & Ayah: 82 90
    Tafsir Ibn Kathir 90
        How Qarun and His Dwelling Place were swallowed up by the Earth 90
        His People learned a Lesson from Him being swallowed up 91
Surah: 28 Ayah: 83 & Ayah: 84 92
    Tafsir Ibn Kathir 92
        The Blessings of the Hereafter for the humble Believers 92
Surah: 28 Ayah: 85, Ayah: 86, Ayah: 87 & Ayah: 88 93
    Tafsir Ibn Kathir 94
        The Command to convey the Message of Tawhid 94

CHAPTER (SURAH) 29: AL-ANKABOOT (THE SPIDER), VERSES 001–045 96

Surah: 29 Ayah: 1, Ayah: 2, Ayah: 3 & Ayah: 4 97
    Tafsir Ibn Kathir 97
        The Believers are tested so that it may be known Who is Sincere and Who is Lying In the beginning of the Tafsir of Surat Al-Baqarah, we discussed the letters which appear at the beginning of some Surahs. 97
        The Evildoers cannot escape from Allah. 98

Table of Contents

Surah: 29 Ayah: 5, Ayah: 6 & Ayah: 7 .... *98*
    Tafsir Ibn Kathir 99
        Allah will fulfill the Hopes of the Righteous 99
Surah: 29 Ayah: 8 & Ayah: 9 .... *100*
    Tafsir Ibn Kathir 100
        The Command to be Good and Dutiful to Parents 100
Surah: 29 Ayah: 10 & Ayah: 11 .... *101*
    Tafsir Ibn Kathir 102
        The Attitudes of the Hypocrites and the Ways in which Allah tests People 102
Surah: 29 Ayah: 12 & Ayah: 13 .... *103*
    Tafsir Ibn Kathir 103
        The Arrogant Claim of the Disbelievers that They would carry the Sins of Others if They would return to Disbelief 103
Surah: 29 Ayah: 14 & Ayah: 15 .... *106*
    Tafsir Ibn Kathir 106
        Nuh and His People 106
Surah: 29 Ayah: 16, Ayah: 17 & Ayah: 18 .... *107*
    Tafsir Ibn Kathir 108
        Ibrahim's preaching to His People 108
Surah: 29 Ayah: 19, Ayah: 20, Ayah: 21, Ayah: 22 & Ayah: 23 .... *109*
    Tafsir Ibn Kathir 110
        The Evidence for Life after Death 110
Surah: 29 Ayah: 24 & Ayah: 25 .... *111*
    Tafsir Ibn Kathir 112
        The Response of Ibrahim's People -- and how Allah controlled the Fire 112
Surah: 29 Ayah: 26 & Ayah: 27 .... *113*
    Tafsir Ibn Kathir 113
        The Faith of Lut and His Emigration with Ibrahim 113
Surah: 29 Ayah: 28, Ayah: 29 & Ayah: 30 .... *115*
    Tafsir Ibn Kathir 116
        The preaching of Lut and what happened between Him and His People 116
Surah: 29 Ayah: 31, Ayah: 32, Ayah: 33, Ayah: 34 & Ayah: 35 .... *116*
    Tafsir Ibn Kathir 117
        The Angels went to Ibrahim and then to Lut, may peace be upon them both 117
Surah: 29 Ayah: 36 & Ayah: 37 .... *118*
    Tafsir Ibn Kathir 119
        Shu`ayb and His People 119
Surah: 29 Ayah: 38, Ayah: 39 & Ayah: 40 .... *119*
    Tafsir Ibn Kathir 120
        The Destruction of Nations Who rejected Their Messengers 120
Surah: 29 Ayah: 41, Ayah: 42 & Ayah: 43 .... *121*
    Tafsir Ibn Kathir 122
        Likening the gods of the Idolators to the House of a Spider 122
Surah: 29 Ayah: 44 & Ayah: 45 .... *122*

Tafsir Ibn Kathir 123
   The Command to convey the Message, to recite the Qur'an and to pray 123

PRELUDE

Opening Serman

Indeed, all praise is due to Allah. We praise Him and seek His help and forgiveness. We seek refuge with Allah from our soul's evil and our wrong doings. He whom Allah guides, no one can misguide; and he whom He misguides, no one can guide

I bear witness that there is no (true) god except Allah – alone without a partner, and I bear witness that Muhammad (peace and blessings of Allah be upon him) is His 'abd (servant) and messenger.

يَٰٓأَيُّهَا ٱلَّذِينَ ءَامَنُوا۟ ٱتَّقُوا۟ ٱللَّهَ حَقَّ تُقَاتِهِۦ وَلَا تَمُوتُنَّ إِلَّا وَأَنتُم مُّسْلِمُونَ ۞

O you who believe! Fear Allâh (by doing all that He has ordered and by abstaining from all that He has forbidden) as He should be feared. (Obey Him, be thankful to Him, and remember Him always), and die not except in a state of Islâm (as Muslims (with complete submission to Allâh)).

يَٰٓأَيُّهَا ٱلنَّاسُ ٱتَّقُوا۟ رَبَّكُمُ ٱلَّذِى خَلَقَكُم مِّن نَّفْسٍ وَٰحِدَةٍ وَخَلَقَ مِنْهَا زَوْجَهَا وَبَثَّ مِنْهُمَا رِجَالًا كَثِيرًا وَنِسَآءً ۚ وَٱتَّقُوا۟ ٱللَّهَ ٱلَّذِى تَسَآءَلُونَ بِهِۦ وَٱلْأَرْحَامَ ۚ إِنَّ ٱللَّهَ كَانَ عَلَيْكُمْ رَقِيبًا ۞

O mankind! Be dutiful to your Lord, Who created you from a single person (Adam), and from him (Adam) He created his wife (Hawwâ (Eve)) and from them both He created many men and women; and fear Allâh through Whom you demand (your mutual rights), and (do not cut the relations of) the wombs (kinship). Surely, Allâh is Ever an All-Watcher over you.

يُصْلِحْ لَكُمْ أَعْمَٰلَكُمْ وَيَغْفِرْ لَكُمْ ذُنُوبَكُمْ ۗ وَمَن يُطِعِ ٱللَّهَ وَرَسُولَهُۥ فَقَدْ فَازَ فَوْزًا عَظِيمًا ۞

He will direct you to do righteous good deeds and will forgive you your sins. And whosoever obeys Allâh and His Messenger (peace be upon him), he has indeed achieved a great achievement (i.e. he will be saved from the Hell-fire and will be admitted to Paradise).

Indeed, the best speech is Allah's Book and the best guidance is Muhammad's () guidance. The worst affairs (of religion) are those innovated (by people), for every such innovation is an act of misguidance leading to the Fire

Our Mission

Our mission is to gather in one place, for the English-speaking public, all relevant information needed to make the Qur'an more understandable and easier to study. This book tries to do this by providing the following:

1. The Arabic Text for those who are able to read Arabic
2. Transliteration of the Arabic text for those who are unable to read the Arabic script. This will give them a sample of the sound of the Qur'an, which they could not otherwise comprehend from reading the English meaning.
3. The meaning of the qur'an (translated by Dr. Muhammad Taqi-ud-Din Al-Hilali, Ph.D. and Dr. Muhammad Muhsin Khan)
4. Explanation (abridged Tafsir) by Ibn Kathir (translated by Safi-ur-Rahman al-Mubarakpuri)

We hope that by doing this an ordinary English-speaker will be able to pick up a copy of this book and study and comprehend The Glorious Qur'an in a way that is acceptable to the understanding of the Rightly-guided Muslim Ummah (Community).

Biography of Hafiz Ibn Kathir (701 H - 774 H)

By the Honored Shaykh `Abdul-Qadir Al-Arna'ut, may Allah protect him.

He is the respected Imam, Abu Al-Fida', `Imad Ad-Din Isma il bin 'Umar bin Kathir Al-Qurashi Al-Busrawi - Busraian in origin; Dimashqi in training, learning and residence.

Ibn Kathir was born in the city of Busra in 701 H. His father was the Friday speaker of the village, but he died while Ibn Kathir was only four years old. Ibn Kathir's brother, Shaykh Abdul-Wahhab, reared him and taught him until he moved to Damascus in 706 H., when he was five years old.

Ibn Kathir's Teachers

Ibn Kathir studied Fiqh - Islamic jurisprudence - with Burhan Ad-Din, Ibrahim bin `Abdur-Rahman Al-Fizari, known as Ibn Al-Firkah (who died in 729 H). Ibn Kathir heard Hadiths from `Isa bin Al-Mutim, Ahmad bin Abi Talib, (Ibn Ash-Shahnah) (who died in 730 H), Ibn Al-Hajjar, (who died in 730 H), and the Hadith narrator of Ash-Sham (modern day Syria and surrounding areas); Baha Ad-Din Al-Qasim bin Muzaffar bin `Asakir (who died in 723 H), and Ibn Ash-Shirdzi, Ishaq bin Yahya Al-Ammuddi, also known as `Afif Ad-Din, the Zahiriyyah Shaykh who died in 725 H, and Muhammad bin Zarrad. He remained with Jamal Ad-Din, Yusuf bin Az-Zaki AlMizzi who died in 724 H, he benefited from his knowledge and also married his daughter. He also read with Shaykh Al-Islam, Taqi Ad-Din Ahmad bin `Abdul-Halim bin `Abdus-Salam bin Taymiyyah who died in 728 H. He also read with the Imam Hafiz and historian Shams Ad-Din, Muhammad bin Ahmad bin Uthman bin Qaymaz Adh-Dhahabi, who died in 748 H. Also, Abu Musa Al-Qarafai, Abu Al-Fath Ad-Dabbusi and

'Ali bin `Umar As-Suwani and others who gave him permission to transmit the knowledge he learned with them in Egypt.

In his book, Al-Mu jam Al-Mukhtas, Al-Hafiz Adh-Dhaliabi wrote that Ibn Kathir was, "The Imam, scholar of jurisprudence, skillful scholar of Hadith, renowned Faqih and scholar of Tafsir who wrote several beneficial books."

Further, in Ad-Durar Al-Kdminah, Al-Hafiz Ibn Hajar AlAsqalani said, "Ibn Kathir worked on the subject of the Hadith in the areas of texts and chains of narrators. He had a good memory, his books became popular during his lifetime, and people benefited from them after his death."

Also, the renowned historian Abu Al-Mahasin, Jamal Ad-Din Yusuf bin Sayf Ad-Din (Ibn Taghri Bardi), said in his book, AlManhal As-Safi, "He is the Shaykh, the Imam, the great scholar `Imad Ad-Din Abu Al-Fida'. He learned extensively and was very active in collecting knowledge and writing. He was excellent in the areas of Fiqh, Tafsfr and Hadith. He collected knowledge, authored (books), taught, narrated Hadith and wrote. He had immense knowledge in the fields of Hadith, Tafsir, Fiqh, the Arabic language, and so forth. He gave Fatawa (religious verdicts) and taught until he died, may Allah grant him mercy. He was known for his precision and vast knowledge, and as a scholar of history, Hadith and Tafsir."

Ibn Kathir's Students

Ibn Hajji was one of Ibn Kathir's students, and he described Ibn Kathir: "He had the best memory of the Hadith texts. He also had the most knowledge concerning the narrators and authenticity, his contemporaries and teachers admitted to these qualities. Every time I met him I gained some benefit from him."

Also, Ibn Al-`Imad Al-Hanbali said in his book, Shadhardt Adh-Dhahab, "He is the renowned Hafiz `Imad Ad-Din, whose memory was excellent, whose forgetfulness was miniscule, whose understanding was adequate, and who had good knowledge in the Arabic language." Also, Ibn Habib said about Ibn Kathir, "He heard knowledge and collected it and wrote various books. He brought comfort to the ears with his Fatwas and narrated Hadith and brought benefit to other people. The papers that contained his Fatwas were transmitted to the various (Islamic) provinces. Further, he was known for his precision and encompassing knowledge."

Ibn Kathir's Books

1 - One of the greatest books that Ibn Kathir wrote was his Tafsir of the Noble Qur'an, which is one of the best Tafsir that rely on narrations [of Ahadith, the Tafsir of the Companions, etc.]. The Tafsir by Ibn Kathir was printed many times and several scholars have summarized it.

2- The History Collection known as Al-Biddyah, which was printed in 14 volumes under the name Al-Bidayah wanNihdyah, and contained the stories of the Prophets and previous nations, the Prophet's Seerah (life story) and Islamic history until his time. He also added a book Al-Fitan, about the Signs of the Last Hour.

3- At-Takmil ft Ma`rifat Ath-Thiqat wa Ad-Du'afa wal Majdhil which Ibn Kathir collected from the books of his two Shaykhs Al-Mizzi and Adh-Dhahabi; Al-Kdmal and Mizan Al-Ftiddl. He added several benefits regarding the subject of Al-Jarh and AtT'adil.

4- Al-Hadi was-Sunan ft Ahadith Al-Masdnfd was-Sunan which is also known by, Jami` Al-Masdnfd. In this book, Ibn Kathir collected the narrations of Imams Ahmad bin Hanbal, Al-Bazzar, Abu Ya`la Al-Mawsili, Ibn Abi Shaybah and from the six collections of Hadith: the Two Sahihs [Al-Bukhari and Muslim] and the Four Sunan [Abu Dawud, At-Tirmidhi, AnNasa and Ibn Majah]. Ibn Kathir divided this book according to areas of Fiqh.

5-Tabaqat Ash-Shaf iyah which also contains the virtues of Imam Ash-Shafi.

6- Ibn Kathir wrote references for the Ahadith of Adillat AtTanbfh, from the Shafi school of Fiqh.

7- Ibn Kathir began an explanation of Sahih Al-Bukhari, but he did not finish it.

8- He started writing a large volume on the Ahkam (Laws), but finished only up to the Hajj rituals.

9- He summarized Al-Bayhaqi's 'Al-Madkhal. Many of these books were not printed.

10- He summarized `Ulum Al-Hadith, by Abu `Amr bin AsSalah and called it Mukhtasar `Ulum Al-Hadith. Shaykh Ahmad Shakir, the Egyptian Muhaddith, printed this book along with his commentary on it and called it Al-Ba'th Al-Hathfth fi Sharh Mukhtasar `Ulum Al-Hadith.

11- As-Sfrah An-Nabawiyyah, which is contained in his book Al-Biddyah, and both of these books are in print.

12- A research on Jihad called Al-Ijtihad ft Talabi Al-Jihad, which was printed several times.

Ibn Kathir's Death

Al-Hafiz Ibn Hajar Al-Asgalani said, "Ibn Kathir lost his sight just before his life ended. He died in Damascus in 774 H." May Allah grant mercy upon Ibn Kathir and make him among the residents of His Paradise.

PREFACE

In the name of Allah, Most Gracious, Most Merciful.

About this book

The previous publication of this book included some background information to the chapters of the Qur'an by an Islamic scholar known as Abul Ala Maududi. This information was used to shed more light on the chapters by giving a summery of why each chapter was given its name, It's period of revelation and the circumstances surrounding its revelatiom. However, some Muslims objected to the inclusion of the contributions of Maududi.

In this new publication of Tafsir Ibn Kathir, we have removed all traces of the contribution of Abul Ala Maududi. Personally, I do not know the reasons for the objections to Maududi, but this work concerns only the tafsir of Ibn Kathir, so we have not included anything from Maududi in it. We have also corrected all the typing and formatting errors found in the previous publication. We have not alter the structure of the book. The reader is still able to read the full Arabic Text of the thirty Parts of the Qur'an and follow its meanings in the English language. The transliteration of the Arabic text should also give the reader a taste of the sound of the original Arabic.

May Almighty Allah accept this effort from us, and make it a source of blessings for us in this world and in the next. I bear witness that there is none worthy of worship but Allah and I bear witness that Muhammad (may the peace and blessings of Allah be upon him) is the slave and messenger of Allah.

Performing Prostration While Reading the Qur'an

Question:

Could you please give a list of the Qur'anic verses when a prostration is recommended? What happens if we read these verses and not perform a prostration?

A. Jalil

Answer:

There are 15 verses in the Qur'an that mention prostration before God Almighty as a good action by God-fearing believers. Therefore, it is strongly recommended to perform such a prostration when we read or listen to any of these verses, whether during prayer or in any situation.

Some scholars are of the view that even if one has not performed ablution, one should prostrate oneself. These verses are given here, starting with the Arabic title of the surah which is followed by two numbers, the first indicating the surah, and the second indicating the verse,: Al-Araf 7: 206; Al-Raad 13: 15; Al-Nahl 16: 50; Al-Isra 17: 109; Maryam 19: 58; Al-Hajj 22: 18 & 22: 77; Al-Furqan 25: 60; Al-Naml 27: 26;

Al-Sajdah 32: 15; Saad 38: 25; Fussilat 41: 38; Al-Najm 53: 62; Al-Inshiqaq 84: 21 and Al-Alaq 96: 19.

If you do not perform a prostration when you read or listen to any of these verses, you have done badly because you miss out on the reward of performing a prostration for God. You incur no sin and violate no divine order.

Reference:
http://archive.arabnews.com/?page=5&section=0&article=97811&d=1&m=7&y=2007

The Glorious Qur'an Juz' 20 (Part 20): Chapter (Surah) 27: An-Nanl (The Ant, The Ants) 056 To Chapter (Surah) 29: Al-Ankaboot (The Spider) 045

PART 20 FULL ARABIC TEXT

Chapter (Surah) 27: An-Naml 056-093

۞ فَمَا كَانَ جَوَابَ قَوْمِهِ إِلَّا أَن قَالُوٓا۟ أَخْرِجُوٓا۟ ءَالَ لُوطٍ مِّن قَرْيَتِكُمْ ۖ إِنَّهُمْ أُنَاسٌ يَتَطَهَّرُونَ ۝٥٦ فَأَنجَيْنَـٰهُ وَأَهْلَهُۥٓ إِلَّا ٱمْرَأَتَهُۥ قَدَّرْنَـٰهَا مِنَ ٱلْغَـٰبِرِينَ ۝٥٧ وَأَمْطَرْنَا عَلَيْهِم مَّطَرًا ۖ فَسَآءَ مَطَرُ ٱلْمُنذَرِينَ ۝٥٨ قُلِ ٱلْحَمْدُ لِلَّهِ وَسَلَـٰمٌ عَلَىٰ عِبَادِهِ ٱلَّذِينَ ٱصْطَفَىٰٓ ۗ ءَآللَّهُ خَيْرٌ أَمَّا يُشْرِكُونَ ۝٥٩ أَمَّنْ خَلَقَ ٱلسَّمَـٰوَٰتِ وَٱلْأَرْضَ وَأَنزَلَ لَكُم مِّنَ ٱلسَّمَآءِ مَآءً فَأَنۢبَتْنَا بِهِۦ حَدَآئِقَ ذَاتَ بَهْجَةٍ مَّا كَانَ لَكُمْ أَن تُنۢبِتُوا۟ شَجَرَهَآ ۗ أَءِلَـٰهٌ مَّعَ ٱللَّهِ ۚ بَلْ هُمْ قَوْمٌ يَعْدِلُونَ ۝٦٠ أَمَّن جَعَلَ ٱلْأَرْضَ قَرَارًا وَجَعَلَ خِلَـٰلَهَآ أَنْهَـٰرًا وَجَعَلَ لَهَا رَوَٰسِىَ وَجَعَلَ بَيْنَ ٱلْبَحْرَيْنِ حَاجِزًا ۗ أَءِلَـٰهٌ مَّعَ ٱللَّهِ ۚ بَلْ أَكْثَرُهُمْ لَا يَعْلَمُونَ ۝٦١ أَمَّن يُجِيبُ ٱلْمُضْطَرَّ إِذَا دَعَاهُ وَيَكْشِفُ ٱلسُّوٓءَ وَيَجْعَلُكُمْ خُلَفَآءَ ٱلْأَرْضِ ۗ أَءِلَـٰهٌ مَّعَ ٱللَّهِ ۚ قَلِيلًا مَّا تَذَكَّرُونَ ۝٦٢ أَمَّن يَهْدِيكُمْ فِى ظُلُمَـٰتِ ٱلْبَرِّ وَٱلْبَحْرِ وَمَن يُرْسِلُ ٱلرِّيَـٰحَ بُشْرًۢا بَيْنَ يَدَىْ رَحْمَتِهِۦٓ ۗ أَءِلَـٰهٌ مَّعَ ٱللَّهِ ۚ تَعَـٰلَى ٱللَّهُ عَمَّا يُشْرِكُونَ ۝٦٣ أَمَّن يَبْدَؤُا۟ ٱلْخَلْقَ ثُمَّ يُعِيدُهُۥ وَمَن يَرْزُقُكُم مِّنَ ٱلسَّمَآءِ وَٱلْأَرْضِ ۗ أَءِلَـٰهٌ مَّعَ ٱللَّهِ ۚ قُلْ هَاتُوا۟ بُرْهَـٰنَكُمْ إِن كُنتُمْ صَـٰدِقِينَ ۝٦٤ قُل لَّا يَعْلَمُ مَن فِى ٱلسَّمَـٰوَٰتِ وَٱلْأَرْضِ ٱلْغَيْبَ إِلَّا ٱللَّهُ ۚ وَمَا يَشْعُرُونَ أَيَّانَ يُبْعَثُونَ ۝٦٥ بَلِ ٱدَّٰرَكَ عِلْمُهُمْ فِى ٱلْءَاخِرَةِ ۚ بَلْ هُمْ فِى شَكٍّ مِّنْهَا ۖ بَلْ هُم مِّنْهَا عَمُونَ ۝٦٦ وَقَالَ ٱلَّذِينَ كَفَرُوٓا۟

أَءِذَا كُنَّا تُرَٰبًا وَءَابَآؤُنَآ أَئِنَّا لَمُخْرَجُونَ ۝ لَقَدْ وُعِدْنَا هَٰذَا نَحْنُ وَءَابَآؤُنَا مِن قَبْلُ إِنْ هَٰذَآ إِلَّآ أَسَٰطِيرُ ٱلْأَوَّلِينَ ۝ قُلْ سِيرُوا۟ فِى ٱلْأَرْضِ فَٱنظُرُوا۟ كَيْفَ كَانَ عَٰقِبَةُ ٱلْمُجْرِمِينَ ۝ وَلَا تَحْزَنْ عَلَيْهِمْ وَلَا تَكُن فِى ضَيْقٍ مِّمَّا يَمْكُرُونَ ۝ وَيَقُولُونَ مَتَىٰ هَٰذَا ٱلْوَعْدُ إِن كُنتُمْ صَٰدِقِينَ ۝ قُلْ عَسَىٰٓ أَن يَكُونَ رَدِفَ لَكُم بَعْضُ ٱلَّذِى تَسْتَعْجِلُونَ ۝ وَإِنَّ رَبَّكَ لَذُو فَضْلٍ عَلَى ٱلنَّاسِ وَلَٰكِنَّ أَكْثَرَهُمْ لَا يَشْكُرُونَ ۝ وَإِنَّ رَبَّكَ لَيَعْلَمُ مَا تُكِنُّ صُدُورُهُمْ وَمَا يُعْلِنُونَ ۝ وَمَا مِنْ غَآئِبَةٍ فِى ٱلسَّمَآءِ وَٱلْأَرْضِ إِلَّا فِى كِتَٰبٍ مُّبِينٍ ۝ إِنَّ هَٰذَا ٱلْقُرْءَانَ يَقُصُّ عَلَىٰ بَنِىٓ إِسْرَٰٓءِيلَ أَكْثَرَ ٱلَّذِى هُمْ فِيهِ يَخْتَلِفُونَ ۝ وَإِنَّهُۥ لَهُدًى وَرَحْمَةٌ لِّلْمُؤْمِنِينَ ۝ إِنَّ رَبَّكَ يَقْضِى بَيْنَهُم بِحُكْمِهِۦ ۚ وَهُوَ ٱلْعَزِيزُ ٱلْعَلِيمُ ۝ فَتَوَكَّلْ عَلَى ٱللَّهِ إِنَّكَ عَلَى ٱلْحَقِّ ٱلْمُبِينِ ۝ إِنَّكَ لَا تُسْمِعُ ٱلْمَوْتَىٰ وَلَا تُسْمِعُ ٱلصُّمَّ ٱلدُّعَآءَ إِذَا وَلَّوْا۟ مُدْبِرِينَ ۝ وَمَآ أَنتَ بِهَٰدِى ٱلْعُمْىِ عَن ضَلَٰلَتِهِمْ ۖ إِن تُسْمِعُ إِلَّا مَن يُؤْمِنُ بِـَٔايَٰتِنَا فَهُم مُّسْلِمُونَ ۩ ۝ وَإِذَا وَقَعَ ٱلْقَوْلُ عَلَيْهِمْ أَخْرَجْنَا لَهُمْ دَآبَّةً مِّنَ ٱلْأَرْضِ تُكَلِّمُهُمْ أَنَّ ٱلنَّاسَ كَانُوا۟ بِـَٔايَٰتِنَا لَا يُوقِنُونَ ۝ وَيَوْمَ نَحْشُرُ مِن كُلِّ أُمَّةٍ فَوْجًا مِّمَّن يُكَذِّبُ بِـَٔايَٰتِنَا فَهُمْ يُوزَعُونَ ۝ حَتَّىٰٓ إِذَا جَآءُو قَالَ أَكَذَّبْتُم بِـَٔايَٰتِى وَلَمْ تُحِيطُوا۟ بِهَا عِلْمًا أَمَّاذَا كُنتُمْ تَعْمَلُونَ ۝ وَوَقَعَ ٱلْقَوْلُ عَلَيْهِم بِمَا ظَلَمُوا۟ فَهُمْ لَا يَنطِقُونَ ۝ أَلَمْ يَرَوْا۟ أَنَّا جَعَلْنَا ٱلَّيْلَ لِيَسْكُنُوا۟ فِيهِ وَٱلنَّهَارَ مُبْصِرًا ۚ إِنَّ فِى ذَٰلِكَ لَءَايَٰتٍ لِّقَوْمٍ يُؤْمِنُونَ ۝ وَيَوْمَ يُنفَخُ فِى ٱلصُّورِ فَفَزِعَ مَن فِى ٱلسَّمَٰوَٰتِ وَمَن فِى ٱلْأَرْضِ إِلَّا مَن شَآءَ ٱللَّهُ ۚ وَكُلٌّ أَتَوْهُ دَٰخِرِينَ ۝ وَتَرَى ٱلْجِبَالَ تَحْسَبُهَا جَامِدَةً وَهِىَ تَمُرُّ مَرَّ ٱلسَّحَابِ ۚ صُنْعَ ٱللَّهِ ٱلَّذِىٓ أَتْقَنَ كُلَّ شَىْءٍ ۚ إِنَّهُۥ خَبِيرٌۢ بِمَا تَفْعَلُونَ

مَن جَاءَ بِٱلْحَسَنَةِ فَلَهُ خَيْرٌ مِّنْهَا وَهُم مِّن فَزَعٍ يَوْمَئِذٍ ءَامِنُونَ ۝ وَمَن جَاءَ بِٱلسَّيِّئَةِ فَكُبَّتْ وُجُوهُهُمْ فِى ٱلنَّارِ هَلْ تُجْزَوْنَ إِلَّا مَا كُنتُمْ تَعْمَلُونَ ۝ إِنَّمَا أُمِرْتُ أَنْ أَعْبُدَ رَبَّ هَٰذِهِ ٱلْبَلْدَةِ ٱلَّذِى حَرَّمَهَا وَلَهُۥ كُلُّ شَىْءٍ وَأُمِرْتُ أَنْ أَكُونَ مِنَ ٱلْمُسْلِمِينَ ۝ وَأَنْ أَتْلُوَاْ ٱلْقُرْءَانَ فَمَنِ ٱهْتَدَىٰ فَإِنَّمَا يَهْتَدِى لِنَفْسِهِۦ وَمَن ضَلَّ فَقُلْ إِنَّمَا أَنَا۠ مِنَ ٱلْمُنذِرِينَ ۝ وَقُلِ ٱلْحَمْدُ لِلَّهِ سَيُرِيكُمْ ءَايَٰتِهِۦ فَتَعْرِفُونَهَا وَمَا رَبُّكَ بِغَٰفِلٍ عَمَّا تَعْمَلُونَ ۝

(An-Naml 056-093)

Chapter (Surah) 28: Al-Qasas 001-088

بِسْمِ ٱللَّهِ ٱلرَّحْمَٰنِ ٱلرَّحِيمِ

طسٓمٓ ۝ تِلْكَ ءَايَٰتُ ٱلْكِتَٰبِ ٱلْمُبِينِ ۝ نَتْلُواْ عَلَيْكَ مِن نَّبَإِ مُوسَىٰ وَفِرْعَوْنَ بِٱلْحَقِّ لِقَوْمٍ يُؤْمِنُونَ ۝ إِنَّ فِرْعَوْنَ عَلَا فِى ٱلْأَرْضِ وَجَعَلَ أَهْلَهَا شِيَعًا يَسْتَضْعِفُ طَآئِفَةً مِّنْهُمْ يُذَبِّحُ أَبْنَآءَهُمْ وَيَسْتَحْىِۦ نِسَآءَهُمْ إِنَّهُۥ كَانَ مِنَ ٱلْمُفْسِدِينَ ۝ وَنُرِيدُ أَن نَّمُنَّ عَلَى ٱلَّذِينَ ٱسْتُضْعِفُواْ فِى ٱلْأَرْضِ وَنَجْعَلَهُمْ أَئِمَّةً وَنَجْعَلَهُمُ ٱلْوَٰرِثِينَ ۝ وَنُمَكِّنَ لَهُمْ فِى ٱلْأَرْضِ وَنُرِىَ فِرْعَوْنَ وَهَٰمَٰنَ وَجُنُودَهُمَا مِنْهُم مَّا كَانُواْ يَحْذَرُونَ ۝ وَأَوْحَيْنَآ إِلَىٰٓ أُمِّ مُوسَىٰٓ أَنْ أَرْضِعِيهِ فَإِذَا خِفْتِ عَلَيْهِ فَأَلْقِيهِ فِى ٱلْيَمِّ وَلَا تَخَافِى وَلَا تَحْزَنِىٓ إِنَّا رَآدُّوهُ إِلَيْكِ وَجَاعِلُوهُ مِنَ ٱلْمُرْسَلِينَ ۝ فَٱلْتَقَطَهُۥٓ ءَالُ فِرْعَوْنَ لِيَكُونَ لَهُمْ عَدُوًّا وَحَزَنًا إِنَّ فِرْعَوْنَ وَهَٰمَٰنَ وَجُنُودَهُمَا كَانُواْ خَٰطِـِٔينَ ۝ وَقَالَتِ ٱمْرَأَتُ فِرْعَوْنَ قُرَّتُ عَيْنٍ لِّى وَلَكَ لَا تَقْتُلُوهُ عَسَىٰٓ أَن يَنفَعَنَآ أَوْ نَتَّخِذَهُۥ وَلَدًا وَهُمْ لَا يَشْعُرُونَ ۝ وَأَصْبَحَ فُؤَادُ أُمِّ مُوسَىٰ فَٰرِغًا إِن كَادَتْ لَتُبْدِى بِهِۦ لَوْلَآ أَن رَّبَطْنَا عَلَىٰ قَلْبِهَا لِتَكُونَ مِنَ ٱلْمُؤْمِنِينَ ۝ وَقَالَتْ لِأُخْتِهِۦ قُصِّيهِ فَبَصُرَتْ بِهِۦ عَن جُنُبٍ وَهُمْ لَا

يَشْعُرُونَ ۝ ‌‌‌‌۞ وَحَرَّمْنَا عَلَيْهِ ٱلْمَرَاضِعَ مِن قَبْلُ فَقَالَتْ هَلْ أَدُلُّكُمْ عَلَىٰٓ أَهْلِ بَيْتٍ يَكْفُلُونَهُۥ لَكُمْ وَهُمْ لَهُۥ نَٰصِحُونَ ۝ فَرَدَدْنَٰهُ إِلَىٰٓ أُمِّهِۦ كَىْ تَقَرَّ عَيْنُهَا وَلَا تَحْزَنَ وَلِتَعْلَمَ أَنَّ وَعْدَ ٱللَّهِ حَقٌّ وَلَٰكِنَّ أَكْثَرَهُمْ لَا يَعْلَمُونَ ۝ وَلَمَّا بَلَغَ أَشُدَّهُۥ وَٱسْتَوَىٰٓ ءَاتَيْنَٰهُ حُكْمًا وَعِلْمًا ۚ وَكَذَٰلِكَ نَجْزِى ٱلْمُحْسِنِينَ ۝ وَدَخَلَ ٱلْمَدِينَةَ عَلَىٰ حِينِ غَفْلَةٍ مِّنْ أَهْلِهَا فَوَجَدَ فِيهَا رَجُلَيْنِ يَقْتَتِلَانِ هَٰذَا مِن شِيعَتِهِۦ وَهَٰذَا مِنْ عَدُوِّهِۦ ۖ فَٱسْتَغَٰثَهُ ٱلَّذِى مِن شِيعَتِهِۦ عَلَى ٱلَّذِى مِنْ عَدُوِّهِۦ فَوَكَزَهُۥ مُوسَىٰ فَقَضَىٰ عَلَيْهِ ۖ قَالَ هَٰذَا مِنْ عَمَلِ ٱلشَّيْطَٰنِ ۖ إِنَّهُۥ عَدُوٌّ مُّضِلٌّ مُّبِينٌ ۝ قَالَ رَبِّ إِنِّى ظَلَمْتُ نَفْسِى فَٱغْفِرْ لِى فَغَفَرَ لَهُۥٓ ۚ إِنَّهُۥ هُوَ ٱلْغَفُورُ ٱلرَّحِيمُ ۝ قَالَ رَبِّ بِمَآ أَنْعَمْتَ عَلَىَّ فَلَنْ أَكُونَ ظَهِيرًا لِّلْمُجْرِمِينَ ۝ فَأَصْبَحَ فِى ٱلْمَدِينَةِ خَآئِفًا يَتَرَقَّبُ فَإِذَا ٱلَّذِى ٱسْتَنصَرَهُۥ بِٱلْأَمْسِ يَسْتَصْرِخُهُۥ ۚ قَالَ لَهُۥ مُوسَىٰٓ إِنَّكَ لَغَوِىٌّ مُّبِينٌ ۝ فَلَمَّآ أَنْ أَرَادَ أَن يَبْطِشَ بِٱلَّذِى هُوَ عَدُوٌّ لَّهُمَا قَالَ يَٰمُوسَىٰٓ أَتُرِيدُ أَن تَقْتُلَنِى كَمَا قَتَلْتَ نَفْسًۢا بِٱلْأَمْسِ ۖ إِن تُرِيدُ إِلَّآ أَن تَكُونَ جَبَّارًا فِى ٱلْأَرْضِ وَمَا تُرِيدُ أَن تَكُونَ مِنَ ٱلْمُصْلِحِينَ ۝ وَجَآءَ رَجُلٌ مِّنْ أَقْصَا ٱلْمَدِينَةِ يَسْعَىٰ قَالَ يَٰمُوسَىٰٓ إِنَّ ٱلْمَلَأَ يَأْتَمِرُونَ بِكَ لِيَقْتُلُوكَ فَٱخْرُجْ إِنِّى لَكَ مِنَ ٱلنَّٰصِحِينَ ۝ فَخَرَجَ مِنْهَا خَآئِفًا يَتَرَقَّبُ ۖ قَالَ رَبِّ نَجِّنِى مِنَ ٱلْقَوْمِ ٱلظَّٰلِمِينَ ۝ وَلَمَّا تَوَجَّهَ تِلْقَآءَ مَدْيَنَ قَالَ عَسَىٰ رَبِّىٓ أَن يَهْدِيَنِى سَوَآءَ ٱلسَّبِيلِ ۝ وَلَمَّا وَرَدَ مَآءَ مَدْيَنَ وَجَدَ عَلَيْهِ أُمَّةً مِّنَ ٱلنَّاسِ يَسْقُونَ وَوَجَدَ مِن دُونِهِمُ ٱمْرَأَتَيْنِ تَذُودَانِ ۖ قَالَ مَا خَطْبُكُمَا ۖ قَالَتَا لَا نَسْقِى حَتَّىٰ يُصْدِرَ ٱلرِّعَآءُ ۖ وَأَبُونَا شَيْخٌ كَبِيرٌ ۝ فَسَقَىٰ لَهُمَا ثُمَّ تَوَلَّىٰٓ إِلَى ٱلظِّلِّ فَقَالَ رَبِّ إِنِّى لِمَآ أَنزَلْتَ إِلَىَّ مِنْ خَيْرٍ فَقِيرٌ ۝ فَجَآءَتْهُ إِحْدَىٰهُمَا تَمْشِى عَلَى ٱسْتِحْيَآءٍ قَالَتْ إِنَّ أَبِى يَدْعُوكَ

لِيَجْزِيَكَ أَجْرَ مَا سَقَيْتَ لَنَا ۚ فَلَمَّا جَاءَهُ وَقَصَّ عَلَيْهِ ٱلْقَصَصَ قَالَ لَا تَخَفْ ۖ نَجَوْتَ مِنَ ٱلْقَوْمِ ٱلظَّٰلِمِينَ ۝ قَالَتْ إِحْدَىٰهُمَا يَٰٓأَبَتِ ٱسْتَـْٔجِرْهُ ۖ إِنَّ خَيْرَ مَنِ ٱسْتَـْٔجَرْتَ ٱلْقَوِيُّ ٱلْأَمِينُ ۝ قَالَ إِنِّىٓ أُرِيدُ أَنْ أُنكِحَكَ إِحْدَى ٱبْنَتَىَّ هَٰتَيْنِ عَلَىٰٓ أَن تَأْجُرَنِى ثَمَٰنِىَ حِجَجٍ ۖ فَإِنْ أَتْمَمْتَ عَشْرًا فَمِنْ عِندِكَ ۖ وَمَآ أُرِيدُ أَنْ أَشُقَّ عَلَيْكَ ۚ سَتَجِدُنِىٓ إِن شَآءَ ٱللَّهُ مِنَ ٱلصَّٰلِحِينَ ۝ قَالَ ذَٰلِكَ بَيْنِى وَبَيْنَكَ ۖ أَيَّمَا ٱلْأَجَلَيْنِ قَضَيْتُ فَلَا عُدْوَٰنَ عَلَىَّ ۖ وَٱللَّهُ عَلَىٰ مَا نَقُولُ وَكِيلٌ ۝ ۞ فَلَمَّا قَضَىٰ مُوسَى ٱلْأَجَلَ وَسَارَ بِأَهْلِهِۦٓ ءَانَسَ مِن جَانِبِ ٱلطُّورِ نَارًا قَالَ لِأَهْلِهِ ٱمْكُثُوٓا۟ إِنِّىٓ ءَانَسْتُ نَارًا لَّعَلِّىٓ ءَاتِيكُم مِّنْهَا بِخَبَرٍ أَوْ جَذْوَةٍ مِّنَ ٱلنَّارِ لَعَلَّكُمْ تَصْطَلُونَ ۝ فَلَمَّآ أَتَىٰهَا نُودِىَ مِن شَٰطِئِ ٱلْوَادِ ٱلْأَيْمَنِ فِى ٱلْبُقْعَةِ ٱلْمُبَٰرَكَةِ مِنَ ٱلشَّجَرَةِ أَن يَٰمُوسَىٰٓ إِنِّىٓ أَنَا ٱللَّهُ رَبُّ ٱلْعَٰلَمِينَ ۝ وَأَنْ أَلْقِ عَصَاكَ ۖ فَلَمَّا رَءَاهَا تَهْتَزُّ كَأَنَّهَا جَآنٌّ وَلَّىٰ مُدْبِرًا وَلَمْ يُعَقِّبْ ۚ يَٰمُوسَىٰٓ أَقْبِلْ وَلَا تَخَفْ ۖ إِنَّكَ مِنَ ٱلْـَٔامِنِينَ ۝ ٱسْلُكْ يَدَكَ فِى جَيْبِكَ تَخْرُجْ بَيْضَآءَ مِنْ غَيْرِ سُوٓءٍ وَٱضْمُمْ إِلَيْكَ جَنَاحَكَ مِنَ ٱلرَّهْبِ ۖ فَذَٰنِكَ بُرْهَٰنَانِ مِن رَّبِّكَ إِلَىٰ فِرْعَوْنَ وَمَلَإِي۟هِۦٓ ۚ إِنَّهُمْ كَانُوا۟ قَوْمًا فَٰسِقِينَ ۝ قَالَ رَبِّ إِنِّى قَتَلْتُ مِنْهُمْ نَفْسًا فَأَخَافُ أَن يَقْتُلُونِ ۝ وَأَخِى هَٰرُونُ هُوَ أَفْصَحُ مِنِّى لِسَانًا فَأَرْسِلْهُ مَعِىَ رِدْءًا يُصَدِّقُنِىٓ ۖ إِنِّىٓ أَخَافُ أَن يُكَذِّبُونِ ۝ قَالَ سَنَشُدُّ عَضُدَكَ بِأَخِيكَ وَنَجْعَلُ لَكُمَا سُلْطَٰنًا فَلَا يَصِلُونَ إِلَيْكُمَا ۚ بِـَٔايَٰتِنَآ أَنتُمَا وَمَنِ ٱتَّبَعَكُمَا ٱلْغَٰلِبُونَ ۝ فَلَمَّا جَآءَهُم مُّوسَىٰ بِـَٔايَٰتِنَا بَيِّنَٰتٍ قَالُوا۟ مَا هَٰذَآ إِلَّا سِحْرٌ مُّفْتَرًى وَمَا سَمِعْنَا بِهَٰذَا فِىٓ ءَابَآئِنَا ٱلْأَوَّلِينَ ۝ وَقَالَ مُوسَىٰ رَبِّىٓ أَعْلَمُ بِمَن جَآءَ بِٱلْهُدَىٰ مِنْ عِندِهِۦ وَمَن تَكُونُ لَهُۥ عَٰقِبَةُ ٱلدَّارِ ۗ إِنَّهُۥ لَا يُفْلِحُ ٱلظَّٰلِمُونَ ۝ وَقَالَ فِرْعَوْنُ يَٰٓأَيُّهَا ٱلْمَلَأُ مَا

عَلِمْتُ لَكُم مِّنْ إِلَٰهٍ غَيْرِى فَأَوْقِدْ لِى يَٰهَٰمَٰنُ عَلَى ٱلطِّينِ فَٱجْعَل لِّى صَرْحًا لَّعَلِّىٓ أَطَّلِعُ إِلَىٰٓ إِلَٰهِ مُوسَىٰ وَإِنِّى لَأَظُنُّهُۥ مِنَ ٱلْكَٰذِبِينَ ۝ وَٱسْتَكْبَرَ هُوَ وَجُنُودُهُۥ فِى ٱلْأَرْضِ بِغَيْرِ ٱلْحَقِّ وَظَنُّوٓا۟ أَنَّهُمْ إِلَيْنَا لَا يُرْجَعُونَ ۝ فَأَخَذْنَٰهُ وَجُنُودَهُۥ فَنَبَذْنَٰهُمْ فِى ٱلْيَمِّ ۖ فَٱنظُرْ كَيْفَ كَانَ عَٰقِبَةُ ٱلظَّٰلِمِينَ ۝ وَجَعَلْنَٰهُمْ أَئِمَّةً يَدْعُونَ إِلَى ٱلنَّارِ ۖ وَيَوْمَ ٱلْقِيَٰمَةِ لَا يُنصَرُونَ ۝ وَأَتْبَعْنَٰهُمْ فِى هَٰذِهِ ٱلدُّنْيَا لَعْنَةً ۖ وَيَوْمَ ٱلْقِيَٰمَةِ هُم مِّنَ ٱلْمَقْبُوحِينَ ۝ وَلَقَدْ ءَاتَيْنَا مُوسَى ٱلْكِتَٰبَ مِنۢ بَعْدِ مَآ أَهْلَكْنَا ٱلْقُرُونَ ٱلْأُولَىٰ بَصَآئِرَ لِلنَّاسِ وَهُدًى وَرَحْمَةً لَّعَلَّهُمْ يَتَذَكَّرُونَ ۝ وَمَا كُنتَ بِجَانِبِ ٱلْغَرْبِىِّ إِذْ قَضَيْنَآ إِلَىٰ مُوسَى ٱلْأَمْرَ وَمَا كُنتَ مِنَ ٱلشَّٰهِدِينَ ۝ وَلَٰكِنَّآ أَنشَأْنَا قُرُونًا فَتَطَاوَلَ عَلَيْهِمُ ٱلْعُمُرُ ۚ وَمَا كُنتَ ثَاوِيًا فِىٓ أَهْلِ مَدْيَنَ تَتْلُوا۟ عَلَيْهِمْ ءَايَٰتِنَا وَلَٰكِنَّا كُنَّا مُرْسِلِينَ ۝ وَمَا كُنتَ بِجَانِبِ ٱلطُّورِ إِذْ نَادَيْنَا وَلَٰكِن رَّحْمَةً مِّن رَّبِّكَ لِتُنذِرَ قَوْمًا مَّآ أَتَىٰهُم مِّن نَّذِيرٍ مِّن قَبْلِكَ لَعَلَّهُمْ يَتَذَكَّرُونَ ۝ وَلَوْلَآ أَن تُصِيبَهُم مُّصِيبَةٌۢ بِمَا قَدَّمَتْ أَيْدِيهِمْ فَيَقُولُوا۟ رَبَّنَا لَوْلَآ أَرْسَلْتَ إِلَيْنَا رَسُولًا فَنَتَّبِعَ ءَايَٰتِكَ وَنَكُونَ مِنَ ٱلْمُؤْمِنِينَ ۝ فَلَمَّا جَآءَهُمُ ٱلْحَقُّ مِنْ عِندِنَا قَالُوا۟ لَوْلَآ أُوتِىَ مِثْلَ مَآ أُوتِىَ مُوسَىٰٓ ۚ أَوَلَمْ يَكْفُرُوا۟ بِمَآ أُوتِىَ مُوسَىٰ مِن قَبْلُ ۖ قَالُوا۟ سِحْرَانِ تَظَٰهَرَا وَقَالُوٓا۟ إِنَّا بِكُلٍّ كَٰفِرُونَ ۝ قُلْ فَأْتُوا۟ بِكِتَٰبٍ مِّنْ عِندِ ٱللَّهِ هُوَ أَهْدَىٰ مِنْهُمَآ أَتَّبِعْهُ إِن كُنتُمْ صَٰدِقِينَ ۝ فَإِن لَّمْ يَسْتَجِيبُوا۟ لَكَ فَٱعْلَمْ أَنَّمَا يَتَّبِعُونَ أَهْوَآءَهُمْ ۚ وَمَنْ أَضَلُّ مِمَّنِ ٱتَّبَعَ هَوَىٰهُ بِغَيْرِ هُدًى مِّنَ ٱللَّهِ ۚ إِنَّ ٱللَّهَ لَا يَهْدِى ٱلْقَوْمَ ٱلظَّٰلِمِينَ ۝ وَلَقَدْ وَصَّلْنَا لَهُمُ ٱلْقَوْلَ لَعَلَّهُمْ يَتَذَكَّرُونَ ۝ ٱلَّذِينَ ءَاتَيْنَٰهُمُ ٱلْكِتَٰبَ مِن قَبْلِهِۦ هُم بِهِۦ يُؤْمِنُونَ ۝ وَإِذَا يُتْلَىٰ عَلَيْهِمْ قَالُوٓا۟ ءَامَنَّا

بِهِۦٓ إِنَّهُ ٱلْحَقُّ مِن رَّبِّنَآ إِنَّا كُنَّا مِن قَبْلِهِۦ مُسْلِمِينَ ۝ أُوْلَٰٓئِكَ يُؤْتَوْنَ أَجْرَهُم مَّرَّتَيْنِ بِمَا صَبَرُواْ وَيَدْرَءُونَ بِٱلْحَسَنَةِ ٱلسَّيِّئَةَ وَمِمَّا رَزَقْنَٰهُمْ يُنفِقُونَ ۝ وَإِذَا سَمِعُواْ ٱللَّغْوَ أَعْرَضُواْ عَنْهُ وَقَالُواْ لَنَآ أَعْمَٰلُنَا وَلَكُمْ أَعْمَٰلُكُمْ سَلَٰمٌ عَلَيْكُمْ لَا نَبْتَغِى ٱلْجَٰهِلِينَ ۝ إِنَّكَ لَا تَهْدِى مَنْ أَحْبَبْتَ وَلَٰكِنَّ ٱللَّهَ يَهْدِى مَن يَشَآءُ وَهُوَ أَعْلَمُ بِٱلْمُهْتَدِينَ ۝ وَقَالُوٓاْ إِن نَّتَّبِعِ ٱلْهُدَىٰ مَعَكَ نُتَخَطَّفْ مِنْ أَرْضِنَآ أَوَلَمْ نُمَكِّن لَّهُمْ حَرَمًا ءَامِنًا يُجْبَىٰٓ إِلَيْهِ ثَمَرَٰتُ كُلِّ شَىْءٍ رِّزْقًا مِّن لَّدُنَّا وَلَٰكِنَّ أَكْثَرَهُمْ لَا يَعْلَمُونَ ۝ وَكَمْ أَهْلَكْنَا مِن قَرْيَةٍۭ بَطِرَتْ مَعِيشَتَهَا فَتِلْكَ مَسَٰكِنُهُمْ لَمْ تُسْكَن مِّنۢ بَعْدِهِمْ إِلَّا قَلِيلًا وَكُنَّا نَحْنُ ٱلْوَٰرِثِينَ ۝ وَمَا كَانَ رَبُّكَ مُهْلِكَ ٱلْقُرَىٰ حَتَّىٰ يَبْعَثَ فِىٓ أُمِّهَا رَسُولًا يَتْلُواْ عَلَيْهِمْ ءَايَٰتِنَا وَمَا كُنَّا مُهْلِكِى ٱلْقُرَىٰٓ إِلَّا وَأَهْلُهَا ظَٰلِمُونَ ۝ وَمَآ أُوتِيتُم مِّن شَىْءٍ فَمَتَٰعُ ٱلْحَيَوٰةِ ٱلدُّنْيَا وَزِينَتُهَا وَمَا عِندَ ٱللَّهِ خَيْرٌ وَأَبْقَىٰٓ أَفَلَا تَعْقِلُونَ ۝ أَفَمَن وَعَدْنَٰهُ وَعْدًا حَسَنًا فَهُوَ لَٰقِيهِ كَمَن مَّتَّعْنَٰهُ مَتَٰعَ ٱلْحَيَوٰةِ ٱلدُّنْيَا ثُمَّ هُوَ يَوْمَ ٱلْقِيَٰمَةِ مِنَ ٱلْمُحْضَرِينَ ۝ وَيَوْمَ يُنَادِيهِمْ فَيَقُولُ أَيْنَ شُرَكَآءِىَ ٱلَّذِينَ كُنتُمْ تَزْعُمُونَ ۝ قَالَ ٱلَّذِينَ حَقَّ عَلَيْهِمُ ٱلْقَوْلُ رَبَّنَا هَٰٓؤُلَآءِ ٱلَّذِينَ أَغْوَيْنَا أَغْوَيْنَٰهُمْ كَمَا غَوَيْنَا تَبَرَّأْنَآ إِلَيْكَ مَا كَانُوٓاْ إِيَّانَا يَعْبُدُونَ ۝ وَقِيلَ ٱدْعُواْ شُرَكَآءَكُمْ فَدَعَوْهُمْ فَلَمْ يَسْتَجِيبُواْ لَهُمْ وَرَأَوُاْ ٱلْعَذَابَ لَوْ أَنَّهُمْ كَانُواْ يَهْتَدُونَ ۝ وَيَوْمَ يُنَادِيهِمْ فَيَقُولُ مَاذَآ أَجَبْتُمُ ٱلْمُرْسَلِينَ ۝ فَعَمِيَتْ عَلَيْهِمُ ٱلْأَنۢبَآءُ يَوْمَئِذٍ فَهُمْ لَا يَتَسَآءَلُونَ ۝ فَأَمَّا مَن تَابَ وَءَامَنَ وَعَمِلَ صَٰلِحًا فَعَسَىٰٓ أَن يَكُونَ مِنَ ٱلْمُفْلِحِينَ ۝ وَرَبُّكَ يَخْلُقُ مَا يَشَآءُ وَيَخْتَارُ مَا كَانَ لَهُمُ ٱلْخِيَرَةُ سُبْحَٰنَ ٱللَّهِ وَتَعَٰلَىٰ عَمَّا يُشْرِكُونَ ۝ وَرَبُّكَ يَعْلَمُ مَا تُكِنُّ صُدُورُهُمْ وَمَا يُعْلِنُونَ ۝ وَهُوَ ٱللَّهُ لَآ إِلَٰهَ إِلَّا هُوَ لَهُ ٱلْحَمْدُ فِى

ٱلْأُولَىٰ وَٱلْآخِرَةِ ۖ وَلَهُ ٱلْحُكْمُ وَإِلَيْهِ تُرْجَعُونَ ۝ قُلْ أَرَءَيْتُمْ إِن جَعَلَ ٱللَّهُ عَلَيْكُمُ ٱلَّيْلَ سَرْمَدًا إِلَىٰ يَوْمِ ٱلْقِيَامَةِ مَنْ إِلَـٰهٌ غَيْرُ ٱللَّهِ يَأْتِيكُم بِضِيَآءٍ ۖ أَفَلَا تَسْمَعُونَ ۝ قُلْ أَرَءَيْتُمْ إِن جَعَلَ ٱللَّهُ عَلَيْكُمُ ٱلنَّهَارَ سَرْمَدًا إِلَىٰ يَوْمِ ٱلْقِيَامَةِ مَنْ إِلَـٰهٌ غَيْرُ ٱللَّهِ يَأْتِيكُم بِلَيْلٍ تَسْكُنُونَ فِيهِ ۖ أَفَلَا تُبْصِرُونَ ۝ وَمِن رَّحْمَتِهِ جَعَلَ لَكُمُ ٱلَّيْلَ وَٱلنَّهَارَ لِتَسْكُنُوا۟ فِيهِ وَلِتَبْتَغُوا۟ مِن فَضْلِهِ وَلَعَلَّكُمْ تَشْكُرُونَ ۝ وَيَوْمَ يُنَادِيهِمْ فَيَقُولُ أَيْنَ شُرَكَآءِيَ ٱلَّذِينَ كُنتُمْ تَزْعُمُونَ ۝ وَنَزَعْنَا مِن كُلِّ أُمَّةٍ شَهِيدًا فَقُلْنَا هَاتُوا۟ بُرْهَـٰنَكُمْ فَعَلِمُوٓا۟ أَنَّ ٱلْحَقَّ لِلَّهِ وَضَلَّ عَنْهُم مَّا كَانُوا۟ يَفْتَرُونَ ۝ ۞ إِنَّ قَـٰرُونَ كَانَ مِن قَوْمِ مُوسَىٰ فَبَغَىٰ عَلَيْهِمْ ۖ وَءَاتَيْنَـٰهُ مِنَ ٱلْكُنُوزِ مَآ إِنَّ مَفَاتِحَهُۥ لَتَنُوٓأُ بِٱلْعُصْبَةِ أُو۟لِى ٱلْقُوَّةِ إِذْ قَالَ لَهُۥ قَوْمُهُۥ لَا تَفْرَحْ ۖ إِنَّ ٱللَّهَ لَا يُحِبُّ ٱلْفَرِحِينَ ۝ وَٱبْتَغِ فِيمَآ ءَاتَىٰكَ ٱللَّهُ ٱلدَّارَ ٱلْآخِرَةَ ۖ وَلَا تَنسَ نَصِيبَكَ مِنَ ٱلدُّنْيَا ۖ وَأَحْسِن كَمَآ أَحْسَنَ ٱللَّهُ إِلَيْكَ ۖ وَلَا تَبْغِ ٱلْفَسَادَ فِى ٱلْأَرْضِ ۖ إِنَّ ٱللَّهَ لَا يُحِبُّ ٱلْمُفْسِدِينَ ۝ قَالَ إِنَّمَآ أُوتِيتُهُۥ عَلَىٰ عِلْمٍ عِندِىٓ ۚ أَوَلَمْ يَعْلَمْ أَنَّ ٱللَّهَ قَدْ أَهْلَكَ مِن قَبْلِهِۦ مِنَ ٱلْقُرُونِ مَنْ هُوَ أَشَدُّ مِنْهُ قُوَّةً وَأَكْثَرُ جَمْعًا ۚ وَلَا يُسْـَٔلُ عَن ذُنُوبِهِمُ ٱلْمُجْرِمُونَ ۝ فَخَرَجَ عَلَىٰ قَوْمِهِۦ فِى زِينَتِهِۦ ۖ قَالَ ٱلَّذِينَ يُرِيدُونَ ٱلْحَيَوٰةَ ٱلدُّنْيَا يَـٰلَيْتَ لَنَا مِثْلَ مَآ أُوتِىَ قَـٰرُونُ إِنَّهُۥ لَذُو حَظٍّ عَظِيمٍ ۝ وَقَالَ ٱلَّذِينَ أُوتُوا۟ ٱلْعِلْمَ وَيْلَكُمْ ثَوَابُ ٱللَّهِ خَيْرٌ لِّمَنْ ءَامَنَ وَعَمِلَ صَـٰلِحًا وَلَا يُلَقَّىٰهَآ إِلَّا ٱلصَّـٰبِرُونَ ۝ فَخَسَفْنَا بِهِۦ وَبِدَارِهِ ٱلْأَرْضَ فَمَا كَانَ لَهُۥ مِن فِئَةٍ يَنصُرُونَهُۥ مِن دُونِ ٱللَّهِ وَمَا كَانَ مِنَ ٱلْمُنتَصِرِينَ ۝ وَأَصْبَحَ ٱلَّذِينَ تَمَنَّوْا۟ مَكَانَهُۥ بِٱلْأَمْسِ يَقُولُونَ وَيْكَأَنَّ ٱللَّهَ يَبْسُطُ ٱلرِّزْقَ لِمَن يَشَآءُ مِنْ عِبَادِهِۦ وَيَقْدِرُ ۖ لَوْلَآ أَن مَّنَّ ٱللَّهُ عَلَيْنَا لَخَسَفَ بِنَا

وَيْكَأَنَّهُ لَا يُفْلِحُ ٱلْكَٰفِرُونَ ۝ تِلْكَ ٱلدَّارُ ٱلْءَاخِرَةُ نَجْعَلُهَا لِلَّذِينَ لَا يُرِيدُونَ عُلُوًّا فِى ٱلْأَرْضِ وَلَا فَسَادًا ۚ وَٱلْعَٰقِبَةُ لِلْمُتَّقِينَ ۝ مَن جَآءَ بِٱلْحَسَنَةِ فَلَهُۥ خَيْرٌ مِّنْهَا ۖ وَمَن جَآءَ بِٱلسَّيِّئَةِ فَلَا يُجْزَى ٱلَّذِينَ عَمِلُوا۟ ٱلسَّيِّـَٔاتِ إِلَّا مَا كَانُوا۟ يَعْمَلُونَ ۝ إِنَّ ٱلَّذِى فَرَضَ عَلَيْكَ ٱلْقُرْءَانَ لَرَآدُّكَ إِلَىٰ مَعَادٍ ۚ قُل رَّبِّىٓ أَعْلَمُ مَن جَآءَ بِٱلْهُدَىٰ وَمَنْ هُوَ فِى ضَلَٰلٍ مُّبِينٍ ۝ وَمَا كُنتَ تَرْجُوٓا۟ أَن يُلْقَىٰٓ إِلَيْكَ ٱلْكِتَٰبُ إِلَّا رَحْمَةً مِّن رَّبِّكَ ۖ فَلَا تَكُونَنَّ ظَهِيرًا لِّلْكَٰفِرِينَ ۝ وَلَا يَصُدُّنَّكَ عَنْ ءَايَٰتِ ٱللَّهِ بَعْدَ إِذْ أُنزِلَتْ إِلَيْكَ ۖ وَٱدْعُ إِلَىٰ رَبِّكَ ۖ وَلَا تَكُونَنَّ مِنَ ٱلْمُشْرِكِينَ ۝ وَلَا تَدْعُ مَعَ ٱللَّهِ إِلَٰهًا ءَاخَرَ ۘ لَآ إِلَٰهَ إِلَّا هُوَ ۚ كُلُّ شَىْءٍ هَالِكٌ إِلَّا وَجْهَهُۥ ۚ لَهُ ٱلْحُكْمُ وَإِلَيْهِ تُرْجَعُونَ ۝

(Al-Qasas 001-088)

Chapter (Surah) 29: Al-'Ankaboot 001-045

بِسْمِ ٱللَّهِ ٱلرَّحْمَٰنِ ٱلرَّحِيمِ

الٓمٓ ۝ أَحَسِبَ ٱلنَّاسُ أَن يُتْرَكُوٓا۟ أَن يَقُولُوٓا۟ ءَامَنَّا وَهُمْ لَا يُفْتَنُونَ ۝ وَلَقَدْ فَتَنَّا ٱلَّذِينَ مِن قَبْلِهِمْ ۖ فَلَيَعْلَمَنَّ ٱللَّهُ ٱلَّذِينَ صَدَقُوا۟ وَلَيَعْلَمَنَّ ٱلْكَٰذِبِينَ ۝ أَمْ حَسِبَ ٱلَّذِينَ يَعْمَلُونَ ٱلسَّيِّـَٔاتِ أَن يَسْبِقُونَا ۚ سَآءَ مَا يَحْكُمُونَ ۝ مَن كَانَ يَرْجُوا۟ لِقَآءَ ٱللَّهِ فَإِنَّ أَجَلَ ٱللَّهِ لَءَاتٍ ۚ وَهُوَ ٱلسَّمِيعُ ٱلْعَلِيمُ ۝ وَمَن جَٰهَدَ فَإِنَّمَا يُجَٰهِدُ لِنَفْسِهِۦٓ ۚ إِنَّ ٱللَّهَ لَغَنِىٌّ عَنِ ٱلْعَٰلَمِينَ ۝ وَٱلَّذِينَ ءَامَنُوا۟ وَعَمِلُوا۟ ٱلصَّٰلِحَٰتِ لَنُكَفِّرَنَّ عَنْهُمْ سَيِّـَٔاتِهِمْ وَلَنَجْزِيَنَّهُمْ أَحْسَنَ ٱلَّذِى كَانُوا۟ يَعْمَلُونَ ۝ وَوَصَّيْنَا ٱلْإِنسَٰنَ بِوَٰلِدَيْهِ حُسْنًا ۖ وَإِن جَٰهَدَاكَ لِتُشْرِكَ بِى مَا لَيْسَ لَكَ بِهِۦ عِلْمٌ فَلَا تُطِعْهُمَآ ۚ إِلَىَّ مَرْجِعُكُمْ فَأُنَبِّئُكُم بِمَا كُنتُمْ تَعْمَلُونَ ۝ وَٱلَّذِينَ ءَامَنُوا۟ وَعَمِلُوا۟ ٱلصَّٰلِحَٰتِ لَنُدْخِلَنَّهُمْ فِى ٱلصَّٰلِحِينَ ۝ وَمِنَ ٱلنَّاسِ مَن يَقُولُ ءَامَنَّا بِٱللَّهِ فَإِذَآ أُوذِىَ فِى ٱللَّهِ جَعَلَ فِتْنَةَ ٱلنَّاسِ كَعَذَابِ ٱللَّهِ وَلَئِن جَآءَ

نَصْرٌ مِّن رَّبِّكَ لَيَقُولُنَّ إِنَّا كُنَّا مَعَكُمْ أَوَلَيْسَ ٱللَّهُ بِأَعْلَمَ بِمَا فِى صُدُورِ ٱلْعَٰلَمِينَ ۝ وَلَيَعْلَمَنَّ ٱللَّهُ ٱلَّذِينَ ءَامَنُوا۟ وَلَيَعْلَمَنَّ ٱلْمُنَٰفِقِينَ ۝ وَقَالَ ٱلَّذِينَ كَفَرُوا۟ لِلَّذِينَ ءَامَنُوا۟ ٱتَّبِعُوا۟ سَبِيلَنَا وَلْنَحْمِلْ خَطَٰيَٰكُمْ وَمَا هُم بِحَٰمِلِينَ مِنْ خَطَٰيَٰهُم مِّن شَىْءٍ إِنَّهُمْ لَكَٰذِبُونَ ۝ وَلَيَحْمِلُنَّ أَثْقَالَهُمْ وَأَثْقَالًا مَّعَ أَثْقَالِهِمْ وَلَيُسْـَٔلُنَّ يَوْمَ ٱلْقِيَٰمَةِ عَمَّا كَانُوا۟ يَفْتَرُونَ ۝ وَلَقَدْ أَرْسَلْنَا نُوحًا إِلَىٰ قَوْمِهِۦ فَلَبِثَ فِيهِمْ أَلْفَ سَنَةٍ إِلَّا خَمْسِينَ عَامًا فَأَخَذَهُمُ ٱلطُّوفَانُ وَهُمْ ظَٰلِمُونَ ۝ فَأَنجَيْنَٰهُ وَأَصْحَٰبَ ٱلسَّفِينَةِ وَجَعَلْنَٰهَآ ءَايَةً لِّلْعَٰلَمِينَ ۝ وَإِبْرَٰهِيمَ إِذْ قَالَ لِقَوْمِهِ ٱعْبُدُوا۟ ٱللَّهَ وَٱتَّقُوهُ ذَٰلِكُمْ خَيْرٌ لَّكُمْ إِن كُنتُمْ تَعْلَمُونَ ۝ إِنَّمَا تَعْبُدُونَ مِن دُونِ ٱللَّهِ أَوْثَٰنًا وَتَخْلُقُونَ إِفْكًا إِنَّ ٱلَّذِينَ تَعْبُدُونَ مِن دُونِ ٱللَّهِ لَا يَمْلِكُونَ لَكُمْ رِزْقًا فَٱبْتَغُوا۟ عِندَ ٱللَّهِ ٱلرِّزْقَ وَٱعْبُدُوهُ وَٱشْكُرُوا۟ لَهُۥٓ إِلَيْهِ تُرْجَعُونَ ۝ وَإِن تُكَذِّبُوا۟ فَقَدْ كَذَّبَ أُمَمٌ مِّن قَبْلِكُمْ وَمَا عَلَى ٱلرَّسُولِ إِلَّا ٱلْبَلَٰغُ ٱلْمُبِينُ ۝ أَوَلَمْ يَرَوْا۟ كَيْفَ يُبْدِئُ ٱللَّهُ ٱلْخَلْقَ ثُمَّ يُعِيدُهُۥٓ إِنَّ ذَٰلِكَ عَلَى ٱللَّهِ يَسِيرٌ ۝ قُلْ سِيرُوا۟ فِى ٱلْأَرْضِ فَٱنظُرُوا۟ كَيْفَ بَدَأَ ٱلْخَلْقَ ثُمَّ ٱللَّهُ يُنشِئُ ٱلنَّشْأَةَ ٱلْءَاخِرَةَ إِنَّ ٱللَّهَ عَلَىٰ كُلِّ شَىْءٍ قَدِيرٌ ۝ يُعَذِّبُ مَن يَشَآءُ وَيَرْحَمُ مَن يَشَآءُ وَإِلَيْهِ تُقْلَبُونَ ۝ وَمَآ أَنتُم بِمُعْجِزِينَ فِى ٱلْأَرْضِ وَلَا فِى ٱلسَّمَآءِ وَمَا لَكُم مِّن دُونِ ٱللَّهِ مِن وَلِىٍّ وَلَا نَصِيرٍ ۝ وَٱلَّذِينَ كَفَرُوا۟ بِـَٔايَٰتِ ٱللَّهِ وَلِقَآئِهِۦٓ أُو۟لَٰٓئِكَ يَئِسُوا۟ مِن رَّحْمَتِى وَأُو۟لَٰٓئِكَ لَهُمْ عَذَابٌ أَلِيمٌ ۝ فَمَا كَانَ جَوَابَ قَوْمِهِۦٓ إِلَّآ أَن قَالُوا۟ ٱقْتُلُوهُ أَوْ حَرِّقُوهُ فَأَنجَىٰهُ ٱللَّهُ مِنَ ٱلنَّارِ إِنَّ فِى ذَٰلِكَ لَءَايَٰتٍ لِّقَوْمٍ يُؤْمِنُونَ ۝ وَقَالَ إِنَّمَا ٱتَّخَذْتُم مِّن دُونِ ٱللَّهِ أَوْثَٰنًا مَّوَدَّةَ بَيْنِكُمْ فِى ٱلْحَيَوٰةِ ٱلدُّنْيَا ثُمَّ يَوْمَ ٱلْقِيَٰمَةِ يَكْفُرُ بَعْضُكُم بِبَعْضٍ

وَيَلْعَنُ بَعْضُكُم بَعْضًا وَمَأْوَىٰكُمُ ٱلنَّارُ وَمَا لَكُم مِّن نَّـٰصِرِينَ ۝ فَـَٔامَنَ لَهُۥ لُوطٌ ۘ وَقَالَ إِنِّى مُهَاجِرٌ إِلَىٰ رَبِّىٓ ۖ إِنَّهُۥ هُوَ ٱلْعَزِيزُ ٱلْحَكِيمُ ۝ وَوَهَبْنَا لَهُۥٓ إِسْحَـٰقَ وَيَعْقُوبَ وَجَعَلْنَا فِى ذُرِّيَّتِهِ ٱلنُّبُوَّةَ وَٱلْكِتَـٰبَ وَءَاتَيْنَـٰهُ أَجْرَهُۥ فِى ٱلدُّنْيَا ۖ وَإِنَّهُۥ فِى ٱلْـَٔاخِرَةِ لَمِنَ ٱلصَّـٰلِحِينَ ۝ وَلُوطًا إِذْ قَالَ لِقَوْمِهِۦٓ إِنَّكُمْ لَتَأْتُونَ ٱلْفَـٰحِشَةَ مَا سَبَقَكُم بِهَا مِنْ أَحَدٍ مِّنَ ٱلْعَـٰلَمِينَ ۝ أَئِنَّكُمْ لَتَأْتُونَ ٱلرِّجَالَ وَتَقْطَعُونَ ٱلسَّبِيلَ وَتَأْتُونَ فِى نَادِيكُمُ ٱلْمُنكَرَ ۖ فَمَا كَانَ جَوَابَ قَوْمِهِۦٓ إِلَّآ أَن قَالُوا۟ ٱئْتِنَا بِعَذَابِ ٱللَّهِ إِن كُنتَ مِنَ ٱلصَّـٰدِقِينَ ۝ قَالَ رَبِّ ٱنصُرْنِى عَلَى ٱلْقَوْمِ ٱلْمُفْسِدِينَ ۝ وَلَمَّا جَآءَتْ رُسُلُنَآ إِبْرَٰهِيمَ بِٱلْبُشْرَىٰ قَالُوٓا۟ إِنَّا مُهْلِكُوٓا۟ أَهْلِ هَـٰذِهِ ٱلْقَرْيَةِ ۖ إِنَّ أَهْلَهَا كَانُوا۟ ظَـٰلِمِينَ ۝ قَالَ إِنَّ فِيهَا لُوطًا ۚ قَالُوا۟ نَحْنُ أَعْلَمُ بِمَن فِيهَا ۖ لَنُنَجِّيَنَّهُۥ وَأَهْلَهُۥٓ إِلَّا ٱمْرَأَتَهُۥ كَانَتْ مِنَ ٱلْغَـٰبِرِينَ ۝ وَلَمَّآ أَن جَآءَتْ رُسُلُنَا لُوطًا سِىٓءَ بِهِمْ وَضَاقَ بِهِمْ ذَرْعًا وَقَالُوا۟ لَا تَخَفْ وَلَا تَحْزَنْ ۖ إِنَّا مُنَجُّوكَ وَأَهْلَكَ إِلَّا ٱمْرَأَتَكَ كَانَتْ مِنَ ٱلْغَـٰبِرِينَ ۝ إِنَّا مُنزِلُونَ عَلَىٰٓ أَهْلِ هَـٰذِهِ ٱلْقَرْيَةِ رِجْزًا مِّنَ ٱلسَّمَآءِ بِمَا كَانُوا۟ يَفْسُقُونَ ۝ وَلَقَد تَّرَكْنَا مِنْهَآ ءَايَةًۢ بَيِّنَةً لِّقَوْمٍ يَعْقِلُونَ ۝ وَإِلَىٰ مَدْيَنَ أَخَاهُمْ شُعَيْبًا فَقَالَ يَـٰقَوْمِ ٱعْبُدُوا۟ ٱللَّهَ وَٱرْجُوا۟ ٱلْيَوْمَ ٱلْـَٔاخِرَ وَلَا تَعْثَوْا۟ فِى ٱلْأَرْضِ مُفْسِدِينَ ۝ فَكَذَّبُوهُ فَأَخَذَتْهُمُ ٱلرَّجْفَةُ فَأَصْبَحُوا۟ فِى دَارِهِمْ جَـٰثِمِينَ ۝ وَعَادًا وَثَمُودَا۟ وَقَد تَّبَيَّنَ لَكُم مِّن مَّسَـٰكِنِهِمْ ۖ وَزَيَّنَ لَهُمُ ٱلشَّيْطَـٰنُ أَعْمَـٰلَهُمْ فَصَدَّهُمْ عَنِ ٱلسَّبِيلِ وَكَانُوا۟ مُسْتَبْصِرِينَ ۝ وَقَـٰرُونَ وَفِرْعَوْنَ وَهَـٰمَـٰنَ ۖ وَلَقَدْ جَآءَهُم مُّوسَىٰ بِٱلْبَيِّنَـٰتِ فَٱسْتَكْبَرُوا۟ فِى ٱلْأَرْضِ وَمَا كَانُوا۟ سَـٰبِقِينَ ۝ فَكُلًّا أَخَذْنَا بِذَنۢبِهِۦ ۖ فَمِنْهُم مَّنْ أَرْسَلْنَا عَلَيْهِ حَاصِبًا وَمِنْهُم

$$\text{مَّنْ أَخَذَتْهُ الصَّيْحَةُ وَمِنْهُم مَّنْ خَسَفْنَا بِهِ الْأَرْضَ وَمِنْهُم مَّنْ أَغْرَقْنَا وَمَا كَانَ اللَّهُ لِيَظْلِمَهُمْ وَلَـٰكِن كَانُوا أَنفُسَهُمْ يَظْلِمُونَ ۝ مَثَلُ الَّذِينَ اتَّخَذُوا مِن دُونِ اللَّهِ أَوْلِيَاءَ كَمَثَلِ الْعَنكَبُوتِ اتَّخَذَتْ بَيْتًا ۖ وَإِنَّ أَوْهَنَ الْبُيُوتِ لَبَيْتُ الْعَنكَبُوتِ ۘ لَوْ كَانُوا يَعْلَمُونَ ۝ إِنَّ اللَّهَ يَعْلَمُ مَا يَدْعُونَ مِن دُونِهِ مِن شَيْءٍ ۚ وَهُوَ الْعَزِيزُ الْحَكِيمُ ۝ وَتِلْكَ الْأَمْثَالُ نَضْرِبُهَا لِلنَّاسِ ۖ وَمَا يَعْقِلُهَا إِلَّا الْعَالِمُونَ ۝ خَلَقَ اللَّهُ السَّمَاوَاتِ وَالْأَرْضَ بِالْحَقِّ ۗ إِنَّ فِي ذَٰلِكَ لَآيَةً لِّلْمُؤْمِنِينَ ۝ اتْلُ مَا أُوحِيَ إِلَيْكَ مِنَ الْكِتَابِ وَأَقِمِ الصَّلَاةَ ۖ إِنَّ الصَّلَاةَ تَنْهَىٰ عَنِ الْفَحْشَاءِ وَالْمُنكَرِ ۗ وَلَذِكْرُ اللَّهِ أَكْبَرُ ۗ وَاللَّهُ يَعْلَمُ مَا تَصْنَعُونَ ۝}$$

(Al-'Ankabut 001–045)

CHAPTER (SURAH) 27: AN-NAML (THE ANT, THE ANTS), VERSES 056–093

Surah: 27 Ayah: 54, Ayah: 55 (end of Part 19; used here to give the fullness the following tafsir), Ayah: 56 (start of Part 20), Ayah: 57 & Ayah: 58

$$\text{وَلُوطًا إِذْ قَالَ لِقَوْمِهِ أَتَأْتُونَ الْفَاحِشَةَ وَأَنتُمْ تُبْصِرُونَ ۝}$$

54. And (remember) Lût (Lot)! When he said to his people. Do you commit Al-Fâhishah (evil, great sin, every kind of unlawful sexual intercourse, sodomy) while you see (one another doing evil without any screen)?"

$$\text{أَئِنَّكُمْ لَتَأْتُونَ الرِّجَالَ شَهْوَةً مِّن دُونِ النِّسَاءِ ۚ بَلْ أَنتُمْ قَوْمٌ تَجْهَلُونَ ۝}$$

55. "Do you practice your lusts on men instead of women? Nay, but you are a people who behave senselessly."

$$\text{۞ فَمَا كَانَ جَوَابَ قَوْمِهِ إِلَّا أَن قَالُوا أَخْرِجُوا آلَ لُوطٍ مِّن قَرْيَتِكُمْ ۖ إِنَّهُمْ أُنَاسٌ يَتَطَهَّرُونَ ۝}$$

56. There was no other answer given by his people except that they said: "Drive out the family of Lût (Lot) from your city Verily, these are men who want to be clean and pure!"

Chapter 27: An-Naml (The Ant, The Ants), Verses 056-093

$$\text{فَأَنجَيْنَاهُ وَأَهْلَهُ إِلَّا امْرَأَتَهُ قَدَّرْنَاهَا مِنَ الْغَابِرِينَ ۝}$$

57. So We saved him and his family, except his wife. We destined her to be of those who remained behind.

$$\text{وَأَمْطَرْنَا عَلَيْهِم مَّطَرًا ۖ فَسَاءَ مَطَرُ الْمُنذَرِينَ ۝}$$

58. And We rained down on them a rain (of stones). So evil was the rain of those who were warned.

Transliteration

54. Walootan ith qala liqawmihi ata/toona alfahishata waantum tubsiroona 55. A-innakum lata/toona alrrijala shahwatan min dooni alnnisa-i bal antum qawmun tajhaloona 56. Fama kana jawaba qawmihi illa an qaloo akhrijoo ala lootin min qaryatikuminnahum onasun yatatahharoona 57. Faanjaynahu waahlahu illa imraatahu qaddarnaha mina alghabireena 58. Waamtarna AAalayhim mataran fasaa mataru almunthareena

Tafsir Ibn Kathir

Lut and His People

Allah tells us about His servant and Messenger Lut, peace be upon him, and how he warned his people of Allah's punishment for committing an act of immorality which no human ever committed before them -- intercourse with males instead of females. This is a major sin, whereby men are satisfied with men and women are with women (i.e., homosexuality). Lut said:

(Do you commit immoral sins while you see) meaning, `while you see one another, and you practice every kind of evil in your meetings.'

(Do you practice your lusts on men instead of women Nay, but you are a people who behave senselessly.) means, `you do not know anything of what is natural or what is prescribed by Allah.' This is like the Ayah:

(Go you in unto the males of mankind, and leave those whom Allah has created for you to be your wives Nay, you are a trespassing people!) (26:165-166)

(There was no other answer given by his people except that they said: "Drive out the family of Lut from your city. Verily, these are men who want to be clean and pure!") means, `they feel embarrassed because of the deeds you are doing, and because you approve of your actions, so expel them from among yourselves, for they are not fit to live among you in your city.' So, the people resolved to do that, and Allah destroyed them, and a similar end awaits the disbelievers. Allah says:

(So, We saved him and his family, except his wife. We destined her to be of those who remained behind.) meaning, she was one of those who were destroyed, with her people, because she was a helper to what they did and she approved of their evil deeds. She told them about the guests of Lut so that they could come to them. She did not do the evil deeds herself, which was because of the honor of Lut and not because of any honor on her part.

(And We rained down on them a rain.) means; stones of Sijjil, in a well-arranged manner one after another. Marked from your Lord; and they are not ever far from the evildoers. Allah said:

(So, evil was the rain of those who were warned.) meaning, those against whom proof was established and whom the warning reached, but they went against the Messenger and denied him, and resolved to drive him out from among them.

Surah: 27 Ayah: 59 & Ayah: 60

قُلِ ٱلْحَمْدُ لِلَّهِ وَسَلَـٰمٌ عَلَىٰ عِبَادِهِ ٱلَّذِينَ ٱصْطَفَىٰٓ ءَآللَّهُ خَيْرٌ أَمَّا يُشْرِكُونَ ۝

59. Say (O Muhammad (peace be upon him)) "Praise and thanks be to Allâh, and peace be on His slaves whom He has chosen (for His Message)! Is Allâh better, or (all) that you ascribe as partners (to Him)?" (Of course, Allâh is Better).

أَمَّنْ خَلَقَ ٱلسَّمَـٰوَٰتِ وَٱلْأَرْضَ وَأَنزَلَ لَكُم مِّنَ ٱلسَّمَآءِ مَآءً فَأَنۢبَتۡنَا بِهِۦ حَدَآئِقَ ذَاتَ بَهْجَةٍ مَّا كَانَ لَكُمْ أَن تُنۢبِتُواْ شَجَرَهَآ ۗ أَءِلَـٰهٌ مَّعَ ٱللَّهِ ۚ بَلْ هُمْ قَوْمٌ يَعْدِلُونَ ۝

60. Is not He (better than your gods) Who created the heavens and the earth, and sends down for you water (rain) from the sky, whereby We cause to grow wonderful gardens full of beauty and delight? It is not in your ability to cause the growth of their trees. Is there any ilâh (god) with Allâh? Nay, but they are a people who ascribe equals (to Him)!

Transliteration

59. Quli alhamdu lillahi wasalamun AAala AAibadihi allatheena istafa allahu khayrun amma yushrikoona 60. Amman khalaqa alssamawati waal-arda waanzala lakum mina alssama-i maan faanbatna bihi hada-iqa thata bahjatin ma kana lakum an tunbitoo shajaraha a-ilahun maAAa Allahi bal hum qawmun yaAAdiloona

Tafsir Ibn Kathir

The Command to praise Allah and send Blessings on His Messengers

Allah commands His Messenger to say:

(Praise and thanks be to Allah,) meaning, for His innumerable blessings upon His servants and for His exalted Attributes and most beautiful Names. And He commands him to send peace upon the servants of Allah whom He chose and selected, i.e., His noble Messengers and Prophets, may the best of peace and blessings from Allah be upon them. This was the view of `Abdur-Rahman bin Zayd bin Aslam and others; the meaning of the servants He has chose is the Prophets. He said, "This like He said in the Ayah;

(Glorified be your Lord, the Lord of honor and power! (He is free) from what they attribute unto Him! And peace be on the Messengers! And all the praises and thanks be to Allah, Lord of all that exists.) (37:180-182)." Ath-Thawri and As-Suddi said, "This refers to the Companions of Muhammad , may Allah be pleased with them all." Something similar was also narrated from Ibn `Abbas, and there is no contradiction between the two views, because they were also among the servants of Allah whom He had chosen, although the description is more befitting of the Prophets.

(Is Allah better, or what they ascribe as partners (to Him)) This is a question aimed at denouncing the idolators for their worship of other gods besides Allah. Some more Proofs of Tawhid Then Allah begins to explain that He is the Only One Who creates, provides and controls, as He says:

(Is not He Who created the heavens) meaning, He created those heavens which are so high and serene, with their shining stars and revolving planets. And He created the earth, with its varying heights and densities, and He created everything in it, mountains, hills, plains, rugged terrain, wildernesses, crops, trees, fruits, seas and animals of all different kinds and colors and shapes, etc.

(and sends down for you water from the sky,) means, He sends it as a provision for His servants,

(whereby We cause to grow wonderful gardens full of beauty and delight) means, beautiful and delightful to behold.

(It is not in your ability to cause the growth of their trees.) meaning, `you are not able to cause their trees to grow. The One Who is able to do that is the Creator and Provider, Who is doing all this Alone and Independent of any idol and other rival.' The idolators themselves admitted this, as Allah says in another Ayah:

(And if you ask them: "Who has created them" they will certainly say: "Allah.") (31:25)

(And if you were to ask them: "Who sends down water from the sky, and gives life therewith to the earth after its death" they will surely reply: "Allah.") (29:63) Meaning they will admit that He is the One Who does all these things, Alone, with no partner or associate, but then they worship others alongside Him, others who they admit cannot create or provide anything. But the Only One Who deserves to be worshipped is the Only One Who can create and provide, Allah says:

(Is there any god with Allah) meaning, `is there any god that can be worshipped alongside Allah, when it is clear to you and anyone who with reason that He is the Creator and Provider, as you yourselves admit' Then Allah says:

(Nay, but they are a people who ascribe equals (to Him)!) meaning, they describe others as being equal and comparable to Allah.

Surah: 27 Ayah: 61

أَمَّن جَعَلَ ٱلْأَرْضَ قَرَارًا وَجَعَلَ خِلَٰلَهَآ أَنْهَٰرًا وَجَعَلَ لَهَا رَوَٰسِىَ وَجَعَلَ بَيْنَ ٱلْبَحْرَيْنِ حَاجِزًا ۗ أَءِلَٰهٌ مَّعَ ٱللَّهِ ۚ بَلْ أَكْثَرُهُمْ لَا يَعْلَمُونَ ۝

61. Is not He (better than your gods) Who has made the earth as a fixed abode, and has placed rivers in its midst, and has placed firm mountains therein, and has set a barrier between the two seas (of salt and sweet water)? Is there any ilâh (god) with Allâh? Nay, but most of them know not.

Transliteration

61. Amman jaAAala al-arda qararan wajaAAala khilalaha anharan wajaAAala laha rawasiya wajaAAala bayna albahrayni hajizan a-ilahun maAAa Allahi bal aktharuhum la yaAAlamoona

Tafsir Ibn Kathir

Allah says:

(Is not He Who has made the earth as a fixed abode,) meaning, stable and stationary, so that it does not move or convulse, because if it were to do so, it would not be a good place for people to live on. But by His grace and mercy, He has made it smooth and calm, and it is not shaken or moved. This is like the Ayah,

(Allah, Who has made for you the earth as a dwelling place and the sky as a canopy) (40:64).

(and has placed rivers in its midst,) means, He has placed rivers which are fresh and sweet, cutting through the earth, and He has made them of different types, large rivers, small rivers and some in between. He has caused them to flow in all directions, east, west, south, north, according to the needs of mankind in different areas and regions, as He has created them throughout the world and sends them their provision according to their needs.

(and has placed firm mountains therein,) means, high mountains which stabilize the earth and make it steadfast, so that it does not shake.

(and has set a barrier between the two seas) means, He has placed a barrier between the fresh water and the salt water, to prevent them from mixing lest they corrupt one another. Divine wisdom dictates that each of them should stay as it is meant to be. The sweet water is that which flows in rivers among mankind, and it is meant to be fresh and palatable so that it may be used to water animals and plants and fruits. The salt water is that which surrounds the continents on all sides, and its water is meant to be salty and undrinkable lest the air be corrupted by its smell, as Allah says:

(And it is He Who has let free the two seas, this is palatable and sweet, and that is salty and bitter; and He has set a barrier and a complete partition between them.) (25:53) Allah says:

(Is there any god with Allah) meaning, any god who could do this, or who deserves to be worshipped Both meanings are indicated by the context.

(Nay, but most of them know not!) means, in that they worship others than Allah.

Surah: 27 Ayah: 62

أَمَّن يُجِيبُ ٱلْمُضْطَرَّ إِذَا دَعَاهُ وَيَكْشِفُ ٱلسُّوٓءَ وَيَجْعَلُكُمْ خُلَفَآءَ ٱلْأَرْضِ ۗ أَءِلَٰهٌ مَّعَ ٱللَّهِ ۚ قَلِيلًا مَّا تَذَكَّرُونَ ۝

62. Is not He (better than your gods) Who responds to the distressed one, when he calls on Him, and Who removes the evil, and makes you inheritors of the earth, generations after generations? Is there any ilâh (god) with Allâh? Little is that you remember!

Transliteration

62. Amman yujeebu almudtarra itha daAAahu wayakshifu alsoo-a wayajAAalukum khulafaa al-ardi a-ilahun maAAa Allahi qaleelan ma tathakkaroona

Tafsir Ibn Kathir

Allah points out that He is the One upon Whom people call in times of difficulty, and He is the One to Whom they turn when calamity strikes, as He says elsewhere:

(And when harm touches you upon the sea, those that you call upon vanish from you except Him) (17:67),

(Then, when harm touches you, unto Him you cry aloud for help) (16:53). Similarly, Allah says here:

(Is not He Who responds to the distressed one, when he calls on Him,) meaning, Who is the only One to Whom the person in desperate need turns, and the only One Who can relieve those who are stricken by harm Imam Ahmad reported that a man of Balhajim said: "O Messenger of Allah, what are you calling for" He said:

«أَدْعُو إِلَى اللهِ وَحْدَهُ الَّذِي إِنْ مَسَّكَ ضُرٌّ فَدَعَوْتَهُ كَشَفَ عَنْكَ، وَالَّذِي إِنْ أَضْلَلْتَ بِأَرْضٍ قَفْرٍ فَدَعَوْتَهُ رَدَّ عَلَيْكَ، وَالَّذِي إِنْ أَصَابَتْكَ سَنَةٌ فَدَعَوْتَهُ أَنْبَتَ لَكَ»

(I am calling people to Allah Alone, the One Who, if you call on Him when harm befalls you, will relieve you; and when you are lost in the wilderness, you call on Him and He brings you back: and when drought (famine) strikes, you call on Him and He makes your crops grow.) He said: "Advise me." He said:

«لَا تَسُبَّنَّ أَحَدًا وَلَا تَزْهَدَنَّ فِي الْمَعْرُوفِ، وَلَوْ أَنْ تَلْقَى أَخَاكَ وَأَنْتَ مُنْبَسِطٌ إِلَيْهِ وَجْهُكَ، وَلَوْ أَنْ تُفْرِغَ مِنْ دَلْوِكَ فِي إِنَاءِ الْمُسْتَقِي، وَاتَّزِرْ إِلَى نِصْفِ السَّاقِ فَإِنْ أَبَيْتَ فَإِلَى الْكَعْبَيْنِ، وَإِيَّاكَ وَإِسْبَالَ الْإِزَارِ فَإِنَّ إِسْبَالَ الْإِزَارِ مِنَ الْمَخِيلَةِ وَإِنَّ اللهَ لَا يُحِبُّ الْمَخِيلَةَ»

(Do not slander anyone and do not think of any good deed as insignificant, even if it is only meeting your brother with a cheerful face or emptying your vessel into the vessel of one who is asking for water. Wear your lower garment at mid-calf length, or -- if you insist -- let it reach your ankles, and beware of lowering the garment below the ankles along the ground, for it is a form of showing-off, and Allah does not like showing-off.)

The Story of a Mujahid who fought for the sake of Allah

In his biography of Fatimah bint Al-Hasan Umm Ahmad Al-`Ajaliyyah, Al-Hafiz bin `Asakir reported that she said: "One day the disbelievers defeated the Muslims in a battle. There was a good horse which belonged to a rich man who was also righteous. The horse just stood there, so its owner said, `What is the matter with you Woe to you! I was only preparing you for a day such as this.' The horse said to him: `How can you expect me not to perform badly, when you delegated my feeding to the grooms, and they mistreated me and only fed me a little' The man said, `I make you a promise before Allah that from this day on, only I will feed you from my own lap.' So the horse began to run, and his owner was saved, and after that he only ever fed the horse from his own lap. This story became well known among the people, and they started to come to him to hear the story from his own lips. News of this reached the king of Byzantium, and he said: `A city where this man is, will be kept safe from harm.' He wanted to bring the man to his own city, so he sent an apostate (a man who had left Islam) who was living in his city to go to him, and when he reached him, he pretended that his intentions towards Islam and its followers were good, so the Mujahid trusted him. One day they went out walking along the shore, but the apostate made a pact with another person, a follower of the Byzantine king, to come and help him take the Mujahid prisoner. When they made their move, he lifted his gaze to the sky and said, `O Allah! He has deceived me by swearing in Your Name, so protect me in whatever way You will.' Then two wild animals came out and seized them, and the Mujahid came back safe and sound. " The Inheritance of the Earth

(and makes you inheritors of the earth,) means, each generation inherits from the generation that came before them, one after the other, as Allah says:

(if He wills, He can destroy you, and in your place make whom He wills as your successors, as He raised you from the seed of other people) (6:133),

(And it is He Who has made you generations coming after generations, replacing each other on the earth. And He has raised you in ranks, some above others) (6:165),

(And (remember) when your Lord said to the angels: "Verily, I am going to place generations after generations on earth.") (2:30) meaning, people who will come after one another, as we have already stated. Allah's saying:

(and makes you inheritors of the earth,) means, nation after nation, generation after generation, people after people. If He had willed, He could have created them all at one time, and not made some of them the offspring of others. If He had willed, He could have created them all together, as He created Adam from dust. If He had willed, He could have made some of them the offspring of others, but not caused any of them to die until they all died at one time; in this case the earth would have become constricted for them and it would be too difficult for them to live and earn a living, and they would have caused inconvenience and harm to one another. But His wisdom and decree ruled that they should be created from one soul, then their numbers should be greatly increased, so He created them on the earth and made them generation after generation, nation after nation, until their time will come to an end and there will be no one left on earth, as Allah has decreed and as He has completely counted out their numbers. Then the Resurrection will come to pass, and each person will be rewarded or punished according to his deeds. Allah says:

(Is not He Who responds to the distressed one, when he calls on Him, and Who removes the evil, and makes you inheritors of the earth, generations after generations Is there any god with Allah) meaning, is there anyone else able to do that, or a god with Allah worth worshipping -- while you know that He is the only one who can do that, having no partners

(Little is that you remember!) meaning, how little they think about that which would guide them to the truth and show them the straight path.

Surah: 27 Ayah: 63

أَمَّن يَهْدِيكُمْ فِى ظُلُمَـٰتِ ٱلْبَرِّ وَٱلْبَحْرِ وَمَن يُرْسِلُ ٱلرِّيَـٰحَ بُشْرًۢا بَيْنَ يَدَىْ رَحْمَتِهِۦٓ ۗ أَءِلَـٰهٌ مَّعَ ٱللَّهِ ۚ تَعَـٰلَى ٱللَّهُ عَمَّا يُشْرِكُونَ ۝

63. Is not He (better than your gods) Who guides you in the darkness of the land and the sea, and Who sends the winds as heralds of glad tidings, going before His Mercy (rain)? Is there any ilâh (god) with Allâh? High Exalted is Allâh above all that they associate as partners (to Him)!

Transliteration

63. Amman yahdeekum fee thulumati albarri waalbahri waman yursilu alrriyaha bushran bayna yaday rahmatihi a-ilahun maAAa Allahi taAAala Allahu AAamma yushrikoona

Tafsir Ibn Kathir

Allah says,

(Is not He Who guides you in the darkness of the land and the sea,) meaning, by means of what He has created of heavenly and earthly signposts. This is like the Ayah,

(And landmarks and by the stars, they guide themselves.) (16:16)

(It is He Who has set the stars for you, so that you may guide your course with their help through the darkness of the land and the sea...) (6:97)

(and Who sends the winds as heralds of glad tidings, going before His mercy) meaning, ahead of the clouds which bring rain, by means of which Allah shows His mercy to His servants who are suffering drought and despair.

(Is there any god with Allah Exalted be Allah above all that they associate as partners!)

Surah: 27 Ayah: 64

أَمَّن يَبْدَؤُاْ ٱلْخَلْقَ ثُمَّ يُعِيدُهُۥ وَمَن يَرْزُقُكُم مِّنَ ٱلسَّمَآءِ وَٱلْأَرْضِ ۗ أَءِلَـٰهٌ مَّعَ ٱللَّهِ ۚ قُلْ هَاتُواْ بُرْهَـٰنَكُمْ إِن كُنتُمْ صَـٰدِقِينَ ۝

64. Is not He (better than your so-called gods) Who originates creation, and shall thereafter repeat it, and Who provides for you from heaven and earth? Is there any ilâh (god) with Allâh? Say: "Bring forth your proofs, if you are truthful."

Transliteration

64. Amman yabdao alkhalqa thumma yuAAeeduhu waman yarzuqukum mina alssama-i waal-ardi a-ilahun maAAa Allahi qul hatoo burhanakum in kuntum sadiqeena

Tafsir Ibn Kathir

He is the One Who, by His might and power, originates creation and then repeats it. This is like the Ayat:

(Verily, the punishment of your Lord is severe and painful. Verily, He it is Who begins and repeats.) (85:12-13)

(And He it is Who originates the creation, then He will repeat it; and this is easier for Him.) (30:27)

(and Who provides for you from heaven and earth) with the rain He sends down from the sky causing the blessings of the earth to grow, as He says elsewhere:

(By the sky which gives rain, again and again. And the earth which splits.) (86:11-12)

(He knows that which goes into the earth and that which comes forth from it, and that which descends from the heaven and that which ascends to it) (34:2). Allah, may He be blessed and exalted, sends down water from the sky as a blessing, and causes it to penetrate the earth, and then come forth as springs. After that, by means of the water He brings forth all kinds of crops, fruits and flowers, in all their different forms and colors.

(Eat and pasture your cattle; verily, in this are signs for men of understanding) (20:54). Allah says:

(Is there any god with Allah) meaning, who did this Or, according to another interpretation: after this (who could be worth worship)

(Say: "Bring forth your proofs, if you are truthful.") Produce the evidence of that. But it is known that they have no proof or evidence, as Allah says:

(And whoever invokes besides Allah, any other god, of whom he has no proof; then his reckoning is only with his Lord. Surely, the disbelievers will not be successful.) (23:117)

Surah: 27 Ayah: 65 & Ayah: 66

قُل لَّا يَعْلَمُ مَن فِي ٱلسَّمَـٰوَٰتِ وَٱلْأَرْضِ ٱلْغَيْبَ إِلَّا ٱللَّهُ ۚ وَمَا يَشْعُرُونَ أَيَّانَ يُبْعَثُونَ ۝

65. Say: "None in the heavens and the earth knows the Ghaib (Unseen) except Allâh, nor can they perceive when they shall be resurrected."

بَلِ ٱدَّٰرَكَ عِلْمُهُمْ فِي ٱلْـَٔاخِرَةِ ۚ بَلْ هُمْ فِي شَكٍّ مِّنْهَا ۖ بَلْ هُم مِّنْهَا عَمُونَ ۝

66. Nay, they have no knowledge of the Hereafter. Nay, they are in doubt about it. Nay, they are in complete blindness about it.

Transliteration

65. Qul la yaAAlamu man fee alssamawati waal-ardi alghayba illa Allahu wama yashAAuroona ayyana yubAAathoona 66. Bali iddaraka AAilmuhum fee al-akhirati bal hum fee shakkin minha bal hum minha AAamoona

Tafsir Ibn Kathir

The One Who knows the Unseen is Allah

Allah commands His Messenger to inform all of creation that no one among the dwellers of heaven and earth knows the Unseen, except Allah.

(except Allah) This is an absolute exception, meaning that no one knows this besides Allah, He is alone in that regard, having no partner in that knowledge. This is like the Ayat:

(And with Him are the keys of the Unseen, none knows them but He) (6:59).

(Verily, Allah, with Him is the knowledge of the Hour, He sends down the rain) (31:34). until the end of the Surah. And there are many Ayat which mention similar things.

(nor can they perceive when they shall be resurrected.) That is, the created beings who dwell in the heavens and on earth do not know when the Hour will occur, as Allah says:

(Heavy is its burden through the heavens and the earth. It shall not come upon you except all of a sudden) (7: 187). meaning, it is a grave matter for the dwellers of heaven and earth.

(Nay, their knowledge will perceive that in the Hereafter. Nay, they are in doubt about it.) means their knowledge and amazement stops short of knowing its time. Other scholars read this with the meaning "their knowledge is all the same with regard to that," which reflects the meaning of the Hadith in Sahih Muslim which states that the Messenger of Allah said to Jibril, when the latter asked him when the Hour would come:

«مَا الْمَسْؤُولُ عَنْهَا بِأَعْلَمَ مِنَ السَّائِلِ»

(The one who is being asked about it does not know any more than the one who is asking.) In other words, they were both equal in the fact that their knowledge did not extend that far.

(Nay, they are in doubt about it.) This refers to the disbelievers in general as Allah says elsewhere:

(And they will be set before your Lord in rows, (and Allah will say:) "Now indeed, you have come to Us as We created you the first time. Nay, but you thought that We had appointed no meeting for you (with Us). ") (18:48) i.e., the disbelievers among you. By the same token, Allah says here:

(Nay, they are in doubt about it.) meaning, they doubt that it will come to pass.

(Nay, they are in complete blindness about it.) They are blind and completely ignorant about it.

Surah: 27 Ayah: 67, Ayah: 68, Ayah: 69 & Ayah: 70

وَقَالَ ٱلَّذِينَ كَفَرُوٓاْ أَءِذَا كُنَّا تُرَٰبًا وَءَابَآؤُنَآ أَئِنَّا لَمُخْرَجُونَ ۝

67. And those who disbelieve say: "When we have become dust - we and our fathers - shall we really be brought forth (again)?

Chapter 27: An-Naml (The Ant, The Ants), Verses 056-093

لَقَدْ وُعِدْنَا هَـٰذَا نَحْنُ وَءَابَآؤُنَا مِن قَبْلُ إِنْ هَـٰذَآ إِلَّآ أَسَـٰطِيرُ ٱلْأَوَّلِينَ ﴿٦٨﴾

68. "Indeed we were promised this - we and our forefathers before (us), Verily, these are nothing but tales of ancients."

قُلْ سِيرُوا۟ فِى ٱلْأَرْضِ فَٱنظُرُوا۟ كَيْفَ كَانَ عَـٰقِبَةُ ٱلْمُجْرِمِينَ ﴿٦٩﴾

69. Say to them (O Muhammad (peace be upon him)) "Travel in the land and see how has been the end of the Mujrimûn (criminals, those who denied Allâh's Messengers and disobeyed Allâh)."

وَلَا تَحْزَنْ عَلَيْهِمْ وَلَا تَكُن فِى ضَيْقٍ مِّمَّا يَمْكُرُونَ ﴿٧٠﴾

70. And grieve you not over them, nor be straitened (in distress) because of what they plot.

Transliteration

67. Waqala allatheena kafaroo a-itha kunna turaban waabaona a-inna lamukhrajoona 68. Laqad wuAAidna hatha nahnu waabaona min qablu in hatha illa asateeru alawwaleena 69. Qul seeroo fee al-ardi faonthuroo kayfa kana AAaqibatu almujrimeena 70. Wala tahzan AAalayhim wala takun fee dayqin mimma yamkuroona

Tafsir Ibn Kathir

Scepticism about the Resurrection and Its Refutation

Allah tells us about the idolators who deny the Resurrection, considering it extremely unlikely that bodies will be re-created after they have become bones and dust. Then He says:

(Indeed we were promised this -- we and our forefathers before,) meaning, `we and our forefathers have been hearing this for a long time, but in reality, we have never seen it happen.'

(verily, these are nothing but tales of ancients.) the promises that bodies will be restored are

(nothing but tales of ancients.) meaning that they were taken by the people who came before us from books which were handed down from one to the other, but they have no basis in reality. Responding to their thoughts of disbelief and their belief that there would be no Resurrection, Allah said,

(Say) `O Muhammad, to these people,'

(Travel in the land and see how has been the end of the criminals.) meaning, those who denied the Messengers and their message of the Resurrection and other matters. See how the punishment and vengeance of Allah struck them and how Allah saved from among them the noble Messengers and the believers who followed them. This will be an indication of the truth of the Message brought by the Messengers. Then, to comfort the Prophet, Allah says:

(And grieve you not over them,) meaning, 'but do not feel sorry for them or kill yourself with regret for them,'

(nor be straitened because of what they plot.) means, 'because they plot against you and reject what you have brought, for Allah will help and support you, and cause your religion to prevail over those who oppose you and stubbornly resist you in the east and in the west.'

Surah: 27 Ayah: 71, Ayah: 72, Ayah: 73, Ayah: 74 & Ayah: 75

وَيَقُولُونَ مَتَىٰ هَـٰذَا ٱلْوَعْدُ إِن كُنتُمْ صَـٰدِقِينَ ۝

71. And they (the disbelievers in the Oneness of Allâh) say: "When (will) this promise (be fulfilled), if you are truthful?"

قُلْ عَسَىٰٓ أَن يَكُونَ رَدِفَ لَكُم بَعْضُ ٱلَّذِى تَسْتَعْجِلُونَ ۝

72. Say: "Perhaps that which you wish to hasten on, may be close behind you.

وَإِنَّ رَبَّكَ لَذُو فَضْلٍ عَلَى ٱلنَّاسِ وَلَـٰكِنَّ أَكْثَرَهُمْ لَا يَشْكُرُونَ ۝

73. "Verily, your Lord is full of Grace for mankind, yet most of them do not give thanks."

وَإِنَّ رَبَّكَ لَيَعْلَمُ مَا تُكِنُّ صُدُورُهُمْ وَمَا يُعْلِنُونَ ۝

74. And verily, your Lord knows what their breasts conceal and what they reveal.

وَمَا مِنْ غَآئِبَةٍ فِى ٱلسَّمَآءِ وَٱلْأَرْضِ إِلَّا فِى كِتَـٰبٍ مُّبِينٍ ۝

75. And there is nothing hidden in the heaven and the earth but it is in a Clear Book (i.e. Al-Lauh Al-Mahfûz).

Transliteration

71. Wayaqooloona mata hatha alwaAAdu in kuntum sadiqeena 72. Qul AAasa an yakoona radifa lakum baAAdu allathee tastaAAjiloona 73. Wa-inna rabbaka lathoo fadlin AAala alnnasi walakinna aktharahum la yashkuroona 74. Wa-inna rabbaka layaAAlamu ma tukinnu sudooruhum wama yuAAlinoona 75. Wama min gha-ibatin fee alssama-i waal-ardi illa fee kitabin mubeenin

Tafsir Ibn Kathir

Allah tells us about how the idolators asked about the Day of Resurrection, but thought it unlikely that it would ever come to pass.

(And they say: "When (will) this promise (be fulfilled), if you are truthful") Allah said, responding to them:

(Say) `O Muhammad,'

(Perhaps that which you wish to hasten on, may be close behind you.) Ibn `Abbas said, "That which you wish to hasten on has come close to you, or some of it has come close." This was also the view of Mujahid, Ad-Dahhak, `Ata Al-Khurasani, Qatadah and As-Suddi. This is also what is meant in the Ayat:

(And they say: "When will that be" Say: "Perhaps it is near!") (17:51)

(They ask you to hasten on the torment. And verily, Hell, of a surety, will encompass the disbelievers) (29:54).

(may be close behind you.) means, it is being hastened for you. This was reported from Mujahid. Then Allah says:

(Verily, your Lord is full of grace for mankind,) meaning, He abundantly bestows His blessings on them even though they wrong themselves, yet despite that they do not give thanks for those blessings, except for a few of them.

(And verily, your Lord knows what their breasts conceal and what they reveal.) means, He knows what is hidden in their hearts just as He knows what is easily visible.

(It is the same (to Him) whether any of you conceals his speech or declares it openly) (13:10),

(He knows the secret and that which is yet more hidden) (20: 7),

(Surely, even when they cover themselves with their garments, He knows what they conceal and what they reveal) (11:5). Then Allah tells us that He is the Knower of the unseen in the heavens and on earth, and that He is the Knower of the unseen and the seen, i.e., that which is unseen by His servants and that which they can see. And Allah says: (and there is nothing hidden) Ibn `Abbas said, "This means, there is nothing

(in the heaven and the earth but it is in a Clear Book.) This is like the Ayah,

(Know you not that Allah knows all that is in the heaven and on the earth Verily, it is (all) in the Book. Verily, that is easy for Allah.) (22:70)

Surah: 27 Ayah: 76, Ayah: 77, Ayah: 78, Ayah: 79, Ayah: 80 & Ayah: 81

إِنَّ هَٰذَا ٱلْقُرْءَانَ يَقُصُّ عَلَىٰ بَنِىٓ إِسْرَٰٓءِيلَ أَكْثَرَ ٱلَّذِى هُمْ فِيهِ يَخْتَلِفُونَ ۝

76. Verily, this Qur'ân narrates to the Children of Israel most of that in which they differ.

$$\text{وَإِنَّهُۥ لَهُدًى وَرَحْمَةٌ لِّلْمُؤْمِنِينَ ﴿٧٧﴾}$$

77. And truly, it (this Qur'ân) is a guide and a mercy for the believers.

$$\text{إِنَّ رَبَّكَ يَقْضِى بَيْنَهُم بِحُكْمِهِۦ ۚ وَهُوَ ٱلْعَزِيزُ ٱلْعَلِيمُ ﴿٧٨﴾}$$

78. Verily, your Lord will decide between them (various sects) by His Judgement. And He is the All-Mighty, the All-Knowing.

$$\text{فَتَوَكَّلْ عَلَى ٱللَّهِ ۖ إِنَّكَ عَلَى ٱلْحَقِّ ٱلْمُبِينِ ﴿٧٩﴾}$$

79. So put your trust in Allâh; surely, you (O Muhammad (peace be upon him)) are on manifest truth.

$$\text{إِنَّكَ لَا تُسْمِعُ ٱلْمَوْتَىٰ وَلَا تُسْمِعُ ٱلصُّمَّ ٱلدُّعَآءَ إِذَا وَلَّوْاْ مُدْبِرِينَ ﴿٨٠﴾}$$

80. Verily, you cannot make the dead to hear nor can you make the deaf to hear the call (i.e. benefit them and similarly the disbelievers), when they flee, turning their backs.

$$\text{وَمَآ أَنتَ بِهَـٰدِى ٱلْعُمْىِ عَن ضَلَـٰلَتِهِمْ ۖ إِن تُسْمِعُ إِلَّا مَن يُؤْمِنُ بِـَٔايَـٰتِنَا فَهُم مُّسْلِمُونَ ﴿٨١﴾}$$

81. Nor can you lead the blind out of their error. You can only make to hear those who believe in Our Ayât (proofs, evidences, verses, lessons, signs, revelations, etc.), and who have submitted (themselves to Allâh in Islâm as Muslims).

Transliteration

76. Inna hatha alqur-ana yaqussu AAala banee isra-eela akthara allathee hum feehi yakhtalifoona

77. Wa-innahu lahudan warahmatun lilmu/mineena

78. Inna rabbaka yaqdee baynahum bihukmihi wahuwa alAAazeezu alAAaleemu

79. Fatawakkal AAala Allahi innaka AAala alhaqqi almubeeni

80. Innaka la tusmiAAu almawta wala tusmiAAu alssumma aldduAAaa itha wallaw mudbireena

81. Wama anta bihadee alAAumyi AAan dalalatihim in tusmiAAu illa man yu/minu biayatina fahum muslimoona

Chapter 27: An-Naml (The Ant, The Ants), Verses 056-093

Tafsir Ibn Kathir

The Qur'an tells the Story of the Differences among the Children of Israel, and Allah judges between Them

Allah tells us about His Book and the guidance, proof and criterion between right and wrong that it contains. He tells us about the Children of Israel, who were the bearers of the Tawrah and Injil.

(most of that in which they differ.) such as their different opinions about `Isa. The Jews lied about him while the Christians exaggerated in praise for him, so the Qur'an came with the moderate word of truth and justice: that he was one of the servants of Allah, and one of His noble Prophets and Messengers, may the best of peace and blessings be upon him, as the Qur'an says: (Such is `Isa, son of Maryam. (It is) a statement of truth, about which they doubt) (19:34).

(And truly, it is a guide and a mercy for the believers.) meaning, it is guidance for the hearts of those who believe in it, and a mercy to them. Then Allah says: (Verily, your Lord will decide between them) meaning, on the Day of Resurrection,

(by His judgement. And He is the All-Mighty,) means, in His vengeance,

(the All-Knowing.) Who knows all that His servants do and say.

The Command to put One's Trust in Allah and to convey the Message

(So, put your trust in Allah;) in all your affairs, and convey the Message of your Lord.

(surely, you are on manifest truth.) meaning, you are following manifest truth, even though you are opposed by those who oppose you because they are doomed. The Word of your Lord has been justified against them, so that they will not believe even if all the signs are brought to them. Allah says:

(Verily, you cannot make the dead to hear) meaning, you cannot cause them to hear anything that will benefit them. The same applies to those over whose hearts is a veil and in whose ears is deafness of disbelief. Allah says:

(nor can you make the deaf to hear the call, when they flee, turning their backs. Nor can you lead the blind out of their error. You can only make to hear those who believe in Our Ayat, so they submit (became Muslims).) meaning, those who have hearing and insight will respond to you, those whose hearing and sight are of benefit to their hearts and who are humble towards Allah and to the Message that comes to them through the mouths of the Messengers, may peace be upon them.

Surah: 27 Ayah: 82

وَإِذَا وَقَعَ ٱلْقَوْلُ عَلَيْهِمْ أَخْرَجْنَا لَهُمْ دَابَّةً مِّنَ ٱلْأَرْضِ تُكَلِّمُهُمْ أَنَّ ٱلنَّاسَ كَانُوا۟ بِـَٔايَٰتِنَا لَا يُوقِنُونَ ۝

82. And when the Word (of torment) is fulfilled against them, We shall bring out from the earth a beast for them, to speak to them because mankind believed not with certainty in Our Ayât (Verses of the Qur'ân and Prophet Muhammad (peace be upon him))

Transliteration

82. Wa-itha waqaAAa alqawlu AAalayhim akhrajna lahum dabbatan mina al-ardi tukallimuhum anna alnnasa kanoo bi-ayatina la yooqinoona

Tafsir Ibn Kathir

The Emergence of the Beast of the Earth

This is the beast which will emerge at the end of time, when mankind has become corrupt and neglected the commands of Allah and changed the true religion. Then Allah will cause a beast to emerge from the earth. It was said that it will be brought from Makkah, or from somewhere else, as we shall discuss in detail below, if Allah wills. The beast will speak to people about matters. Ibn `Abbas, Al-Hasan and Qatadah said, and it was also narrated from `Ali, may Allah be pleased with him, that it will speak words, meaning, it will address them. Many Hadiths and reports have been narrated about the beast, and we will narrate as many of them as Allah enables us to, for He is the One Whose help we seek. Imam Ahmad recorded that Hudhayfah bin Asid Al-Ghifari said, "The Messenger of Allah came out from his room while we were discussing the matter of the Hour. He said:

«لَا تَقُومُ السَّاعَةُ حَتَّى تَرَوْا عَشْرَ آيَاتٍ: طُلُوعُ الشَّمْسِ مِنْ مَغْرِبِهَا، وَالدُّخَانُ وَالدَّابَّةُ وَخُرُوجُ يَأْجُوجَ وَمَأْجُوجَ، وَخُرُوجُ عِيسَى ابْنِ مَرْيَمَ عَلَيْهِ السَّلَامُ، وَالدَّجَّالُ، وَثَلَاثَةُ خُسُوفٍ: خَسْفٌ بِالْمَغْرِبِ، وَخَسْفٌ بِالْمَشْرِقِ، وَخَسْفٌ بِجَزِيرَةِ الْعَرَبِ، وَنَارٌ تَخْرُجُ مِنْ قَعْرِ عَدَنٍ تَسُوقُ أَوْ تَحْشُرُ النَّاسَ، تَبِيتُ مَعَهُمْ حَيْثُ بَاتُوا وَتَقِيلُ مَعَهُمْ حَيْثُ قَالُوا»

(The Hour will not come until you see ten signs: the rising of the sun from the west; the smoke (Ad-Dukhan); emergence of the beast; the emergence of Ya'juj and Ma'juj; the appearance of `Isa bin Maryam, upon him be peace; the Dajjal; and three land cave-ins, one in the west, one in the east and one in the Arabian Peninsula; and a Fire which will emerge from the midst of Yemen, and will drive or gather the people, stopping with them whenever they stop for the night or to rest during the day.)" This was also recorded by Muslim and the Sunan compilers from Hudhayfah, in a Mawquf report. At-Tirmidhi said, "It is Hasan Sahih." It was also recorded by Muslim from Hudhayfah in a Marfu` report. And Allah knows best.

Chapter 27: An-Naml (The Ant, The Ants), Verses 056-093

Another Hadith

Muslim bin Al-Hajjaj recorded that `Abdullah bin `Amr said, "I memorized a Hadith from the Messenger of Allah which I never forgot afterwards. I heard the Messenger of Allah say:

«إِنَّ أَوَّلَ الْآيَاتِ خُرُوجًا طُلُوعُ الشَّمْسِ مِنْ مَغْرِبِهَا، وَخُرُوجُ الدَّابَّةِ عَلَى النَّاسِ ضُحًى، وَأَيَّتُهُمَا مَا كَانَتْ قَبْلَ صَاحِبَتِهَا فَالْأُخْرَى عَلَى إِثْرِهَا قَرِيبًا»

(The first of the signs to appear will be the rising of the sun from the west, and the emergence of the beast to mankind in the forenoon. Whichever of them appears first, the other will follow close behind it.)

Another Hadith

In his Sahih, Muslim recorded that Abu Hurayrah, may Allah be pleased with him, said that the Messenger of Allah said:

«بَادِرُوا بِالْأَعْمَالِ سِتًّا، طُلُوعَ الشَّمْسِ مِنْ مَغْرِبِهَا، وَالدُّخَانَ، وَالدَّجَّالَ، وَالدَّابَّةَ، وَخَاصَّةَ أَحَدِكُمْ، وَأَمْرَ الْعَامَّةِ»

(Hasten to do good deeds before six things appear: the rising of the sun from the west; the smoke; the Dajjal; the beast; the (death) of one of your favorite, or general affliction.) This was recorded by Muslim alone.

Muslim also recorded that Abu Hurayrah, may Allah be pleased with him, said that the the Prophet said:

«بَادِرُوا بِالْأَعْمَالِ سِتًّا: الدَّجَّالَ، وَالدُّخَانَ، وَدَابَّةَ الْأَرْضِ، وَطُلُوعَ الشَّمْسِ مِنْ مَغْرِبِهَا، وَأَمْرَ الْعَامَّةِ، وَخُوَيْصَّةَ أَحَدِكُمْ»

(Hasten to do good deeds before six things appear: the Dajjal; the smoke; the beast of the earth; the rising of the sun from the west; and the (death of one of your favorite) or general affliction.)

Another Hadith

Ibn Majah recorded from Anas bin Malik that the Messenger of Allah said:

«بَادِرُوا بِالْأَعْمَالِ سِتًّا: طُلُوعَ الشَّمْسِ مِنْ مَغْرِبِهَا، وَالدُّخَانَ، وَالدَّابَّةَ،

«الدَّجَّالَ، وَخُوَيْصَّةَ أَحَدِكُمْ، وَأَمْرَ الْعَامَّةِ»

(Hasten to do good deeds before six things appear: the rising of the sun from the west; the smoke; the beast; the Dajjal; and the (death of one of your favorite) or general affliction.) He was the only one who recorded this version.

Another Hadith

Abu Dawud At-Tayalisi recorded from Abu Hurayrah, may Allah be pleased with him, that the Messenger of Allah said:

«تَخْرُجُ دَابَّةُ الْأَرْضِ وَمَعَهَا عَصَا مُوسَى وَخَاتَمُ سُلَيْمَانَ عَلَيْهِمَا السَّلَامُ، فَتَخْطِمُ أَنْفَ الْكَافِرِ بِالْعَصَا، وَتُجَلِّي وَجْهَ الْمُؤْمِنِ بِالْخَاتَمِ، حَتَّى يَجْتَمِعَ النَّاسُ عَلَى الْخِوَانِ يُعْرَفُ الْمُؤْمِنُ مِنَ الْكَافِرِ»

(A beast will emerge from the earth, and with it will be the staff of Musa and the ring of Sulayman, peace be upon them both. It will strike the nose of the disbelievers with the staff, and it will make the face of the believer bright with the ring, until when people gather to eat, they will be able to recognize the believers from the disbelievers.) It also was recorded by Imam Ahmad, with the wording:

«فَتَخْطِمُ أَنْفَ الْكَافِرِ بِالْخَاتَمِ، وَتَجْلُو وَجْهَ الْمُؤْمِنِ بِالْعَصَا، حَتَّى إِنَّ أَهْلَ الْخِوَانِ الْوَاحِدِ لَيَجْتَمِعُونَ فَيَقُولُ هَذَا: يَا مُؤْمِنُ، وَيَقُولُ هَذَا: يَا كَافِرُ»

(It will strike the nose of the disbelievers with the ring, and will make the face of the believer bright with the staff, until when people gather for a meal, they will say to one another, O believer, or O disbeliever.) It was also recorded by Ibn Majah. Ibn Jurayj reported that Ibn Az-Zubayr described the beast and said, "Its head is like the head of a bull, its eyes are like the eyes of a pig, its ears are like the ears of an elephant, its horns are like the horns of a stag, its neck is like the neck of an ostrich, its chest is like the chest of a lion, its color is like the colour of a tiger, its haunches are like the haunches of a cat, its tail is like the tail of a ram, and its legs are like the legs of a camel. Between each pair of its joints is a distance of twelve cubits. It will bring out with it the staff of Musa and the ring of Sulayman. There will be no believer left without it making a white spot on his face, which will spread until all his face is shining white as a result; and there will be no disbeliever left without it making a black spot on his face, which will spread until all his face is black as a result, then when the people trade with one another in the marketplace, they will say, `How much is this, O believer' `How much is this, O disbeliever' And when the members of one household sit down together to eat, they will know who is a believer and who is a

Chapter 27: An-Naml (The Ant, The Ants), Verses 056-093

disbeliever. Then the beast will say: `O so-and-so, enjoy yourself, for you are among the people of Paradise.' And it will say: `O so-and-so, you are among the people of Hell,' This is what Allah says:

(And when the Word is fulfilled against them, We shall bring out from the earth a beast for them, to speak to them because mankind believed not with certainty in Our Ayat.)

Surah: 27 Ayah: 83, Ayah: 84, Ayah: 85 & Ayah: 86

وَيَوْمَ نَحْشُرُ مِن كُلِّ أُمَّةٍ فَوْجًا مِّمَّن يُكَذِّبُ بِـَٔايَـٰتِنَا فَهُمْ يُوزَعُونَ ۝

83. And (remember) the Day when We shall gather out of every nation a troop of those who denied Our Ayât (proofs, evidences, verses, lessons, signs, revelations, etc.), and (then) they (all) shall be set in array (and driven to the place of reckoning),

حَتَّىٰٓ إِذَا جَآءُو قَالَ أَكَذَّبْتُم بِـَٔايَـٰتِى وَلَمْ تُحِيطُوا۟ بِهَا عِلْمًا أَمَّاذَا كُنتُمْ تَعْمَلُونَ ۝

84. Till, when they come (before their Lord at the place of reckoning), He will say: "Did you deny My Ayât (proofs, evidences, verses, lessons, signs, revelations, etc.) whereas you comprehended them not by knowledge (of their truth or falsehood), or what (else) was it that you used to do?"

وَوَقَعَ ٱلْقَوْلُ عَلَيْهِم بِمَا ظَلَمُوا۟ فَهُمْ لَا يَنطِقُونَ ۝

85. And the Word (of torment) will be fulfilled against them, because they have done wrong, and they will be unable to speak (in order to defend themselves).

أَلَمْ يَرَوْا۟ أَنَّا جَعَلْنَا ٱلَّيْلَ لِيَسْكُنُوا۟ فِيهِ وَٱلنَّهَارَ مُبْصِرًا ۚ إِنَّ فِى ذَٰلِكَ لَـَٔايَـٰتٍ لِّقَوْمٍ يُؤْمِنُونَ ۝

86. See they not that We have made the night for them to rest therein, and the day sight-giving? Verily, in this are Ayât (proofs, evidences, verses, lessons, signs, revelations, etc.) for the people who believe.

Transliteration

83. Wayawma nahshuru min kulli ommatin fawjan mimman yukaththibu bi-ayatina fahum yoozaAAoona 84. Hatta itha jaoo qala akaththabtum bi-ayatee walam tuheetoo biha AAilman ammatha kuntum taAAmaloona 85. WawaqaAAa alqawlu AAalayhim bima thalamoo fahum la yantiqoona 86. Alam yaraw anna jaAAalna allayla liyaskunoo feehi waalnnahara mubsiran inna fee thalika laayatin liqawmin yu/minoona

Tafsir Ibn Kathir

Gathering the Wrongdoers on the Day of Resurrection

Allah tells us about the Day of Resurrection when the wrongdoers who disbelieved in the signs and Messengers of Allah will be gathered before Allah, so that He will ask them about what they did in this world, rebuking, scolding and belittling them.

(And the Day when We shall gather out of every nation, a Fawj) means, from every people and generation a group

(of those who denied Our Ayat). This is like the Ayat:

("Assemble those who did wrong, together with their companions (from the devils).") (37:22)

(And when the souls are joined with their bodies) (81:7).

(and they shall be driven,) Ibn `Abbas, may Allah be pleased with him, said: "They will be pushed." `Abdur-Rahman bin Zayd bin Aslam said: "They will be driven."

(Till, when they come,) and stand before Allah, may He be glorified and exalted, in the place of reckoning,

(He will say: "Did you deny My Ayat whereas you comprehended them not by knowledge, or what was it that you used to do") meaning they will be asked about their beliefs and their deeds. Since they are among the doomed and, as Allah says:

(He neither believed nor performed Salah! But on the contrary, he denied and turned away!) (75:31-32) Then the proof will be established against them and they will have no excuse whatsoever, as Allah says:

(That will be a Day when they shall not speak. And they will not be permitted to put forth any excuse) (77:35-36). Similarly, Allah says here:

(And the Word will be fulfilled against them, because they have done wrong, and they will be unable to speak.) They will be stunned and speechless, unable to give any answer. This is because they wronged themselves in the world, and now they have returned to the One Who sees the unseen and the seen, from Whom nothing can be hidden. Then Allah points out His complete power, immense authority and greatness, all dictating that He is to be obeyed and that His commands must be followed, and that the message of inescapable truth brought by His Prophets must be believed in. Allah says:

(See they not that We have made the night for them to rest therein,) Due to the darkness of the night they halt their activities and calm themselves down, to recover from the exhausting efforts of the day.

(and the day sight-giving) meaning filled with light, so that they can work and earn a living, and travel and engage in business, and do other things that they need to do.

(Verily, in this are Ayat for the people who believe.)

Surah: 27 Ayah: 87, Ayah: 88, Ayah: 89 & Ayah: 90

$$\text{وَيَوْمَ يُنفَخُ فِى ٱلصُّورِ فَفَزِعَ مَن فِى ٱلسَّمَٰوَٰتِ وَمَن فِى ٱلْأَرْضِ إِلَّا مَن شَآءَ ٱللَّهُ ۚ وَكُلٌّ أَتَوْهُ دَٰخِرِينَ ۝}$$

87. And (remember) the Day on which the Trumpet will be blown - and all who are in the heavens and all who are on the earth, will be terrified except him whom Allâh will (exempt). And all shall come to Him, humbled.

$$\text{وَتَرَى ٱلْجِبَالَ تَحْسَبُهَا جَامِدَةً وَهِىَ تَمُرُّ مَرَّ ٱلسَّحَابِ ۚ صُنْعَ ٱللَّهِ ٱلَّذِىٓ أَتْقَنَ كُلَّ شَىْءٍ ۚ إِنَّهُۥ خَبِيرٌۢ بِمَا تَفْعَلُونَ ۝}$$

88. And you will see the mountains and think them solid, but they shall pass away as the passing away of the clouds. The Work of Allâh, Who perfected all things, verily He is Well-Acquainted with what you do.

$$\text{مَن جَآءَ بِٱلْحَسَنَةِ فَلَهُۥ خَيْرٌ مِّنْهَا وَهُم مِّن فَزَعٍ يَوْمَئِذٍ ءَامِنُونَ ۝}$$

89. Whoever brings a good deed (i.e. Belief in the Oneness of Allâh along with every deed of righteousness), will have better than its worth; and they will be safe from the terror on that Day.

$$\text{وَمَن جَآءَ بِٱلسَّيِّئَةِ فَكُبَّتْ وُجُوهُهُمْ فِى ٱلنَّارِ هَلْ تُجْزَوْنَ إِلَّا مَا كُنتُمْ تَعْمَلُونَ ۝}$$

90. And whoever brings an evil deed (i.e. Shirk - polytheism, disbelief in the Oneness of Allâh and every evil sinful deed), they will be cast down (prone) on their faces in the Fire. (And it will be said to them) "Are you being recompensed anything except what you used to do?"

Transliteration

87. Wayawma yunfakhu fee alssoori fafaziAAa man fee alssamawati waman fee al-ardi illa man shaa Allahu wakullun atawhu dakhireena 88. Watara aljibala tahsabuha jamidatan wahiya tamurru marra alssahabi sunAAa Allahi allathee atqana kulla shay-in innahu khabeerun bima tafAAaloona 89. Man jaa bialhasanati falahu khayrun minha wahum min fazaAAin yawma-ithin aminoona 90. Waman jaa bialssayyi-ati fakubbat wujoohuhum fee alnnari hal tujzawna illa ma kuntum taAAmaloona

Tafsir Ibn Kathir

The Terrors of the Day of Resurrection, the Rewards for Good Deeds and the Punishments for Evil Deeds

Allah tells us about the terrors of the Day when the Sur will be blown. The Sur, as described in the Hadith, is,

$$«قَرْنٌ يُنْفَخُ فِيهِ»$$

(a horn which is blown into.) According to the Hadith about the Sur (Trumpet), it is (the angel) Israfil who will blow into it by the command of Allah, may He be exalted. He will blow into it for the first time, for a long time. This will signal the end of the life of this world, and the Hour will come upon the most evil of people ever to live. Everyone who is in the heavens and on earth will be terrified,

(except him whom Allah wills.) these are the martyrs, for they are alive, with their Lord, and being provided for. Imam Muslim bin Al-Hajjaj recorded that `Abdullah bin `Amr, may Allah be pleased with him, said that a man came to him and said, "What is this Hadith that you are narrating, that the Hour will come upon such and such people" He said, "Subhan Allah or `La Ilaha Illallah (or something similar), I had decided that I would not narrate anything to anyone now. I had only said that after a little while, you will see a major event which will destroy the House (the Ka`bah), and such and such will happen." Then he said, "The Messenger of Allah said:

$$«يَخْرُجُ الدَّجَّالُ فِي أُمَّتِي فَيَمْكُثُ أَرْبَعِينَ لَا أَدْرِي أَرْبَعِينَ يَوْمًا أَوْ أَرْبَعِينَ شَهْرًا أَوْ أَرْبَعِينَ عَامًا فَيَبْعَثُ اللهُ عِيسَى ابْنَ مَرْيَمَ كَأَنَّهُ عُرْوَةُ بْنُ مَسْعُودٍ فَيَطْلُبُهُ فَيُهْلِكُهُ، ثُمَّ يَمْكُثُ النَّاسُ سَبْعَ سِنِينَ لَيْسَ بَيْنَ اثْنَيْنِ عَدَاوَةٌ، ثُمَّ يُرْسِلُ اللهُ رِيحًا بَارِدَةً مِنْ قِبَلِ الشَّامِ، فَلَا يَبْقَى عَلَى وَجْهِ الْأَرْضِ أَحَدٌ فِي قَلْبِهِ مِثْقَالُ ذَرَّةٍ مِنْ خَيْرٍ أَوْ إِيمَانٍ إِلَّا قَبَضَتْهُ، حَتَّى لَوْ أَنَّ أَحَدَكُمْ دَخَلَ فِي كَبِدِ جَبَلٍ لَدَخَلَتْهُ عَلَيْهِ حَتَّى تَقْبِضَهُ»$$

(The Dajjal will emerge in my Ummah, and will remain for forty -- I do not know whether he said forty days, or forty months, or forty years -- then Allah will send `Isa son of Maryam, who looks like `Urwah bin Mas`ud, and he will search for him and destroy him. Then mankind will remain for seven years during which there will not be any enmity between any two people. Then Allah will send a cool wind from the direction of Syria, and no one will be left on the face of the earth who has even a speck of goodness or faith in his heart, but it will take him. Even if he entered into the

Chapter 27: An-Naml (The Ant, The Ants), Verses 056-093   35

heart of a mountain, the wind would follow him and seize him.)" He said, "I heard it from the Messenger of Allah who said:

«فَيَبْقَى شِرَارُ النَّاسِ فِي خِفَّةِ الطَّيْرِ وَأَحْلَامِ السِّبَاعِ لَا يَعْرِفُونَ مَعْرُوفًا، وَلَا يُنْكِرُونَ مُنْكَرًا، فَيَتَمَثَّلُ لَهُمُ الشَّيْطَانُ فَيَقُولُ: أَلَا تَسْتَجِيبُونَ؟ فَيَقُولُونَ: فَمَا تَأْمُرُنَا؟ فَيَأْمُرُهُمْ بِعِبَادَةِ الْأَوْثَانِ، وَهُمْ فِي ذَلِكَ دَارٌّ رِزْقُهُمْ حَسَنٌ عَيْشُهُمْ، ثُمَّ يُنْفَخُ فِي الصُّورِ فَلَا يَسْمَعُهُ أَحَدٌ إِلَّا أَصْغَى لِيتًا وَرَفَعَ لِيتًا قَالَ وَأَوَّلُ مَنْ يَسْمَعُهُ رَجُلٌ يَلُوطُ حَوْضَ إِبِلِهِ، قَالَ: فَيَصْعَقُ وَيَصْعَقُ النَّاسُ، ثُمَّ يُرْسِلُ اللهُ أَوْ قَالَ يُنْزِلُ اللهُ مَطَرًا كَأَنَّهُ الطَّلُّ أَوْ قَالَ: الظِّلُّ نُعْمَانُ الشَّاكُّ فَتَنْبُتُ مِنْهُ أَجْسَادُ النَّاسِ، ثُمَّ يُنْفَخُ فِيهِ أُخْرَى فَإِذَا هُمْ قِيَامٌ يَنْظُرُونَ، ثُمَّ يُقَالُ: يَا أَيُّهَا النَّاسُ هَلُمُّوا إِلَى رَبِّكُمْ وَقِفُوهُمْ إِنَّهُمْ مَسْؤُولُونَ، ثُمَّ يُقَالُ: أَخْرِجُوا بَعْثَ النَّارِ، فَيُقَالُ: مِنْ كَمْ؟ فَيُقَالُ: مِنْ كُلِّ أَلْفٍ تِسْعَمِائَةٍ وَتِسْعَةً وَتِسْعِينَ، قَالَ: فَذَلِكَ يَوْمَ يَجْعَلُ الْوِلْدَانَ شِيبًا، وَذَلِكَ يَوْمَ يُكْشَفُ عَنْ سَاقٍ»

(Then the most evil of people will remain, and they will be as nimble as birds and will be more temperamental than wild beasts. They will not recognize anything good or denounce anything evil. The Shaytan will appear to them and will say, "Will you do as I tell you" They will say, "What do you command us to do" He will command them to worship idols but in spite of this their provision will be plentiful and they will lead comfortable lives. Then the Sur (Trumpet) will be blown, and no one will hear it but he will tilt his head to hear the sound. The first person to hear it will be a man who is setting up the tank for watering his camels. He will fall down, and all the other people will also fall down. Then Allah will send -- or send down -- rain like dew -- or he said, like shade (Nu'man was the one who was not sure) -- from which will grow the bodies of the people. Then the Trumpet will be blown again, and they will get up and look around. Then it will be said: "O mankind! Go to your Lord!" And they will be stopped, for they are to be questioned. Then it will be said: "Bring forth the people who are to be sent to the Fire." It will be asked: "How many are they" It will be said, "Out of every thousand, nine hundred and ninety-nine." That will be the Day which will make the children grey-headed, and that will be the Day when the Shin shall be uncovered.) His saying;

«ثُمَّ يُنْفَخُ فِي الصُّورِ فَلَا يَسْمَعُهُ أَحَدٌ إِلَّا أَصْغَى لِيتًا وَرَفَعَ لِيتًا»

(Then the Sur (Trumpet) will be blown, and no one will hear it but he will tilt his head to hear the sound.) means that they will tilt their heads so that they can better hear the sound coming from the heavens. That is the blast of the Sur which will terrify everyone, then after that will come the blast which will cause them to die, then the blast which will resurrect them to meet the Lord of the worlds -- this is when all of the creation will be brought forth from their graves. Allah says:

(And all shall come to Him, humbled.) meaning, humbling themselves and obeying Him, and no one will go against His command. This is like the Ayat:

(On the Day when He will call you, and you will answer with His praise and obedience) (17:52).

(Then afterwards when He will call you by a single call, behold, you will come out from the earth) (30:25). According to the Hadith about the Sur, when it is blown for the third time, Allah will command the souls to be put into the hole of the Sur (Trumpet), then Israfil will blow into it, after the bodies have grown in their graves and resting places, and when he blows into the Sur (Trumpet), the souls will fly, the believers' souls glowing with light, and the disbelievers' souls looking like darkness. And Allah will say: "By My might and majesty, every soul will go back to its body." And the souls will come back to their bodies and go through them like poison going through a person who is bitten or stung by a poisonous creature. Then they will get up, brushing off the dirt of their graves. Allah says:

(The Day when they will come out of the graves quickly as racing to a goal.) (70:43)

(And you will see the mountains and think them solid, but they shall pass away as the passing away of the clouds.) (27:88) meaning, you will see them as if they are fixed and as if they will remain as they are, but they will pass away as the passing away of the clouds, i.e., they will move away from their places. This is like the Ayat:

(On the Day when the heaven will shake with a dreadful shaking, And the mountains will move away with a (horrible) movement.) (52:9-10)

(And they ask you concerning the mountains: say, "My Lord will blast them and scatter them as particles of dust. Then He shall leave them as a level smooth plain. You will see therein nothing crooked or curved.") (20:105-107),

(And (remember) the Day We shall cause the mountains to pass away, and you will see the earth as a leveled plain.) (18:47).

(The work of Allah, Who perfected all things,) means, He does that by His great power.

(Who perfected all things,) means, He has perfected all that He has created, and has fashioned it according to His wisdom.

(verily, He is well-acquainted with what you do) means, He knows all that His servants do, good or evil, and He will reward or punish them accordingly. Then Allah describes the state of the blessed and the doomed on that Day, and says:

(Whoever brings a good deed, will have better than its worth.) Qatadah said, "That is sincerely for Allah alone." Allah has explained elsewhere in the Qur'an that He will give ten like it.

(and they will be safe from the terror on that Day.) This is like the Ayah,

(The greatest terror will not grieve them) (21:103) and Allah said:

(Is he who is cast into the Fire better or he who comes secure on the Day of Resurrection) (41:40),

(and they will reside in the high dwellings in peace and security) (34:37).

(And whoever brings an evil deed, they will be cast down on their faces in the Fire.) means, whoever comes to Allah with evil deeds, and with no good deeds to his credit, or whose evil deeds outweigh his good deeds. Allah says:

((And it will be said to them) "Are you being recompensed anything except what you used to do")

Surah: 27 Ayah: 91, Ayah: 92 & Ayah: 93

إِنَّمَآ أُمِرْتُ أَنْ أَعْبُدَ رَبَّ هَـٰذِهِ ٱلْبَلْدَةِ ٱلَّذِى حَرَّمَهَا وَلَهُۥ كُلُّ شَىْءٍ ۖ وَأُمِرْتُ أَنْ أَكُونَ مِنَ ٱلْمُسْلِمِينَ ۞

91. I (Muhammad (peace be upon him)) have been commanded only to worship the Lord of this city (Makkah), Who has sanctified it and to Whom belongs everything. And I am commanded to be from among the Muslims (those who submit to Allâh in Islâm).

وَأَنْ أَتْلُوَاْ ٱلْقُرْءَانَ ۖ فَمَنِ ٱهْتَدَىٰ فَإِنَّمَا يَهْتَدِى لِنَفْسِهِۦ ۖ وَمَن ضَلَّ فَقُلْ إِنَّمَآ أَنَا۠ مِنَ ٱلْمُنذِرِينَ ۞

92. And that I should recite the Qur'ân, then whosoever receives guidance, receives it for the good of his own self, and whosoever goes astray, say (to him): "I am only one of the warners."

وَقُلِ ٱلْحَمْدُ لِلَّهِ سَيُرِيكُمْ ءَايَـٰتِهِۦ فَتَعْرِفُونَهَا ۚ وَمَا رَبُّكَ بِغَـٰفِلٍ عَمَّا تَعْمَلُونَ ۞

93. And say ((O Muhammad (peace be upon him)) to these polytheists and pagans.): "All the praises and thanks are to Allâh. He will show you His Ayât (signs, in yourselves, and in the universe or punishments), and you shall recognize them. And your Lord is not unaware of what you do."

Transliteration

91. Innama omirtu an aAAbuda rabba hathihi albaldati allathee harramaha walahu kullu shay-in waomirtu an akoona mina almuslimeena 92. Waan atluwa alqur-ana famani ihtada fa-innama yahtadee linafsihi waman dalla faqul innama ana mina almunthireena 93. Waquli alhamdu lillahi sayureekum ayatihi fataAArifoonaha wama rabbuka bighafilin AAamma taAAmaloona

Tafsir Ibn Kathir

The Command to worship Allah and to call People with the Qur'an

Allah commands His Messenger to say:

(I have been commanded only to worship the Lord of this city, Who has sanctified it and to Whom belongs everything.) This is like the Ayah,

(Say: "O you mankind! If you are in doubt as to my religion, then (know that) I will never worship those whom you worship besides Allah. But I worship Allah Who causes you to die.) (10:104) The fact that the word "Rabb" (Lord) is connected to the word city (in the phrase "the Lord of this city") is a sign of honor and divine care for that city. This is like the Ayah,

(So let them worship the Lord of this House (the Ka`bah), Who has fed them against hunger, and has made them safe from fear.) (106:3-4)

(Who has sanctified it) means, the One Who made it a sanctuary by His Law and by His decree, making it sanctified. It was recorded in the Two Sahihs that Ibn `Abbas said: "On the day of the conquest of Makkah, the Messenger of Allah said:

«إِنَّ هَذَا الْبَلَدَ حَرَّمَهُ اللهُ يَوْمَ خَلَقَ السَّمَوَاتِ وَالْأَرْضَ، فَهُوَ حَرَامٌ بِحُرْمَةِ اللهِ إِلَى يَوْمِ الْقِيَامَةِ، لَا يُعْضَدُ شَوْكُهُ، وَلَا يُنَفَّرُ صَيْدُهُ وَلَا يَلْتَقِطُ لُقَطَتَهُ إِلَّا مَنْ عَرَّفَهَا وَلَا يُخْتَلَى خَلَاهَا»

(Verily, this city was made sacred by Allah the day He created the heavens and the earth, so it is sacred by the sanctity of Allah until the Day of Resurrection. Its thorny bushes should not be cut, its game should not be chased, and its lost property should not be picked up except by one who would announce it publicly and none is allowed to uproot its thorny shrubs...)" This was reported in Sahih, Hasan, Musnad narrations, through various routes, by such a large group that it is absolutely unquestionable, as has been explained in the appropriate place in the book Al-Ahkam, to Allah is the praise and thanks.

(and to Whom belongs everything.) This is a statement of general application following a specific statement, i.e., He is the Lord of this city, and the Lord and Sovereign of all things, there is no god worthy of worship besides Him.

(And I am commanded to be from among the Muslims.) means, those who believe in Allah alone, who are sincere towards Him and who obediently follow His commands.

(And that I should recite the Qur'an,) means, to people, so as to convey it to them. This is like the Ayah,

(This is what We recite to you of the Ayat and the Wise Reminder.) (3:58)

(We recite to you some of the news of Musa and Fir`awn in truth.) (28:3) meaning, `I am a conveyer and a warner.'

(then whosoever receives guidance, receives it for the good of himself; and whosoever goes astray, say (to him): "I am only one of the warners.") meaning, `I have an example to follow in the Messengers who warned their people, and did what they had to do in order to convey the Message to them and fulfil the covenant they had made.' Allah will judge their nations to whom they were sent, as He says:

(your duty is only to convey and on Us is the reckoning) (13: 40).

(But you are only a warner. And Allah is a Protector over all thing) (11:12).

(And say: "All the praises and thanks be to Allah. He will show you His Ayat (signs), and you shall recognize them.) means, praise be to Allah, Who does not punish anyone except after establishing plea against him, warning him (and leaving him with no excuse). Allah says:

(He will show you His Ayat (signs), and you shall recognize them.) This is like the Ayah,

(We will show them Our signs in the universe, and in themselves, until it becomes manifest to them that this is the truth) (41:53).

(And your Lord is not unaware of what you do.) means, on the contrary, He witnesses and sees all things. It was recorded that Imam Ahmad, may Allah have mercy upon him, used to recite the following two lines of verse, whether they were written by him or someone else: "If you are alone one day, do not say, `I am alone.' Rather say, `Someone is watching me.' Do not think that Allah will let His attention wander for even an instant, or that anything is hidden from Him." This is the end of the Tafsir of Surat An-Naml. All praise and thanks be to Allah.

INTRODUCTION TO CHAPTER (SURAH) 28: AL-QASAS (THE STORY, STORIES)

Ibn kathir's Introduction

Imam Ahmad bin Hanbal, may Allah have mercy on him, recorded that Ma`diykarib said: "We came to `Abdullah and asked him to recite to us:

(Ta Sin Mim.) the two hundred. He said, `I do not know it; you should go to someone who learned it from the Messenger of Allah Khabbab bin Al-Aratt.' So we went to Khabbab bin Al-Aratt and he recited it to us, may Allah be pleased with him."

CHAPTER (SURAH) 28: AL-QASAS (THE STORY, STORIES), VERSES 001–088

(بِسْمِ اللَّهِ الرَّحْمَـنِ الرَّحِيمِ)

In the Name of Allah, the Most Gracious, the Most Merciful.

Surah: 28 Ayah: 1, Ayah: 2, Ayah: 3, Ayah: 4, Ayah: 5 & Ayah: 6

طسم

1. Tâ-Sîn-Mîm [These letters are one of the miracles of the Qur'ân, and none but Allâh (Alone) knows their meanings]

تِلْكَ ءَايَـتُ ٱلْكِتَـٰبِ ٱلْمُبِينِ

2. These are the Verses of the manifest Book (that makes clear truth from falsehood, good from evil).

نَتْلُوا۟ عَلَيْكَ مِن نَّبَإِ مُوسَىٰ وَفِرْعَوْنَ بِٱلْحَقِّ لِقَوْمٍ يُؤْمِنُونَ

3. We recite to you some of the news of Mûsâ (Moses) and Fir'aun (Pharaoh) in truth, for a people who believe (in this Qur'ân, and in the Oneness of Allâh).

إِنَّ فِرْعَوْنَ عَلَا فِى ٱلْأَرْضِ وَجَعَلَ أَهْلَهَا شِيَعًا يَسْتَضْعِفُ طَآئِفَةً مِّنْهُمْ يُذَبِّحُ أَبْنَآءَهُمْ وَيَسْتَحْىِۦ نِسَآءَهُمْ إِنَّهُۥ كَانَ مِنَ ٱلْمُفْسِدِينَ

4. Verily, Fir'aun (Pharaoh) exalted himself in the land and made its people sects, weakening (oppressing) a group (i.e. Children of Israel) among them: killing their sons, and letting their females live. Verily, he was of the Mufsidûn (i.e. those who commit great sins and crimes, oppressors, tyrants).

وَنُرِيدُ أَن نَّمُنَّ عَلَى ٱلَّذِينَ ٱسْتُضْعِفُوا۟ فِى ٱلْأَرْضِ وَنَجْعَلَهُمْ أَئِمَّةً وَنَجْعَلَهُمُ ٱلْوَٰرِثِينَ

5. And We wished to do a favor to those who were weak (and oppressed) in the land, and to make them rulers and to make them the inheritors,

Chapter 28: Al-Qasas (The story, Stories), Verses 001–088

$$\text{وَنُمَكِّنَ لَهُمْ فِى ٱلْأَرْضِ وَنُرِىَ فِرْعَوْنَ وَهَـٰمَـٰنَ وَجُنُودَهُمَا مِنْهُم مَّا كَانُوا۟ يَحْذَرُونَ ۝}$$

6. And to establish them in the land, and We let Fir'aun (Pharaoh) and Hâmân and their hosts receive from them that which they feared.

Transliteration

1. Ta-seen-meem 2. Tilka ayatu alkitabi almubeeni 3. Natloo AAalayka min naba-i moosa wafirAAawna bialhaqqi liqawmin yu/minoona 4. Inna firAAawna AAala fee al-ardi wajaAAala ahlaha shiyaAAan yastadAAifu ta-ifatan minhum yuthabbihu abnaahum wayastahyee nisaahum innahu kana mina almufsideena 5. Wanureedu an namunna AAala allatheena istudAAifoo fee al-ardi wanajAAalahum aimmatan wanajAAalahumu alwaritheena   6. Wanumakkina lahum fee al-ardi wanuriya firAAawna wahamana wajunoodahuma minhum ma kanoo yahtharoona

Tafsir Ibn Kathir

The Story of Musa and Fir`awn, and what Allah intended for Their Peoples

We have already discussed the significance of the separate letters.

(These are the Ayat of the manifest Book.) means the Book which is clear and makes plain the true reality of things, and tells us about what happened and what will happen.

(We recite to you some of the news of Musa and Fir`awn in truth,) This is like the Ayah,

(We relate unto you the best of stories) (12:3). which means, `We tell you about things as they really were, as if you are there and are seeing them yourself.' Then Allah says:

(Verily, Fir`awn exalted himself in the land) means, he was an arrogant oppressor and tyrant.

(and made its people Shiya`) means, he made them into different classes, each of which he used to do whatever he wanted of the affairs of his state.

(weakening a group among them.) This refers to the Children of Israel, who at that time were the best of people, even though this tyrant king overpowered them, using them to do the most menial work and forcing them to hard labor night and day for him and his people. At the same time, he was killing their sons and letting their daughters live, to humiliate them and because he feared that there might appear among them the boy who would be the cause of his destruction and the downfall of his kingdom. So Fir`awn took precautions against that happening, by ordering that all boys born to the Children of Israel should be killed, but this precaution did not protect him against the divine decree, because when the term of Allah comes, it cannot be delayed, and for each and every matter there is a decree from Allah. Allah says:

(And We wished to do a favor to those who were weak in the land,) until His saying;

(which they feared.) And Allah did indeed do this to them, as He says:

(And We made the people who were considered weak) until His saying;

(they erected) (7:137). And Allah said:

(Thus and We caused the Children of Israel to inherit them) (26: 59). Fir`awn hoped that by his strength and power he would be saved from Musa, but that did not help him in the slightest. Despite his great power as a king he could not oppose the decree of Allah, which can never be overcome. On the contrary, Allah's ruling was carried out, for it had been written and decreed from past eternity that Fir`awn would meet his doom at the hands of Musa.

Surah: 28 Ayah: 7, Ayah: 8 & Ayah: 9

وَأَوْحَيْنَآ إِلَىٰٓ أُمِّ مُوسَىٰٓ أَنْ أَرْضِعِيهِ ۖ فَإِذَا خِفْتِ عَلَيْهِ فَأَلْقِيهِ فِى ٱلْيَمِّ وَلَا تَخَافِى وَلَا تَحْزَنِىٓ ۖ إِنَّا رَآدُّوهُ إِلَيْكِ وَجَاعِلُوهُ مِنَ ٱلْمُرْسَلِينَ ۝

7. And We inspired the mother of Mûsâ (Moses): (saying): "Suckle him (Mûsâ (Moses)) but when you fear for him, then cast him into the river and fear not, nor grieve. Verily, We shall bring him back to you, and shall make him one of (Our) Messengers."

فَٱلْتَقَطَهُۥٓ ءَالُ فِرْعَوْنَ لِيَكُونَ لَهُمْ عَدُوًّا وَحَزَنًا ۗ إِنَّ فِرْعَوْنَ وَهَـٰمَـٰنَ وَجُنُودَهُمَا كَانُوا۟ خَـٰطِـِٔينَ ۝

8. Then the household of Fir'aun (Pharaoh) picked him up, that he might become for them an enemy and a (cause of) grief. Verily, Fir'aun (Pharaoh), Hâmân and their hosts were sinners.

وَقَالَتِ ٱمْرَأَتُ فِرْعَوْنَ قُرَّتُ عَيْنٍ لِّى وَلَكَ ۖ لَا تَقْتُلُوهُ عَسَىٰٓ أَن يَنفَعَنَآ أَوْ نَتَّخِذَهُۥ وَلَدًا وَهُمْ لَا يَشْعُرُونَ ۝

9. And the wife of Fir'aun (Pharaoh) said: "A comfort of the eye for me and for you. Kill him not, perhaps he may be of benefit to us, or we may adopt him as a son." And they perceive not (the result of that).

Transliteration

7. Waawhayna ila ommi moosa an ardiAAeehi fa-itha khifti AAalayhi faalqeehi fee alyammi wala takhafee wala tahzanee inna raddoohu ilayki wajaAAiloohu mina almursaleena 8. Failtaqatahu alu firAAawna liyakoona lahum AAaduwwan wahazanan inna firAAawna wahamana wajunoodahuma kanoo khati-eena 9. Waqalati imraatu

firAAawna qurratu AAaynin lee walaka la taqtuloohu AAasa an yanfaAAana aw nattakhithahu waladan wahum la yashAAuroona

Tafsir Ibn Kathir

How Musa's Mother was inspired and shown what to do

It was mentioned that when Fir`awn killed so many of the males of the Children of Israel, the Copts were scared that the Children of Israel would die out, and they themselves would have to do the heavy labor that the Children of Israel used to do. So they said to Fir`awn, "If this continues, and their old men die and the young men are killed, their women will not be able to do the work that the men are doing, and we will end up having to do it." So Fir`awn issued orders that the boys should be killed one year, and left alone the following year. Harun, peace be upon him, was born in a year when the boys were not killed, and Musa was born in a year when the boys were being killed. Fir`awn had people who were entrusted with this task. There were midwives who would go around and check on the women, and if they noticed that any woman was pregnant, they would write her name down. When the time came for her to give birth, no one was allowed to attend her except for Coptic women. If the woman gave birth to a girl, they would leave her alone and go away, but if she gave birth to a boy, the killers would come in with their sharp knives and kill the child, then they would go away; may Allah curse them. When the mother of Musa became pregnant with him, she did not show any signs of pregnancy as other women did, and none of the midwives noticed. But when she gave birth to a boy, she became very distressed and did not know what to do with him. She was extremely scared for him, because she loved him very much. No one ever saw Musa, peace be upon him, but they loved him, and the blessed ones were those who loved him both as a natural feeling and because he was a Prophet. Allah says:

(And I endued you with love from Me) (20:39).

Musa, peace be upon him, in the House of Fir`awn

When Musa's mother became so worried and confused, it was inspired into her heart and mind what she should do, as Allah says:

(And We inspired the mother of Musa (telling): "Suckle him, but when you fear for him, then cast him into the river and fear not, nor grieve. Verily, We shall bring him back to you, and shall make him one of (Our) Messengers.") Her house was on the banks of the Nile, so she took a box and made it into a cradle, and started to nurse her child. When someone came to her that she was afraid of, she would go and put him in that box and put it in the river, and she would tie it with a rope. One day someone that she was afraid of came to the house, so she went and put the child in that box and put it in the river, but she forgot to tie it. The water carried him away, past the house of Fir`awn, where some servant women picked the box up and took it to Fir`awn's wife. They did not know what was inside, and they were afraid that they would be in trouble if they opened it without her. When the box was opened, they saw it was a child with the most beautiful features. Allah filled her heart with love for him when she saw him; this was because she was blessed and because Allah wanted to honor her and cause her husband's doom. Allah says:

(Then the household of Fir`awn picked him up, that he might become for them an enemy and a (cause of) grief.) Allah says:

(Verily, Fir`awn, Haman and their armies were sinners.)

(And the wife of Fir`awn said: "A comfort of the eye for me and for you...") means, when Fir`awn saw him, he wanted to kill him, fearing that he was one of the Children of Israel. But his wife Asiyah bint Muzahim came to the child's defence and tried to endear him to Fir`awn, saying,

(A comfort of the eye for me and for you.) Fir`awn said: "For you he may be, but not for me. And this was indeed the case: Allah guided her because of him, and destroyed him at his hands.

(perhaps he may be of benefit to us,) This is indeed what happened in her case, for Allah guided her through him and caused her to dwell in Paradise because of him. (or we may adopt him as a son.) She wanted to take him and adopt him as a son, because she had no children from Fir`awn.

(And they perceived not.) means, they did not know what Allah planned for them when they picked him up, by His great wisdom and definitive proof.

Surah: 28 Ayah: 10, Ayah: 11, Ayah: 12 & Ayah: 13

وَأَصْبَحَ فُؤَادُ أُمِّ مُوسَىٰ فَٰرِغًا إِن كَادَتْ لَتُبْدِى بِهِۦ لَوْلَآ أَن رَّبَطْنَا عَلَىٰ قَلْبِهَا لِتَكُونَ مِنَ ٱلْمُؤْمِنِينَ ۝

10. And the heart of the mother of Mûsâ (Moses) became empty (from every thought, except the thought of Mûsâ (Moses)) She was very near to disclose his (case, i.e. the child is her son), had We not strengthened her heart (with Faith), so that she might remain as one of the believers.

وَقَالَتْ لِأُخْتِهِۦ قُصِّيهِ فَبَصُرَتْ بِهِۦ عَن جُنُبٍ وَهُمْ لَا يَشْعُرُونَ ۝

11. And she said to his (Mûsâ's (Moses)) sister: "Follow him." So she (his sister) watched him from a far place secretly, while they perceived not.

۞ وَحَرَّمْنَا عَلَيْهِ ٱلْمَرَاضِعَ مِن قَبْلُ فَقَالَتْ هَلْ أَدُلُّكُمْ عَلَىٰ أَهْلِ بَيْتٍ يَكْفُلُونَهُۥ لَكُمْ وَهُمْ لَهُۥ نَٰصِحُونَ ۝

12. And We had already forbidden (other) foster suckling mothers for him, until she (his sister came up and) said: "Shall I direct you to a household who will rear him for you, and look after him in a good manner?"

فَرَدَدْنَٰهُ إِلَىٰٓ أُمِّهِۦ كَىْ تَقَرَّ عَيْنُهَا وَلَا تَحْزَنَ وَلِتَعْلَمَ أَنَّ وَعْدَ ٱللَّهِ حَقٌّ وَلَٰكِنَّ أَكْثَرَهُمْ لَا يَعْلَمُونَ ۞

13. So did We restore him to his mother, that her eye might be comforted, and that she might not grieve, and that she might know that the Promise of Allâh is true. But most of them know not.

Transliteration

10. Waasbaha fu-adu ommi moosa farighan in kadat latubdee bihi lawla an rabatna AAala qalbiha litakoona mina almu/mineena 11. Waqalat li-okhtihi qusseehi fabasurat bihi AAan junubin wahum la yashAAuroona 12. Waharramna AAalayhi almaradiAAa min qablu faqalat hal adullukum AAala ahli baytin yakfuloonahu lakum wahum lahu nasihoona 13. Faradadnahu ila ommihi kay taqarra AAaynuha wala tahzana walitaAAlama anna waAAda Allahi haqqun walakinna aktharahum la yaAAlamoona

Tafsir Ibn Kathir

The intense Grief of Musa's Mother, and how He was returned to Her

Allah tells us how, when her child was lost in the river, the heart of Musa's mother became empty, i.e., she could not think of any matter in this world except Musa. This was the view of Ibn `Abbas, Mujahid, `Ikrimah, Sa`id bin Jubayr, Abu `Ubaydah, Ad-Dahhak, Al-Hasan Al-Basri, Qatadah and others.

(She was very near to disclose his (case),) means, because of the intensity of her grief, she almost told people that she had lost a son. She would have disclosed her situation, if Allah had not given her strength and patience. Allah says:

(had We not strengthened her heart, so that she might remain as one of the believers. And she said to his sister: "Follow him.") means, she told her daughter, who was older and was of an age to understand things,

(Follow him.) means, follow his traces and look for information about him, try to find out about him around the city. So she went out to do that.

(So she watched him from a far place (secretly),) Ibn `Abbas said, "Off to the side." Mujahid said, "It means she looked from afar. Qatadah said: "She started to look at him as if she was not really interested." When Musa had settled into the house of Fir`awn, after the king's wife had begun to love him and asked Fir`awn not to kill him, they brought to him the wet nurses who were to be found in their household, and he did not accept any of them, refusing to take milk from them. So they took him out to the marketplace, hoping to find a woman who would be suitable to nurse him. When (his sister) saw him in their arms, she recognized him, but she did not give any indication nor did they suspect her. Allah says:

(And We had already forbidden foster suckling mothers for him,) Because of his honored status with Allah, it was forbidden by divine decree. It was decreed that no one should nurse him except his own mother, and Allah caused this to be the means reuniting him with his mother so that she could nurse him and feel safe after having felt such fear. When (his sister) saw that they were confused over who should nurse the child,

(she said: "Shall I direct you to a household who will rear him for you, and look after him in a good manner") Ibn `Abbas said: When she said that, they had some doubts about her, so they seized her and asked her, How do you know these people will be sincere and will care for him" She said to them, "They will be sincere and will care for him because they want the king to be happy and because they hope for some reward." So they let her go. After what she said, being safe from their harm, they took her to their house and brought the baby to his mother. She gave him her breast and he accepted it, so they rejoiced and sent the glad tidings to the wife of Fir`awn. She called for Musa's mother, treating her kindly and rewarding her generously. She did not realize that she was his real mother, but she saw that the baby accepted her breast. Then Asiyah asked her to stay with her and nurse the baby, but she refused, saying, "I have a husband and children, and I cannot stay with you, but if you would like me to nurse him in my own home, I will do that." The wife of Fir`awn agreed to that, and paid her a regular salary and gave her extra gifts and clothing and treated her kindly. The mother of Musa came back with her child, happy that after a time of fear Allah granted her security, prestige, and ongoing provision. There was only a short time between the distress and the way out, a day and night, or thereabouts -- and Allah knows best. Glory be to the One in Whose hands are all things; what He wills happens and what He does not will does not happen. He is the One Who grants those who fear Him, a way out from every worry and distress, Allah said:

(So We restored him to his mother, that her eye might be comforted,) means, by him,

(and that she might not grieve,) means, for him.

(and that she might know that the promise of Allah is true.) meaning, `We had promised her to return him to her and to make him one of the Messengers.' When he was returned to her, she realized that he was one of the Messengers, so as she brought him up, she treated him both as a child (with kindness) and as a Messenger (with respect).

(But most of them know not.) means, they do not know the wisdom of Allah in His actions and their good consequences, for which He is to be praised in this world and the Hereafter. For a thing may happen that people do not like, but its consequences are good, as Allah says:

(and it may be that you dislike a thing which is good for you and that you like a thing which is bad for you) (2:216).

(it may be that you dislike a thing and Allah brings through it a great deal of good) (4:19).

Chapter 28: Al-Qasas (The story, Stories), Verses 001–088

Surah: 28 Ayah: 14, Ayah: 15, Ayah: 16 & Ayah: 17

وَلَمَّا بَلَغَ أَشُدَّهُ وَٱسْتَوَىٰٓ ءَاتَيْنَٰهُ حُكْمًا وَعِلْمًا ۚ وَكَذَٰلِكَ نَجْزِى ٱلْمُحْسِنِينَ ۝

14. And when he attained his full strength, and was perfect (in manhood), We bestowed on him Hukm (Prophethood and right judgement of the affairs) and religious knowledge (of the religion of his forefathers i.e. Islâmic Monotheism). And thus do We reward the Muhsinûn (i.e. good doers).

وَدَخَلَ ٱلْمَدِينَةَ عَلَىٰ حِينِ غَفْلَةٍ مِّنْ أَهْلِهَا فَوَجَدَ فِيهَا رَجُلَيْنِ يَقْتَتِلَانِ هَٰذَا مِن شِيعَتِهِۦ وَهَٰذَا مِنْ عَدُوِّهِۦ ۖ فَٱسْتَغَٰثَهُ ٱلَّذِى مِن شِيعَتِهِۦ عَلَى ٱلَّذِى مِنْ عَدُوِّهِۦ فَوَكَزَهُ مُوسَىٰ فَقَضَىٰ عَلَيْهِ ۖ قَالَ هَٰذَا مِنْ عَمَلِ ٱلشَّيْطَٰنِ ۖ إِنَّهُۥ عَدُوٌّ مُّضِلٌّ مُّبِينٌ ۝

15. And he entered the city at a time of unawareness of its people: and he found there two men fighting, - one of his party (his religion - from the Children of Israel), and the other of his foes. The man of his (own) party asked him for help against his foe, so Mûsâ (Moses) struck him with his fist and killed him. He said: "This is of Shaitân's (Satan) doing: verily, he is a plain misleading enemy."

قَالَ رَبِّ إِنِّى ظَلَمْتُ نَفْسِى فَٱغْفِرْ لِى فَغَفَرَ لَهُۥٓ ۚ إِنَّهُۥ هُوَ ٱلْغَفُورُ ٱلرَّحِيمُ

16. He said: "My Lord! Verily, I have wronged myself, so forgive me." Then He forgave him. Verily, He is the Oft-Forgiving, the Most Merciful.

قَالَ رَبِّ بِمَآ أَنْعَمْتَ عَلَىَّ فَلَنْ أَكُونَ ظَهِيرًا لِّلْمُجْرِمِينَ ۝

17. He said: "My Lord! For that with which You have favored me, I will never more be a helper of the Mujrimûn (criminals, disbelievers, polytheists, sinners)!"

Transliteration

14. Walamma balagha ashuddahu waistawa ataynahu hukman waAAilman wakathalika najzee almuhsineena 15. Wadakhala almadeenata AAala heeni ghaflatin min ahliha fawajada feeha rajulayni yaqtatilani hatha min sheeAAatihi wahatha min AAaduwwihi faistaghathahu allathee min sheeAAatihi AAala allathee min AAaduwwihi fawakazahu moosa faqada AAalayhi qala hatha min AAamali alshshaytani innahu AAaduwwun mudillun mubeenun 16. Qala rabbi innee thalamtu nafsee faighfir lee faghafara lahu innahu huwa alghafooru alrraheemu 17. Qala rabbi bima anAAamta AAalayya falan akoona thaheeran lilmujrimeena

Tafsir Ibn Kathir

How Musa killed a Coptic Man

Having described Musa's beginnings, Allah then tells us that when he reached maturity, and was complete in stature, Allah gave him Hukm and religious knowledge. Mujahid said that this means prophethood.

(And thus do We reward the doers of good.) Then Allah describes how Musa reached the status that was decreed for him, that of Prophethood and speaking to Allah, as a direct consequence of killing the Coptic, which was the reason why he left Egypt and went to Madyan. Allah says:

(And he entered the city when its people were unaware.) Ibn Jurayj narrated from `Ata' Al-Khurasani, from Ibn `Abbas, "That was between Maghrib and `Isha'." Ibn Al-Munkadir narrated from `Ata' bin Yasar from Ibn `Abbas, "That was in the middle of the day." This was also the view of Sa`id bin Jubayr, `Ikrimah, As-Suddi and Qatadah.

(and he found there two men fighting,) meaning, hitting one another and struggling with one another.

(one of his party,) meaning, an Israelite,

(and the other of his foes.) meaning, a Coptic. This was the view of Ibn `Abbas, Qatadah, As-Suddi and Muhammad bin Ishaq. The Israelite man asked Musa, peace be upon him, for help, and Musa took advantage of the fact that people were not paying attention, so he went to the Coptic man and

(so Musa struck him with his fist and he died.) Mujahid said, "This means he punched him with his fist." And then he died.

(He said) refers to Musa.

("This is of Shaytan's doing, verily, he is a plain misleading enemy." He said: "My Lord! Verily, I have wronged myself, so forgive me." Then He forgave him. Verily, He is the Oft-Forgiving, the Most Merciful. He said: "My Lord! For that with which You have favored me,) meaning, `what You have given me of prestige, power and blessings -- '

(I will nevermore be a helper of the criminals!) `those who disbelieve in You and go against Your commands.'

Surah: 28 Ayah: 18 & Ayah: 19

فَأَصْبَحَ فِى ٱلْمَدِينَةِ خَآئِفًا يَتَرَقَّبُ فَإِذَا ٱلَّذِى ٱسْتَنصَرَهُۥ بِٱلْأَمْسِ يَسْتَصْرِخُهُۥ قَالَ لَهُۥ مُوسَىٰٓ إِنَّكَ لَغَوِىٌّ مُّبِينٌ ۝

Chapter 28: Al-Qasas (The story, Stories), Verses 001–088

18. So he became afraid, looking about in the city (waiting as to what will be the result of his crime of killing), when behold, the man who had sought his help the day before, called for his help (again). Mûsâ (Moses) said to him: "Verily, you are a plain misleader!"

فَلَمَّآ أَنْ أَرَادَ أَن يَبْطِشَ بِٱلَّذِى هُوَ عَدُوٌّ لَّهُمَا قَالَ يَـٰمُوسَىٰٓ أَتُرِيدُ أَن تَقْتُلَنِى كَمَا قَتَلْتَ نَفْسًۢا بِٱلْأَمْسِ ۖ إِن تُرِيدُ إِلَّآ أَن تَكُونَ جَبَّارًۭا فِى ٱلْأَرْضِ وَمَا تُرِيدُ أَن تَكُونَ مِنَ ٱلْمُصْلِحِينَ ۝

19. Then when he decided to seize the man who was an enemy to both of them, the man said: "O Mûsâ (Moses)! Is it your intention to kill me as you killed a man yesterday? Your aim is nothing but to become a tyrant in the land, and not to be one of those who do right."

Transliteration

18. Faasbaha fee almadeenati kha-ifan yataraqqabu fa-itha allathee istansarahu bialamsi yastasrikhuhu qala lahu moosa innaka laghawiyyun mubeenun 19. Falamma an arada an yabtisha biallathee huwa AAaduwwun lahuma qala ya moosa atureedu an taqtulanee kama qatalta nafsan bial-amsi in tureedu illa an takoona jabbaran fee al-ardi wama tureedu an takoona mina almusliheena

Tafsir Ibn Kathir

How the Secret of this Killing became known

Allah tells us that when Musa killed that Coptic,

(he became afraid in the city) meaning, of the consequences of his action,

(looking about) means, turning around and watching out, waiting for the consequences of his action to befall him. He went out and about, and saw the man who sought his help the day before, fighting with another Coptic. When Musa passed by him, he called for his help again, against this other Coptic. Musa said to him:

(Verily, you are a plain misleader!) meaning, `you obviously lead people astray and are very evil.' Then Musa intended to attack that Coptic, but the Israelite -- because of his own cowardice and weakness -- thought that Musa wanted to hit him because of what he had said, so he said, in self-defence --

(O Musa! Is it your intention to kill me as you killed a man yesterday) Nobody except him and Musa, peace be upon him, knew about it, but when the other Coptic heard this, he took the news to Fir`awn's gate and told him about it. So Fir`awn came to know of it, and he became very angry and resolved to kill Musa, so he sent people after him to bring him to him.

Surah: 28 Ayah: 20

وَجَآءَ رَجُلٌ مِّنْ أَقْصَا ٱلْمَدِينَةِ يَسْعَىٰ قَالَ يَـٰمُوسَىٰٓ إِنَّ ٱلْمَلَأَ يَأْتَمِرُونَ بِكَ لِيَقْتُلُوكَ فَٱخْرُجْ إِنِّى لَكَ مِنَ ٱلنَّـٰصِحِينَ ۝

20. And there came a man running, from the farthest end of the city. He said: "O Mûsâ (Moses)! Verily, the chiefs are taking counsel together about you, to kill you, so escape. Truly, I am to you of the good advisers to you."

Transliteration

20. Wajaa rajulun min aqsa almadeenati yasAAa qala ya moosa inna almalaa ya/tamiroona bika liyaqtulooka faokhruj innee laka mina alnnasiheena

Tafsir Ibn Kathir

(And there came a man) He is described as being a man because he had the courage to take a different route, a shorter route than those who were sent after Musa, so he reached Musa first and said to him: "O Musa,

(Verily, the chiefs are taking counsel together about you.)," meaning, `they are consulting with one another about you.'

(to kill you, so escape.) means, from this land.

(Truly, I am one of the good advisers to you.)

Surah: 28 Ayah: 21, Ayah: 22, Ayah: 23 & Ayah: 24

فَخَرَجَ مِنْهَا خَآئِفًا يَتَرَقَّبُ قَالَ رَبِّ نَجِّنِى مِنَ ٱلْقَوْمِ ٱلظَّـٰلِمِينَ ۝

21. So he escaped from there, looking about in a state of fear. He said: "My Lord! Save me from the people who are Zâlimûn (polytheists and wrong-doers)!"

وَلَمَّا تَوَجَّهَ تِلْقَآءَ مَدْيَنَ قَالَ عَسَىٰ رَبِّىٓ أَن يَهْدِيَنِى سَوَآءَ ٱلسَّبِيلِ ۝

22. And when he went towards (the land of) Madyan (Midian), he said: "It may be that my Lord guides me to the Right Way."

وَلَمَّا وَرَدَ مَآءَ مَدْيَنَ وَجَدَ عَلَيْهِ أُمَّةً مِّنَ ٱلنَّاسِ يَسْقُونَ وَوَجَدَ مِن دُونِهِمُ ٱمْرَأَتَيْنِ تَذُودَانِ قَالَ مَا خَطْبُكُمَا قَالَتَا لَا نَسْقِى حَتَّىٰ يُصْدِرَ ٱلرِّعَآءُ وَأَبُونَا شَيْخٌ كَبِيرٌ ۝

23. And when he arrived at the water (a well) of Madyan (Midian) he found there a group of men watering (their flocks), and besides them he found two women who were keeping back (their flocks). He said: "What is the matter with you?"

They said: "We cannot water (our flocks) until the shepherds take (their flocks). And our father is a very old man."

فَسَقَىٰ لَهُمَا ثُمَّ تَوَلَّىٰٓ إِلَى ٱلظِّلِّ فَقَالَ رَبِّ إِنِّى لِمَآ أَنزَلْتَ إِلَىَّ مِنْ خَيْرٍ فَقِيرٌ ۝

24. So he watered (their flocks) for them, then he turned back to shade, and said: "My Lord! Truly, I am in need of whatever good that You bestow on me!"

Transliteration

21. Fakharaja minha kha-ifan yataraqqabu qala rabbi najjinee mina alqawmi alththalimeena 22. Walamma tawajjaha tilqaa madyana qala AAasa rabbee an yahdiyanee sawaa alssabeeli 23. Walamma warada maa madyana wajada AAalayhi ommatan mina alnnasi yasqoona wawajada min doonihimu imraatayni tathoodani qala ma khatbukuma qalata la nasqee hatta yusdira alrriAAao waaboona shaykhun kabeerun 24. Fasaqa lahuma thumma tawalla ila alththilli faqala rabbi innee lima anzalta ilayya min khayrin faqeerun

Tafsir Ibn Kathir

Musa, peace be upon him, in Madyan, and how He watered the Flocks of the Two Women

When the man told Musa about how Fir`awn and his chiefs were conspiring against him, he left Egypt on his own. He was not used to being alone, because before that he had been living a life of luxury and ease, in a position of leadership.

(So he escaped from there, looking about in a state of fear.) meaning, turning around and watching.

(My Lord! Save me from the people who are wrongdoers!) means, from Fir`awn and his chiefs. It was mentioned that Allah sent to him an angel riding a horse, who showed him the way. And Allah knows best.

(And when he went towards (the land of) Madyan,) means, he took a smooth and easy route -- and he rejoiced because of that.

(he said: "It may be that my Lord guides me to the right way.") meaning, the most straight route. And Allah did indeed do that, for He guided him to the straight path in this world and the Hereafter, and caused him to be guided and to guide others.

(And when he arrived at the water (a well) of Madyan,) means, when he reached Madyan and went to drink from its water, for it had a well where shepherds used to water their flocks,

(he found there a group of men watering, and besides them he found two women who were keeping back.) means, they were stopping their sheep from drinking with the sheep of those shepherds, lest some harm come to them. When Musa, peace be upon him, saw them, he felt sorry for them and took pity on them.

(He said: "What is the matter with you") meaning, 'why do you not water your flocks with these people'

(They said: "We cannot water until the shepherds take...") meaning, 'we cannot water our flocks until they finish.'

(And our father is a very old man.) means, 'this is what has driven us to what you see.'

(So he watered (their flocks) for them,)

(then he turned back to shade, and said: "My Lord! Truly, I am in need of whatever good that You bestow on me!")

(to shade,) Ibn `Abbas, Ibn Mas`ud and As-Suddi said: "He sat beneath a tree." `Ata' bin As-Sa'ib said: "When Musa said:

("My Lord! Truly, I am in need of whatever good that You bestow on me!") the women heard him."

Surah: 28 Ayah: 25, Ayah: 26, Ayah: 27 & Ayah: 28

فَجَآءَتْهُ إِحْدَىٰهُمَا تَمْشِى عَلَى اسْتِحْيَآءٍ قَالَتْ إِنَّ أَبِى يَدْعُوكَ لِيَجْزِيَكَ أَجْرَ مَا سَقَيْتَ لَنَا ۚ فَلَمَّا جَآءَهُ وَقَصَّ عَلَيْهِ الْقَصَصَ قَالَ لَا تَخَفْ نَجَوْتَ مِنَ الْقَوْمِ الظَّٰلِمِينَ ۝

25. Then there came to him one of the two women, walking shyly. She said: "Verily, my father calls you that he may reward you for having watered (our flocks) for us." So when he came to him and narrated the story, he said: "Fear you not. You have escaped from the people who are Zâlimûn (polytheists, disbelievers, and wrong-doers)."

قَالَتْ إِحْدَىٰهُمَا يَٰٓأَبَتِ اسْتَـْٔجِرْهُ ۖ إِنَّ خَيْرَ مَنِ اسْتَـْٔجَرْتَ الْقَوِىُّ الْأَمِينُ ۝

26. And said one of them (the two women): "O my father! Hire him! Verily, the best of men for you to hire is the strong, the trustworthy."

قَالَ إِنِّى أُرِيدُ أَنْ أُنكِحَكَ إِحْدَى ابْنَتَىَّ هَٰتَيْنِ عَلَىٰٓ أَن تَأْجُرَنِى ثَمَٰنِىَ حِجَجٍ ۖ فَإِنْ أَتْمَمْتَ عَشْرًا فَمِنْ عِندِكَ ۖ وَمَآ أُرِيدُ أَنْ أَشُقَّ عَلَيْكَ ۚ سَتَجِدُنِىٓ إِن شَآءَ اللَّهُ مِنَ الصَّٰلِحِينَ ۝

27. He said: "I intend to wed one of these two daughters of mine to you, on condition that you serve me for eight years; but if you complete ten years, it will

be (a favor) from you. But I intend not to place you under a difficulty. If Allâh will, you will find me one of the righteous."

قَالَ ذَٰلِكَ بَيْنِى وَبَيْنَكَ ۖ أَيَّمَا ٱلْأَجَلَيْنِ قَضَيْتُ فَلَا عُدْوَانَ عَلَىَّ ۖ وَٱللَّهُ عَلَىٰ مَا نَقُولُ وَكِيلٌ ﴿٢٨﴾

28. He (Mûsâ (Moses)) said: "That (is settled) between me and you: whichever of the two terms I fulfil , there will be no injustice to me, and Allâh is Surety over what we say."

Transliteration

25. Fajaat-hu ihdahuma tamshee AAala istihya-in qalat inna abee yadAAooka liyajziyaka ajra ma saqayta lana falamma jaahu waqassa AAalayhi alqasasa qala la takhaf najawta mina alqawmi alththalimeena 26. Qalat ihdahuma ya abati ista/jirhu inna khayra mani ista/jarta alqawiyyu al-ameenu 27. Qala innee oreedu an onkihaka ihda ibnatayya hatayni AAala an ta/juranee thamaniya hijajin fa-in atmamta AAashran famin AAindika wama oreedu an ashuqqa AAalayka satajidunee in shaa Allahu mina alssaliheena 28. Qala thalika baynee wabaynaka ayyama al-ajalayni qadaytu fala AAudwana AAalayya waAllahu AAala ma naqoolu wakeelun

Tafsir Ibn Kathir

Musa, the Father of the Two Women, and His Marriage to One of Them

When the two women came back quickly with the sheep, their father was surprised that they returned so soon. He asked them what had happened, and they told him what Musa, peace be upon him, had done. So he sent one of them to call him to meet her father. Allah says:

(Then there came to him one of them, walking shyly.) meaning, she was walking like a free woman, as it was narrated from the Commander of the faithful, `Umar, may Allah be pleased with him: "She was covering herself from them with the folds of her garment." Ibn Abi Hatim recorded that `Amr bin Maymun said, `Umar, may Allah be pleased with him, said: "She came walking shyly, putting her garment over her face. She was not one of those audacious women who come and go as they please." This chain of narrators is Sahih.

(She said: "Verily, my father calls you that he may reward you for having watered (our flocks) for us.") This is an example of good manners: she did not invite him directly lest he have some suspicious thoughts about her. Rather she said: "My father is inviting you so that he may reward you for watering our sheep," i.e., give you some payment for that.

(So when he came to him and narrated the story,) means, he told him about his story and why he had to leave his country.

(he said: "Fear you not. You have escaped from the people who are wrongdoers.") He was saying: `calm down and relax, for you have left their kingdom and they have no authority in our land.' So he said:

(You have escaped from the people who are wrongdoers.)

(And said one of them: "O my father! Hire him! Verily, the best of men for you to hire is the strong, the trustworthy.") One of the two daughters of the man said this, and it was said that she was the one who had walked behind Musa, peace be upon him. She said to her father:

(O my father! Hire him!) as a shepherd to look after the sheep. `Umar, Ibn `Abbas, Shurayh Al-Qadi, Abu Malik, Qatadah, Muhammad bin Ishaq and others said: "When she said:

(Verily, the best of men for you to hire is the strong, the trustworthy.) her father said to her, `What do you know about that' She said to him, `He lifted a rock which could only be lifted by ten men, and when I came back with him, I walked ahead of him, but he said to me, walk behind me, and if I get confused about the route, throw a pebble so that I will know which way to go.'" `Abdullah (Ibn Mas`ud) said, "The people who had the most discernment were three: Abu Bakr's intuition about `Umar; the companion of Yusuf when he said, `Make his stay comfortable'; and the companion of Musa, when she said:

(O my father! Hire him! Verily, the best of men for you to hire is the strong, the trustworthy.)."

(I intend to wed one of these two daughters of mine to you,) means, this old man asked him to take care of his flocks, then he would marry one of his two daughters to him.

(on condition that you serve me for eight years; but if you complete ten years, it will be (a favor) from you.) meaning, `on the condition that you tend my flocks for eight years, and if you want to give me two extra years, that is up to you, but if you do not want to, then eight years is enough.'

(But I intend not to place you under a difficulty. If Allah wills, you will find me one of the righteous.) means, `I do not want to put pressure on you or cause you any inconvenience or argue with you.' Ibn Abi Hatim recorded that `Ali bin Rabah Al-Lakhmi said, "I heard `Utbah bin An-Nadar As-Sulami, the Companion of the Messenger of Allah narrating that the Messenger of Allah said:

«إِنَّ مُوسَى عَلَيْهِ السَّلَامُ آجَرَ نَفْسَهُ بِعِفَّةِ فَرْجِهِ وَطُعْمَةِ بَطْنِهِ»

(Musa, peace be upon him, hired himself out for the purpose of keeping chaste and to feed himself.) And Allah tells us about Musa, peace be upon him:

Chapter 28: Al-Qasas (The story, Stories), Verses 001–088

(He said: "That (is settled) between me and you: whichever of the two terms I fulfill, there will be no injustice to me, and Allah is Surety over what we say.") Musa said to his father-in-law, "The matter is as you say. You have hired me for eight years, and if I complete ten years, that is my choice, but if I do the lesser amount, I will still have fulfilled the covenant and met the conditions." So he said: (whichever of the two terms I fulfill, there will be no injustice to me,) meaning, `there will be no blame on me. The complete term is permissible but it is still regarded as something extra.' This is like the Ayah,

(But whosoever hastens to leave in two days, there is no sin on him and whosoever stays on, there is no sin on him) (2:203). And the Messenger of Allah said to Hamzah bin `Amr Al-Aslami, may Allah be pleased with him, who used to fast a great deal and who asked him about fasting while traveling:

«إِنْ شِئْتَ فَصُمْ، وَإِنْ شِئْتَ فَأَفْطِرْ»

(If you wish, then fast, and if you wish, do not fast.) even though it is better to fast, according to the evidence of other reports. And there is evidence which indicates that Musa, peace be upon him, fulfilled the longer of the two terms. Al-Bukhari recorded that Sa`id bin Jubayr said: "A Jew from the people of Hirah asked me; `Which of the two terms did Musa fulfill' I said, `I do not know until I go to the scholar of the Arabs and ask him.' So I went to Ibn `Abbas, may Allah be pleased with him, and asked him. He said: `He fulfilled the longer and better of them, for when a Messenger of Allah said he would do a thing, he did it.'" This is how it was recorded by Al-Bukhari.

Surah: 28 Ayah: 29, Ayah: 30, Ayah: 31 & Ayah: 32

فَلَمَّا قَضَىٰ مُوسَى ٱلْأَجَلَ وَسَارَ بِأَهْلِهِۦ ءَانَسَ مِن جَانِبِ ٱلطُّورِ نَارًا قَالَ لِأَهْلِهِ ٱمْكُثُوٓا۟ إِنِّىٓ ءَانَسْتُ نَارًا لَّعَلِّىٓ ءَاتِيكُم مِّنْهَا بِخَبَرٍ أَوْ جَذْوَةٍ مِّنَ ٱلنَّارِ لَعَلَّكُمْ تَصْطَلُونَ ۝

29. Then, when Mûsâ (Moses) had fulfilled the term, and was travelling with his family, he saw a fire in the direction of Tûr (Mount). He said to his family: "Wait, I have seen a fire; perhaps I may bring to you from there some information, or a burning fire-brand that you may warm yourselves."

فَلَمَّآ أَتَىٰهَا نُودِىَ مِن شَـٰطِئِ ٱلْوَادِ ٱلْأَيْمَنِ فِى ٱلْبُقْعَةِ ٱلْمُبَـٰرَكَةِ مِنَ ٱلشَّجَرَةِ أَن يَـٰمُوسَىٰٓ إِنِّىٓ أَنَا ٱللَّهُ رَبُّ ٱلْعَـٰلَمِينَ ۝

30. So when he reached it (the fire), he was called from the right side of the valley, in the blessed place, from the tree: "O Mûsâ (Moses)! Verily I am Allâh, the Lord of the 'Alamîn (mankind, jinn and all that exists)!

$$وَأَنْ أَلْقِ عَصَاكَ ۖ فَلَمَّا رَآهَا تَهْتَزُّ كَأَنَّهَا جَانٌّ وَلَّىٰ مُدْبِرًا وَلَمْ يُعَقِّبْ ۚ يَٰمُوسَىٰ أَقْبِلْ وَلَا تَخَفْ ۖ إِنَّكَ مِنَ ٱلْآمِنِينَ ۝$$

31. "And throw your stick!" But when he saw it moving as if it were a snake, he turned in flight, and looked not back. (It was said): "O Mûsâ (Moses)! Draw near, and fear not. Verily, you are of those who are secure.

$$ٱسْلُكْ يَدَكَ فِى جَيْبِكَ تَخْرُجْ بَيْضَآءَ مِنْ غَيْرِ سُوٓءٍ وَٱضْمُمْ إِلَيْكَ جَنَاحَكَ مِنَ ٱلرَّهْبِ ۖ فَذَٰنِكَ بُرْهَٰنَانِ مِن رَّبِّكَ إِلَىٰ فِرْعَوْنَ وَمَلَإِيْهِ ۚ إِنَّهُمْ كَانُوا۟ قَوْمًا فَٰسِقِينَ ۝$$

32. "Put your hand in your bosom, it will come forth white without a disease; and draw your hand close to your side to be free from fear (which you suffered from the snake, and also your hand will return to its original state). These are two Burhâns (signs, miracles, evidences, proofs) from your Lord to Fir'aun (Pharaoh) and his chiefs. Verily, they are the people who are Fâsiqûn (rebellious, disobedient to Allâh).

Transliteration

29. Falamma qada moosa al-ajala wasara bi-ahlihi anasa min janibi alttoori naran qala li-ahlihi omkuthoo innee anastu naran laAAallee ateekum minha bikhabarin aw jathwatin mina alnnari laAAallakum tastaloona 30. Falamma ataha noodiya min shati-i alwadi al-aymani fee albuqAAati almubarakati mina alshshajarati an ya moosa innee ana Allahu rabbu alAAalameena 31. Waan alqi AAasaka falamma raaha tahtazzu kaannaha jannun walla mudbiran walam yuAAaqqib ya moosa aqbil wala takhaf innaka mina al-amineena 32. Osluk yadaka fee jaybika takhruj baydaa min ghayri soo-in waodmum ilayka janahaka mina alrrahbi fathanika burhanani min rabbika ila firAAawna wamala-ihi innahum kanoo qawman fasiqeena

Tafsir Ibn Kathir

Musa's Return to Egypt and how he was honored with the Mission and Miracles on the Way

In the explanation of the previous Ayah, we have already seen that Musa completed the longer and better of the two terms, which may also be understood from the Ayah where Allah says:

(Then, when Musa had fulfilled the term,) meaning, the longer of the two; and Allah knows best.

(and was traveling with his family,) They said: "Musa missed his country and his relatives, so he resolved to visit them in secret, without Fir`awn and his people knowing. So he gathered up his family and the flocks which his father-in-law had given to him, and set out on a cold, dark, rainy night. They stopped to camp, and whenever he tried to start a fire, he did not succeed. He was surprised by this, and while he was in this state,

(he saw a fire in the direction of At-Tur) he saw a fire burning from a far.

(He said to his family: "Wait, I have seen a fire...") meaning, `wait while I go there, '

(perhaps I may bring to you from there some information,) This was because they lost their way.

(or a burning firebrand that you may warm yourselves.) so that they could get warm and find relief from the cold.

(So when he reached it (the fire), he was called from the right side of the valley,) From the side of the valley that adjoined the mountain on his right, to the west. This is like the Ayah,

(And you were not on the western side, when We made clear to Musa the commandment) (20:44). This indicates that when Musa headed for the fire, he headed in the direction of the Qiblah with the western mountain on his right. He found the fire burning in a green bush on the side of the mountain adjoining the valley, and he stood there amazed at what he was seeing. Then his Lord called him:

(from the right side of the valley, in the blessed place, from the tree.)

(O Musa! Verily, I am Allah, the Lord of all that exits!) meaning, `the One Who is addressing you and speaking to you is the Lord of all that exits, the One Who does what He wills, the One apart from Whom there is no other god or lord, may He be exalted and sanctified, the One Who by His very nature, attributes, words and deeds is far above any resemblance to His creation, may He be glorified.

(And throw your stick!) `the stick that is in your hand' -- as was stated in the Ayah,

("And what is that in your right hand, O Musa" He said: "This is my stick, whereon I lean, and wherewith I beat down branches for my sheep, and wherein I find other uses.") (20:17-18). The meaning is: `this stick, which you know so well;'

("Cast it down, O Musa!" He cast it down, and behold! It was a snake, moving quickly.) (20:19-20). Musa knew that the One Who was speaking to him was the One Who merely says to a thing, "Be!" and it is, as we have already stated in (the explanation of) Surah Ta Ha. And here Allah says:

(But when he saw it moving as if it were a snake, he turned in flight,) It moved so quickly, even though it was so big, and its mouth was so huge, with its jaws snapping. It swallowed every rock it passed, and every rock that fell into its mouth fell with a sound like a rock falling into a valley. When he saw that:

(he turned in flight, and looked not back.) he did not turn around, because it is human nature to flee from such a thing. But when Allah said to him:

(O Musa! Draw near, and fear not. Verily, you are of those who are secure.) he came back to his original position. Then Allah said:

(Put your hand into the opening of your garment, it will come forth white without a disease;) meaning, `when you put your hand in your garment and then draw it out, it will be shining white as if it were a piece of the moon or a flash of lightning.' Allah said:

(without a disease) i.e., with no trace of leukoderma.

(and draw your hand close to your side to be free from the fear.) Mujahid said, "To be free from terror." Qatadah said, "To be free from fear." Musa was commanded, when he felt afraid of anything, to draw his hand close to his side to be free from the fear. If he did that, whatever fear he felt would be gone. Perhaps if a person does this, following the example of Musa, and puts his hand over his heart, his fear will disappear or be lessened, if Allah wills; in Allah we place our trust.

(These are two proofs from your Lord) This refers to the throwing down of his stick, whereupon it turned into a moving snake, and his putting his hand into his garment and bringing it forth white without a disease. These were two clear and definitive proofs of the power of the One Who does as He chooses, and of the truth of the prophethood of the one at whose hands these miracles occurred. Allah said:

(to Fir`awn and his chiefs.) meaning his leaders and prominent followers.

(Verily, they are the people who are rebellious.) means, who are disobedient towards Allah and who go against His commands and His religion.

Surah: 28 Ayah: 33, Ayah: 34 & Ayah: 35

قَالَ رَبِّ إِنِّى قَتَلْتُ مِنْهُمْ نَفْسًا فَأَخَافُ أَن يَقْتُلُونِ ﴿٣٣﴾

33. He said: "My Lord! I have killed a man among them, and I fear that they will kill me.

وَأَخِى هَـرُونُ هُوَ أَفْصَحُ مِنِّى لِسَانًا فَأَرْسِلْهُ مَعِىَ رِدْءًا يُصَدِّقُنِى إِنِّى أَخَافُ أَن يُكَذِّبُونِ ﴿٣٤﴾

34. "And my brother Hârûn (Aaron) - he is more eloquent in speech than me: so send him with me as a helper to confirm me. Verily I fear that they will belie me."

قَالَ سَنَشُدُّ عَضُدَكَ بِأَخِيكَ وَنَجْعَلُ لَكُمَا سُلْطَنًا فَلَا يَصِلُونَ إِلَيْكُمَا بِـَايَتِنَآ أَنتُمَا وَمَنِ اتَّبَعَكُمَا الْغَلِبُونَ ﴿٣٥﴾

35. Allâh said: "We will strengthen your arm through your brother, and give you both power, so they shall not be able to harm you: with Our Ayât (proofs, evidences,

verses, lessons, signs, revelations, etc.), you two as well as those who follow you will be the victors."

Transliteration

33. Qala rabbi innee qataltu minhum nafsan faakhafu an yaqtulooni 34. Waakhee haroonu huwa afsahu minnee lisanan faarsilhu maAAiya rid-an yusaddiqunee innee akhafu an yukaththibooni 35. Qala sanashuddu AAadudaka bi-akheeka wanajAAalu lakuma sultanan fala yasiloona ilaykuma bi-ayatina antuma wamani ittabaAAakuma alghaliboona

Tafsir Ibn Kathir

How Musa asked for the Support of His Brother and was granted that by Allah

When Allah commanded him to go to Fir`awn, the one who he had run away from and whose vengeance he feared,

(Musa said: My Lord! I have killed a man among them,) meaning, that Coptic,

(and I fear that they will kill me.) i.e., `when they see me.'

(And my brother Harun -- he is more eloquent in speech than me,) Musa, peace be upon him, had a speech defect, because when he had been given the choice between a date and a pearl, he mistakenly picked up a coal and placed it on his tongue, so he found it difficult to speak clearly. Musa said:

("And loose the knot (the defect) from my tongue. That they understand my speech. And appoint for me a helper from my family, Harun, my brother. Increase my strength with him, And let him share my task.") (20:27-32) meaning, `give me someone to keep me company in this immense task of prophethood and conveying the Message to this arrogant, tyrannical and stubborn king. ' Hence Musa said:

(And my brother Harun -- he is more eloquent in speech than me: so send him with me as a helper) meaning, as a support to give strength to my cause and confirm what I say and convey from Allah, because the word of two carries more weight in people's minds than the word of one. So he said:

(Verily, I fear that they will deny me.) Muhammad bin Ishaq said: c

(as a helper to confirm me.) means, `to explain to them what I say, for he can understand me where they may not.' When Musa asked for this, Allah said to him:

(We will strengthen your arm through your brother,) meaning, `We will add strength to your cause and give you help through your brother, who you have asked to be made a Prophet alongside you.' This is like the Ayat;

(You are granted your request, O Musa!) (20:36)

(And We granted him his brother Harun, (also) a Prophet, out of Our mercy) (19:53). One of the Salaf said, "There is no one who has ever done a greater favor to his brother than Musa did for Harun, may peace be upon them both, for he interceded for him until Allah made him a Prophet and Messenger with him to Fir`awn and his chiefs. Allah said concerning Musa:

(he was honorable before Allah) (33:69).

(and (We will) give you both power) means, overwhelming evidence.

(so they shall not be able to harm you, with Our Ayat;) means, `they will have no way or means of harming you because you are conveying the signs of Allah.' This is like the Ayat:

(O Messenger! Proclaim (the Message) which has been sent down to you from your Lord.) until His saying:

(Allah will protect you from mankind) (5:67).

(Those who convey the Message of Allah) until His saying:

(And sufficient is Allah as a Reckoner) (33:39). And sufficient is Allah as a Helper and Supporter. And Allah told them the consequences in this world and the next, for them and for those who followed them,

(you two as well as those who follow you will be the victors.) This is like the Ayat:

(Allah has decreed: "Verily, it is I and My Messengers who shall be the victorious." Verily, Allah is All-Powerful, All-Mighty.) (58:21)

(Verily, We will indeed make victorious Our Messengers and those who believe in this world's life) (40:51) to the end of the Ayah.

Surah: 28 Ayah: 36 & Ayah: 37

فَلَمَّا جَآءَهُم مُّوسَىٰ بِـَٔايَـٰتِنَا بَيِّنَـٰتٍ قَالُوا۟ مَا هَـٰذَآ إِلَّا سِحْرٌ مُّفْتَرًى وَمَا سَمِعْنَا بِهَـٰذَا فِىٓ ءَابَآئِنَا ٱلْأَوَّلِينَ ۝

36. Then when Mûsâ (Moses) came to them with Our Clear Ayât (proofs, evidences, verses, lessons, signs, revelations, etc.), they said: "This is nothing but invented magic. Never did we hear of this among our fathers of old."

وَقَالَ مُوسَىٰ رَبِّىٓ أَعْلَمُ بِمَن جَآءَ بِٱلْهُدَىٰ مِنْ عِندِهِۦ وَمَن تَكُونُ لَهُۥ عَـٰقِبَةُ ٱلدَّارِ إِنَّهُۥ لَا يُفْلِحُ ٱلظَّـٰلِمُونَ ۝

37. Mûsâ (Moses) said: "My Lord knows best him who came with guidance from Him, and whose will be the happy end in the Hereafter. Verily, the Zâlimûn (wrong-

doers, polytheists and disbelievers in the Oneness of Allâh) will not be successful."

Transliteration

36. Falamma jaahum moosa bi-ayatina bayyinatin qaloo ma hatha illa sihrun muftaran wama samiAAna bihatha fee aba-ina al-awwaleena 37. Waqala moosa rabbee aAAlamu biman jaa bialhuda min AAindihi waman takoonu lahu AAaqibatu alddari innahu la yuflihu alththalimoona

Tafsir Ibn Kathir

Musa before Fir`awn and His People

Allah tells us how Musa and his brother Harun came before Fir`awn and his chiefs, and showed them the clear miracles and overwhelming proof that Allah had given them to confirm the truth of what they were saying about Allah being One and that His commandments were to be followed. Fir`awn and his chiefs saw that with their own eyes and realized that it was certainly from Allah, but because of their disbelief and sin they resorted to stubbornness and false arguments. This was because they were too evil and arrogant to follow the truth. They said:

(This is nothing but invented magic.) meaning, fabricated and made up. They wanted to oppose him by means of their own tricks and their position and power, but this did not work.

(Never did we hear of this among our fathers of old.) They were referring worshipping Allah Alone, with no partner or associate. They said: "We have never seen anyone among our forefathers following this religion; we have only ever seen people associating other gods in worship with Allah. Musa said in response to them:

(My Lord knows best him who came with guidance from Him,) meaning, `of me and you, and He will decide between me and you.' So he said:

(and whose will be the happy end in the Hereafter.) meaning, who will be supported and will prevail.

(Verily, the wrongdoers will not be successful.) refers to the idolators who associate others in worship with Allah.

Surah: 28 Ayah: 38, Ayah: 39, Ayah: 40, Ayah: 41 & Ayah: 42

وَقَالَ فِرْعَوْنُ يَٰٓأَيُّهَا ٱلْمَلَأُ مَا عَلِمْتُ لَكُم مِّنْ إِلَٰهٍ غَيْرِى فَأَوْقِدْ لِى يَٰهَٰمَٰنُ عَلَى ٱلطِّينِ فَٱجْعَل لِّى صَرْحًا لَّعَلِّى أَطَّلِعُ إِلَىٰٓ إِلَٰهِ مُوسَىٰ وَإِنِّى لَأَظُنُّهُۥ مِنَ ٱلْكَٰذِبِينَ ۝

38. Fir'aun (Pharaoh) said: "O chiefs! I know not that you have an ilâh (a god) other than me. So kindle for me (a fire), O Hâmân, to bake (bricks out of) clay, and set

up for me a Sarh (a lofty tower, or palace) in order that I may look at (or look for) the Ilâh (God) of Mûsâ (Moses); and verily, I think that he (Mûsâ (Moses)) is one of the liars."

$$\text{وَٱسْتَكْبَرَ هُوَ وَجُنُودُهُۥ فِى ٱلْأَرْضِ بِغَيْرِ ٱلْحَقِّ وَظَنُّوٓا۟ أَنَّهُمْ إِلَيْنَا لَا يُرْجَعُونَ ۝}$$

39. And he and his hosts were arrogant in the land, without right, and they thought that they would never return to Us.

$$\text{فَأَخَذْنَٰهُ وَجُنُودَهُۥ فَنَبَذْنَٰهُمْ فِى ٱلْيَمِّ ۖ فَٱنظُرْ كَيْفَ كَانَ عَٰقِبَةُ ٱلظَّٰلِمِينَ ۝}$$

40. So We seized him and his hosts, and We threw them all into the sea (and drowned them). So behold (O Muhammad (peace be upon him)) what was the end of the Zâlimûn (wrong-doers, polytheists and those who disbelieved in the Oneness of their Lord (Allâh), or rejected the advice of His Messenger Mûsâ (Moses) peace be upon him).

$$\text{وَجَعَلْنَٰهُمْ أَئِمَّةً يَدْعُونَ إِلَى ٱلنَّارِ ۖ وَيَوْمَ ٱلْقِيَٰمَةِ لَا يُنصَرُونَ ۝}$$

41. And We made them leaders inviting to the Fire: and on the Day of Resurrection, they will not be helped.

$$\text{وَأَتْبَعْنَٰهُمْ فِى هَٰذِهِ ٱلدُّنْيَا لَعْنَةً ۖ وَيَوْمَ ٱلْقِيَٰمَةِ هُم مِّنَ ٱلْمَقْبُوحِينَ ۝}$$

42. And We made a curse to follow them in this world, and on the Day of Resurrection, they will be among Al-Maqbuhûn (those who are prevented from receiving Allâh's Mercy or any good; despised or destroyed).

Transliteration

38. Waqala firAAawnu ya ayyuha almalao ma AAalimtu lakum min ilahin ghayree faawqid lee ya hamanu AAala altteeni faijAAal lee sarhan laAAallee attaliAAu ila ilahi moosa wa-innee laathunnuhu mina alkathibeena 39. Waistakbara huwa wajunooduhu fee al-ardi bighayri alhaqqi wathannoo annahum ilayna la yurjaAAoona 40. Faakhathnahu wajunoodahu fanabathnahum fee alyammi faonthur kayfa kana AAaqibatu alththalimeena 41. WajaAAalnahum a-immatan yadAAoona ila alnnari wayawma alqiyamati la yunsaroona 42. WaatbaAAnahum fee hathihi alddunya laAAnatan wayawma alqiyamati hum mina almaqbooheena

Tafsir Ibn Kathir

The Arrogance of Fir`awn and His ultimate Destiny

Allah tells us of Fir`awn's disbelief and wrongdoing, and how he falsely claimed divinity for his evil self, may Allah curse him.

Chapter 28: Al-Qasas (The story, Stories), Verses 001–088

(Thus he fooled his people, and they obeyed him.) (43:54) He called on his people to recognize his divinity, and they responded, because of their weak and foolish minds. So, he said:

(O chiefs! I know not that you have a god other than me.) Allah tells us about Fir`awn:

(Then he gathered (his people) and cried aloud, saying: "I am your lord, most high." So Allah, seized him with punishment for his last and first transgression. Verily, in this is an instructive admonition for whosoever fears Allah.) (79:23-26) meaning: he brought his people together and called to them in a loud voice, shouting that, and they responded to him obediently. So Allah took revenge on him, and made him a lesson to others in this world and the Hereafter. He even confronted Musa with that, and said:

(If you choose a god other than me, I will certainly put you among the prisoners) (26:29).

(So kindle for me (a fire), O Haman, to bake (bricks out of) clay, and set up for me a Sarh in order that I may look at the God of Musa;) He commanded his minister and adviser Haman to bake bricks for him, i.e., to make bricks in order to build a Sarh, a exalted towering palace. This is like the Ayah,

(And Fir`awn said: "O Haman! Build me a Sarh that I may arrive at the ways -- the ways of the heavens, and I may look upon the God of Musa, but verily, I think him to be a liar." Thus it was made fair seeming, in Fir`awn's eyes, the evil of his deeds, and he was hindered from the path; and the plot of Fir`awn led to nothing but loss and destruction) (40:36-37). Fir`awn built this tower, which was the highest structure ever seen on earth, because he wanted to show his people that Musa was lying when he claimed that there was a God other than Fir`awn. Fir`awn said:

(and verily, I think that he (Musa) is one of the liars.) meaning, `when he says that there is a lord other than me.' The issue was not whether Allah had sent Musa, because he did not acknowledge the existence of the Creator in the first place. On the contrary, he said:

(And what is the Lord of Al-`Alamin) (26:23) and:

(If you choose a god other than me, I will certainly put you among the prisoners.) (26:29) and he said:

(O chiefs! I know not that you have a god other than me.) This was the view of Ibn Jarir.

(And he and his armies were arrogant in the land, without right, and they thought that they would never return to Us.) means, they were arrogant oppressors who spread much mischief in the land, and they believed that there would be no Resurrection.

(So, your Lord poured on them different kinds of severe torment. Verily, your Lord is Ever Watchful (over them).) (89:13-14). Allah says here:

(So, We seized him and his armies, and We threw them all into the sea.) meaning, `We drowned them in the sea in a single morning, and not one of them was left.'

(So, behold what was the end of the wrongdoers. And We made them leaders inviting to the Fire) for those who followed them and took the same path as they did, rejecting the Messengers and denying the Creator.

(and on the Day of Resurrection, they will not be helped.) their humiliation in this world is combined with and connected to their humiliation in the Hereafter, as Allah says:

(We have destroyed them. And there was none to help them) (47:13).

(And We made a curse to follow them in this world,) Allah decreed that they and their king Fir`awn should be cursed by the believers among His servants who follow His Messengers, just as in this world they were cursed by the Prophets and their followers.

(and on the Day of Resurrection, they will be among disgraced.) Qatadah said, "This Ayah is like the Ayah,

(They were pursued by a curse in this (life) and on the Day of Resurrection. Evil indeed is the gift given.) (11:99)."

Surah: 28 Ayah: 43

وَلَقَدْ ءَاتَيْنَا مُوسَى ٱلْكِتَـٰبَ مِنۢ بَعْدِ مَآ أَهْلَكْنَا ٱلْقُرُونَ ٱلْأُولَىٰ بَصَآئِرَ لِلنَّاسِ وَهُدًى وَرَحْمَةً لَّعَلَّهُمْ يَتَذَكَّرُونَ ۝

43. And indeed We gave Mûsâ (Moses)- after We had destroyed the generations of old -the Scripture (the Taurât (Torah)) as an enlightenment for mankind, and a guidance and a mercy, that they might remember (or receive admonition).

Transliteration

43. Walaqad atayna moosa alkitaba min baAAdi ma ahlakna alquroona al-oola basa-ira lilnnasi wahudan warahmatan laAAallahum yatathakkaroona

Tafsir Ibn Kathir

The Blessings which Allah bestowed upon Musa

Allah tells us about the blessings which He gave His servant and Messenger Musa, the speaker, may the best of peace and blessings from his Lord be upon him, He revealed the Tawrah to him after He destroyed Fir`awn and his chiefs.

(after We had destroyed the generations of old) After the revelation of the Tawrah, no nation would again be punished with an overwhelming calamity; instead the believers were now commanded to fight the enemies of Allah among the idolators, as Allah says:

(And Fir`awn, and those before him, and the cities overthrown committed sin. And they disobeyed their Lord's Messenger, so He seized them with a strong punishment) (69:9-10).

(as an enlightenment for mankind, and a guidance and a mercy,) guidance from blindness and error. A guidance to the truth and a mercy means, to show the way towards doing righteous deeds.

(that they might remember.) means, that the people might be reminded and guided by it.

Surah: 28 Ayah: 44, Ayah: 45, Ayah: 46 & Ayah: 47

وَمَا كُنتَ بِجَانِبِ ٱلْغَرْبِيِّ إِذْ قَضَيْنَآ إِلَىٰ مُوسَى ٱلْأَمْرَ وَمَا كُنتَ مِنَ ٱلشَّٰهِدِينَ ۞

44. And you (O Muhammad (peace be upon him)) were not on the western side (of the Mount), when We made clear to Mûsâ (Moses) the commandment, and you were not among the witnesses.

وَلَٰكِنَّآ أَنشَأْنَا قُرُونًا فَتَطَاوَلَ عَلَيْهِمُ ٱلْعُمُرُ وَمَا كُنتَ ثَاوِيًا فِىٓ أَهْلِ مَدْيَنَ تَتْلُواْ عَلَيْهِمْ ءَايَٰتِنَا وَلَٰكِنَّا كُنَّا مُرْسِلِينَ ۞

45. But We created generations (after generations i.e. after Mûsâ (Moses) peace be upon him), and long were the ages that passed over them. And you (O Muhammad (peace be upon him)) were not a dweller among the people of Madyan (Midian), reciting Our Verses to them. But it is We Who kept sending (Messengers).

وَمَا كُنتَ بِجَانِبِ ٱلطُّورِ إِذْ نَادَيْنَا وَلَٰكِن رَّحْمَةً مِّن رَّبِّكَ لِتُنذِرَ قَوْمًا مَّآ أَتَىٰهُم مِّن نَّذِيرٍ مِّن قَبْلِكَ لَعَلَّهُمْ يَتَذَكَّرُونَ ۞

46. And you (O Muhammad (peace be upon him)) were not at the side of the Tûr (Mount) when We did call: (it is said that Allâh called the followers of Muhammad (peace be upon him) and they answered His Call, or that Allâh called Mûsâ (Moses)) But (you are sent) as a mercy from your Lord, to give warning to a people to whom no warner had come before you: in order that they may remember or receive admonition. (Tafsir At-Tabarî).

$$\text{وَلَوْلَآ أَن تُصِيبَهُم مُّصِيبَةٌ بِمَا قَدَّمَتْ أَيْدِيهِمْ فَيَقُولُواْ رَبَّنَا لَوْلَآ أَرْسَلْتَ إِلَيْنَا رَسُولاً فَنَتَّبِعَ ءَايَـٰتِكَ وَنَكُونَ مِنَ ٱلْمُؤْمِنِينَ ۝}$$

47. And if (We had) not (sent you to the people of Makkah) - in case a calamity should seize them for (the deeds) that their hands have sent forth, they would have said: "Our Lord! Why did You not send us a Messenger? We should then have followed Your Ayât (Verses of the Qur'ân) and would have been among the believers."

Transliteration

44. Wama kunta bijanibi algharbiyyi ith qadayna ila moosa al-amra wama kunta mina alshshahideena 45. Walakinna ansha-na quroonan fatatawala AAalayhimu alAAumuru wama kunta thawiyan fee ahli madyana tatloo AAalayhim ayatina walakinna kunna mursileena 46. Wama kunta bijanibi alttoori ith nadayna walakin rahmatan min rabbika litunthira qawman ma atahum min natheerin min qablika laAAallahum yatathakkaroona 47. Walawla an tuseebahum museebatun bima qaddamat aydeehim fayaqooloo rabbana lawla arsalta ilayna rasoolan fanattabiAAa ayatika wanakoona mina almu/mineena

Tafsir Ibn Kathir

Proof of the Prophethood of Muhammad

Allah points out the proof of the prophethood of Muhammad, whereby he told others about matters of the past, and spoke about them as if he were hearing and seeing them for himself. But he was an illiterate man who could not read books, and he grew up among a people who knew nothing of such things. Similarly, Allah told him about Maryam and her story, as Allah said:

(You were not with them, when they cast lots with their pens as to which of them should be charged with the care of Maryam; nor were you with them when they disputed) (3:44), meaning, `you were not present then, but Allah has revealed this to you.' Similarly, Allah told him about Nuh and his people, and how He saved Nuh and drowned his people, then He said:

(This is of the news of the Unseen which We reveal unto you; neither you nor your people knew it before this. So, be patient. Surely, the (good) end is for those who have Taqwa) (11:49). And at the end of the same Surah (Hud) Allah says:

(That is some of the news of the towns which We relate unto you) (11: 100). And here, after telling the story of Musa from beginning to end and how Allah began His revelation to him and spoke with him, Allah says:

(And you were not on the western side (of the Mount), when We made clear to Musa the commandment,) meaning, `you -- O Muhammad -- were not on the western side of the mountain where Allah spoke to Musa from the tree which was to the east of it, in the valley.'

Chapter 28: Al-Qasas (The story, Stories), Verses 001–088

(and you were not among the witnesses.) `to that event, but Allah has revealed this to you,' so that it may be evidence and proof of events which happened centuries ago, for people have forgotten the evidence that Allah established against them and what was revealed to the earlier Prophets.

(And you were not a dweller among the people of Madyan, reciting Our Ayat to them.) meaning, `you were not living among the people of Madyan reciting Our Ayat to them, when you started to tell about Our Prophet Shu`ayb and what he said to his people and how they responded.'

(But it is We Who kept sending.) means, `but We revealed that to you and sent you to mankind as a Messenger.'

(And you were not at the side of At-Tur when We called.) Qatadah said that:

(And you were not at the side of At-Tur when We did call.) refers to Musa, and this -- and Allah knows best -- is like the Ayah:

(And you were not on the western side (of the Mount), when We made clear to Musa the commandment,) Here Allah puts it in a different and more specific way by describing it as a call. This is like the Ayat:

(And (remember) when your Lord called Musa) (26:10).

(When his Lord called him in the sacred valley of Tuwa) (79:16).

(And We called him from the right side of At-Tur, and made him draw near to Us for a talk with him) (19:52).

(But (you are sent) as a mercy from your Lord,) means, `you were not a witness to any of those things, but Allah has revealed them to you and told you about them as a mercy from Him to you and to His servants, by sending you to them,'

(to give warning to a people to whom no warner had come before you, in order that they may remember or receive admonition.) means, `so that they may be guided by that which you bring from Allah.'

(And if (We had) not (sent you to the people of Makkah) -- in case a calamity should seize them for (the deeds) that their hands have sent forth, they would have said: "Our Lord! Why did You not send us a Messenger) meaning: `and We have sent you to them to establish proof against them, and to give them no excuse when the punishment of Allah comes to them because of their disbelief, lest they offer the excuse that no Messenger or warner came to them.' This is like what Allah says about the situation after He revealed His blessed Book the Qur'an:

(Lest you should say: "The Book was sent down only to two sects before us, and for our part, we were in fact unaware of what they studied." Or lest you should say: "If only the Book had been sent down to us, we would surely have been better guided than they." So, now has come unto you a clear proof from your Lord, and a guidance and a mercy) (6:156-157).

(Messengers as bearers of good news as well as warning in order that mankind should have no plea against Allah after the Messengers) (4:165).

(O People of the Scripture! Now has come to you Our Messenger making (things) clear unto you, after a break in (the series of) Messengers, lest you say: "There came unto us no bringer of glad tidings and no warner." But now has come unto you a bringer of glad tidings and a warner) (5:19). And there are many similar Ayat.

Surah: 28 Ayah: 48, Ayah: 49, Ayah: 50 & Ayah: 51

فَلَمَّا جَآءَهُمُ ٱلْحَقُّ مِنْ عِندِنَا قَالُوا۟ لَوْلَآ أُوتِىَ مِثْلَ مَآ أُوتِىَ مُوسَىٰٓ ۚ أَوَلَمْ يَكْفُرُوا۟ بِمَآ أُوتِىَ مُوسَىٰ مِن قَبْلُ ۖ قَالُوا۟ سِحْرَانِ تَظَٰهَرَا وَقَالُوٓا۟ إِنَّا بِكُلٍّ كَٰفِرُونَ

48. But when the truth (i.e. Muhammad (peace be upon him) with his Message) has come to them from Us, they say: "Why is he not given the like of what was given to Mûsâ (Moses)? Did they not disbelieve in that which was given to Mûsâ (Moses) of old? They say: "Two kinds of magic (the Taurât (Torah) and the Qur'ân), each helping the other!" And they say: "Verily in both we are disbelievers."

قُلْ فَأْتُوا۟ بِكِتَٰبٍ مِّنْ عِندِ ٱللَّهِ هُوَ أَهْدَىٰ مِنْهُمَآ أَتَّبِعْهُ إِن كُنتُمْ صَٰدِقِينَ

49. Say (to them, O Muhammad (peace be upon him)) "Then bring a Book from Allâh, which is a better guide than these two (the Taurât (Torah) and the Qur'ân), that I may follow it, if you are truthful."

فَإِن لَّمْ يَسْتَجِيبُوا۟ لَكَ فَٱعْلَمْ أَنَّمَا يَتَّبِعُونَ أَهْوَآءَهُمْ ۚ وَمَنْ أَضَلُّ مِمَّنِ ٱتَّبَعَ هَوَىٰهُ بِغَيْرِ هُدًى مِّنَ ٱللَّهِ ۚ إِنَّ ٱللَّهَ لَا يَهْدِى ٱلْقَوْمَ ٱلظَّٰلِمِينَ

50. But if they answer you not (i.e. do not bring the Book nor believe in your doctrine of Islâmic Monotheism), then know that they only follow their own lusts. And who is more astray than one who follows his own lusts, without guidance from Allâh? Verily Allâh guides not the people who are Zâlimûn (wrong-doers, disobedient to Allâh, and polytheists).

۞ وَلَقَدْ وَصَّلْنَا لَهُمُ ٱلْقَوْلَ لَعَلَّهُمْ يَتَذَكَّرُونَ

51. And indeed now We have conveyed the Word (this Qur'ân in which is the news of everything) to them, in order that they may remember (or receive admonition).

Transliteration

48. Falamma jaahumu alhaqqu min AAindina qaloo lawla ootiya mithla ma ootiya moosa awa lam yakfuroo bima ootiya moosa min qablu qaloo sihrani tathahara waqaloo inna bikullin kafiroona 49. Qul fa/too bikitabin min AAindi Allahi huwa ahda minhuma attabiAAhu in kuntum sadiqeena 50. Fa-in lam yastajeeboo laka faiAAlam annama yattabiAAoona ahwaahum waman adallu mimmani ittabaAAa hawahu bighayri hudan mina Allahi inna Allaha la yahdee alqawma alththalimeena 51. Walaqad wassalna lahumu alqawla laAAallahum yatathakkaroona

Tafsir Ibn Kathir

The stubborn Response of the Disbelievers

Allah tells us that if people were to be punished before proof was established against them, they would use the excuse that no Messenger came to them, but when the truth did come to them through Muhammad , in their stubbornness, disbelief, ignorance and misguided thinking, they said:

(Why is he not given the like of what was given to Musa) Meaning -- and Allah knows best -- many signs like the staff, the hand, the flood, the locusts, the lice, the frogs, the blood, the destruction of crops and fruits -- which made things difficult for the enemies of Allah -- and the parting of the sea, the clouds (following the Children of Israel in the wilderness and) shading them, the manna and quails, and other clear signs and definitive proof, miracles which Allah wrought at the hands of Musa as evidence and proof against Fir`awn and his chiefs and the Children of Israel. But all of this had no effect on Fir`awn and his chiefs; on the contrary, they denied Musa and his brother Harun, as Allah tells us:

(Have you come to us to turn us away from what we found our fathers following, and that you two may have greatness in the land We are not going to believe you two!) (10:78)

(So they denied them both and became of those who were destroyed.) (23:48)

The Rebellious do not believe in Miracles

Allah says here:

(Did they not disbelieve in that which was given to Musa of old) Did not mankind disbelieve in those mighty signs which were given to Musa

(They say: "Two kinds of magic, each helping the other!") cooperating or working one with the other.

(And they say: "Verily, in both we are disbelievers.") meaning, `we disbelieve in each of them.' Because of the close relationship between Musa and Harun, mention of one includes the other.

False Accusation that Musa and Harun (peace be upon them both) practiced Magic

Mujahid bin Jabr said, "The Jews told Quraysh to say this to Muhammad , then Allah said: `Did they not disbelieve in that which was given to Musa of old They say: Two kinds of magic, each helping the other!' This refers to Musa and Harun, may the peace and blessings of Allah be upon them both,

(each helping the other) i.e., working together and supporting one another." This was also the view of Sa`id bin Jubayr and Abu Razin that the phrase "two kinds of magic" referred to Musa and Harun. This is a good suggestion. And Allah knows best.

The Response to this False Accusation

(Two kinds of magic, each helping the other!) `Ali bin Abi Talhah and Al-`Awfi reported that Ibn `Abbas said that this refers to the Tawrah and the Qur'an, because Allah says next:

(Say: "Then bring a Book from Allah, which is a better guide than these two that I may follow it.") Allah often mentions the Tawrah and the Qur'an together, as in the Ayat:

(Say: "Who then sent down the Book which Musa brought, a light and a guidance to mankind...) until:

(And this is a blessed Book which We have sent down.") (6:91-92) And at the end of the same Surah, Allah says:

(Then, We gave Musa the Book, to complete (Our favor) upon those who would do right) (6: 154).

(And this is a blessed Book which We have sent down, so follow it and have Taqwa of Allah, that you may receive mercy) (6:155). And the Jinn said:

(Verily, we have heard a Book sent down after Musa, confirming what came before it) (46:30). Waraqah bin Nawfal said, "This is An-Namus, who came down to Musa." And those who are possessed of insight know instinctively that among the many Books which He has sent down to His Prophets, there is no Book more perfect, more eloquent or more noble than the Book which He revealed to Muhammad , which is the Qur'an. Next to it in status and greatness is the Book which Allah revealed to Musa bin `Imran, which is the Book concerning which Allah says:

(Verily, We did send down the Tawrah, therein was guidance and light, by which the Prophets, who submitted themselves to Allah's will, judged for the Jews. And the rabbis and the priests, for to them was entrusted the protection of Allah's Book, and they were witnesses thereto) (5:44). The Injil was revealed as a continuation and complement of the Tawrah and to permit some of the things that had been forbidden to the Children of Israel. Allah says:

(Then bring a Book from Allah, which is a better guide than these two, that I may follow it, if you are truthful.) meaning, `in your efforts to refute the truth with false arguments.'

(But if they answer you not,) means, `if they do not respond to what you tell them, and do not follow the truth,'

(then know that they only follow their own lusts.) means, with no basis or evidence. p

(And who is more astray than one who follows his own lusts, without guidance from Allah) means, with no guidance taken from the Book of Allah.

(Verily, Allah guides not the people who are wrongdoers.)

(And indeed now We have conveyed the Word) Mujahid said: "We have explained the Word to them." As-Suddi said something similar. Qatadah said: "Allah is saying, `He has told them what He did in the past and what He will do in the future.'"

(in order that they may remember.) Mujahid and others said:

(We have conveyed the Word) means, to Quraysh.

Surah: 28 Ayah: 52, Ayah: 53, Ayah: 54 & Ayah: 55

ٱلَّذِينَ ءَاتَيْنَٰهُمُ ٱلْكِتَٰبَ مِن قَبْلِهِۦ هُم بِهِۦ يُؤْمِنُونَ ۝

52. Those to whom We gave the Scripture (i.e. the Taurât (Torah) and the Injeel (Gospel)) before it, they believe in it (the Qur'ân).

وَإِذَا يُتْلَىٰ عَلَيْهِمْ قَالُوٓاْ ءَامَنَّا بِهِۦٓ إِنَّهُ ٱلْحَقُّ مِن رَّبِّنَآ إِنَّا كُنَّا مِن قَبْلِهِۦ مُسْلِمِينَ ۝

53. And when it is recited to them, they say: "We believe in it. Verily, it is the truth from our Lord. Indeed even before it we have been from those who submit themselves to Allâh in Islâm as Muslims (like 'Abdullâh bin Salâm and Salmân Al-Farisî).

أُوْلَٰٓئِكَ يُؤْتَوْنَ أَجْرَهُم مَّرَّتَيْنِ بِمَا صَبَرُواْ وَيَدْرَءُونَ بِٱلْحَسَنَةِ ٱلسَّيِّئَةَ وَمِمَّا رَزَقْنَٰهُمْ يُنفِقُونَ ۝

54. These will be given their reward twice over, because they are patient, and repel evil with good, and spend (in charity) out of what We have provided them.

وَإِذَا سَمِعُواْ ٱللَّغْوَ أَعْرَضُواْ عَنْهُ وَقَالُواْ لَنَآ أَعْمَٰلُنَا وَلَكُمْ أَعْمَٰلُكُمْ سَلَٰمٌ عَلَيْكُمْ لَا نَبْتَغِى ٱلْجَٰهِلِينَ ۝

55. And when they hear Al-Laghw (dirty, false, evil vain talk), they withdraw from it and say: "To us our deeds, and to you your deeds. Peace be to you. We seek not (the way of)the ignorant."

Transliteration

52. Allatheena ataynahumu alkitaba min qablihi hum bihi yu/minoona 53. Wa-itha yutla AAalayhim qaloo amanna bihi innahu alhaqqu min rabbina inna kunna min qablihi muslimeena 54. Ola-ika yu/tawna ajrahum marratayni bima sabaroo wayadraoona bialhasanati alssayyi-ata wamimma razaqnahum yunfiqoona 55. Wa-itha samiAAoo allaghwa aAAradoo AAanhu waqaloo lana aAAmaluna walakum aAAmalukum salamun AAalaykum la nabtaghee aljahileena

Tafsir Ibn Kathir

The Believers among the People of the Book

Allah tells us that the pious scholars among the People of the Book believe in the Qur'an, as He says:

(Those to whom We gave the Book recite it as it should be recited, they are the ones who believe therein) (2:121).

(And there are, certainly, among the People of the Scripture, those who believe in Allah and in that which has been revealed to you, and in that which has been revealed to them, humbling themselves before Allah) (3:199).

(Verily, those who were given knowledge before it, when it is recited to them, fall down on their faces in humble prostration. And they say: "Glory be to our Lord! Truly, the promise of our Lord must be fulfilled.") (17:107-108)

(And you will find the nearest in love to the believers those who say: "We are Christians. ") until:

(so write us down among the witnesses) (5:82-83). Sa`id bin Jubayr said, "This was revealed concerning seventy priests who were sent by An-Najashi (ruler of Ethiopia). When they came to the Prophet , he recited to them:

(Ya Sin. By the Qur'an, full of wisdom.) (36:1-2) until he completed the Surah. They began to weep, and they embraced Islam. These other Ayat were revealed concerning them:

(Those to whom We gave the Scripture before it, they believe in it. And when it is recited to them, they say: "We believe in it. Verily, it is the truth from our Lord. Indeed even before it we have been from Muslims.") meaning, `even befor e the Qur'an came we were Muslims, i.e., we believed in One God and were sincerely responding to Allah's commands.'

(These will be given their reward twice over, because they are patient,) means, those who have this characteristic -- that they believed in the first Book and then in the second. Allah says:

(because they are patient,) meaning, in their adherence to the truth, for taking such thing upon oneself is not easy for people. It was reported in the Sahih from the Hadith of `Amir Ash-Sha`bi from Abu Burdah that Abu Musa Al-Ash`ari, may Allah be pleased with him, said that the Messenger of Allah said:

«ثَلَاثَةٌ يُؤْتَوْنَ أَجْرَهُمْ مَرَّتَيْنِ: رَجُلٌ مِنْ أَهْلِ الْكِتَابِ آمَنَ بِنَبِيِّهِ ثُمَّ آمَنَ بِي، وَعَبْدٌ مَمْلُوكٌ أَدَّى حَقَّ اللهِ وَحَقَّ مَوَالِيهِ، وَرَجُلٌ كَانَتْ لَهُ أَمَةٌ، فَأَدَّبَهَا فَأَحْسَنَ تَأْدِيبَهَا، ثُمَّ أَعْتَقَهَا فَتَزَوَّجَهَا»

(There are three who will be given their reward twice: a man among the People of the Book who believed in his Prophet then believed in me; a slave who fulfills his duty towards Allah and towards his master; and a man who has a slave woman and educates her and teaches her good manners, then he frees her and marries her.) Imam Ahmad recorded that Abu Umamah said: "On the day of the Conquest (of Makkah) I was walking alongside the Messenger of Allah as he was riding, and he said some very beautiful words, including the following:

«مَنْ أَسْلَمَ مِنْ أَهْلِ الْكِتَابَيْنِ فَلَهُ أَجْرُهُ مَرَّتَيْنِ وَلَهُ مَا لَنَا وَعَلَيْهِ مَا عَلَيْنَا وَمَنْ أَسْلَمَ مِنَ الْمُشْرِكِينَ فَلَهُ أَجْرُهُ وَلَهُ مَا لَنَا وَعَلَيْهِ مَا عَلَيْنَا»

(Whoever among the people of the two Books becomes Muslim, he will have his reward twice, and he has the same rights and duties as we do. Whoever among the idolators becomes Muslim will have one reward, and he has the same rights and duties as we do.)" Allah's saying:

(and repel evil with good,) means, they do not respond to evil in kind, rather they forgive and overlook.

(and spend out of what We have provided for them.) meaning, `from the lawful provision that We have given them, they spend on their families and relatives as they are required to do, and they pay Zakah and give voluntary charity.'

(And when they hear evil vain talk, they withdraw from it) meaning, they do not mix with the people who indulge in such talk, rather they do as Allah says:

(and if they pass by some evil vain talk, they pass by it with dignity) (25:72).

(and they say: "To us our deeds, and to you your deeds. Peace be to you. We seek not (the way of) the ignorant.") means, if some foolish person speaks to them in a foolish manner and says something to which it does not befit them to respond, they turn away from him and do not respond in kind with ugly speech. They never say anything but good words. Allah says of them that they say:

(To us our deeds, and to you your deeds. Peace be to you. We seek not (the way of) the ignorant.) meaning, 'we do not seek the way of the ignorant and we do not like it.'

Surah: 28 Ayah: 56 & Ayah: 57

إِنَّكَ لَا تَهْدِى مَنْ أَحْبَبْتَ وَلَكِنَّ ٱللَّهَ يَهْدِى مَن يَشَآءُ وَهُوَ أَعْلَمُ بِٱلْمُهْتَدِينَ ۝

56. Verily you (O Muhammad (peace be upon him)) guide not whom you like, but Allâh guides whom He wills. And He knows best those who are the guided.

وَقَالُوٓا۟ إِن نَّتَّبِعِ ٱلْهُدَىٰ مَعَكَ نُتَخَطَّفْ مِنْ أَرْضِنَآ ۚ أَوَلَمْ نُمَكِّن لَّهُمْ حَرَمًا ءَامِنًا يُجْبَىٰٓ إِلَيْهِ ثَمَرَٰتُ كُلِّ شَىْءٍ رِّزْقًا مِّن لَّدُنَّا وَلَكِنَّ أَكْثَرَهُمْ لَا يَعْلَمُونَ ۝

57. And they say: "If we follow the guidance with you, we would be snatched away from our land." Have We not established for them a secure sanctuary (Makkah), to which are brought fruits of all kinds, a provision from Ourselves, but most of them know not.

Transliteration

56. Innaka la tahdee man ahbabta walakinna Allaha yahdee man yashao wahuwa aAAlamu bialmuhtadeena 57. Waqaloo in nattabiAAi alhuda maAAaka nutakhattaf min ardina awa lam numakkin lahum haraman aminan yujba ilayhi thamaratu kulli shay-in rizqan min ladunna walakinna aktharahum la yaAAlamoona

Tafsir Ibn Kathir

Allah guides Whom He wills

Allah says to His Messenger : `O Muhammad:

(Verily, you guide not whom you like)' meaning, 'the matter does not rest with you; all that you have to do is convey the Message, and Allah will guide whom He wills, and His is the ultimate wisdom,' as He says:

(Not upon you is their guidance, but Allah guides whom He wills.) (2:272)

(And most of mankind will not believe even if you desire it eagerly.) (12:103) This Ayah is even more specific than the following:

(Verily, you guide not whom you like, but Allah guides whom He wills. And He knows best those who are the guided.) meaning: Allah knows best who deserves to be guided and who deserves to be misguided. It was recorded in the Two Sahihs that this Ayah was revealed concerning Abu Talib, the paternal uncle of the Messenger of Allah . He used to protect the Prophet, support him and stand by him. He loved the Prophet dearly, but this love was a natural love, i.e., born of kinship, not a love that was born of the fact that he was the Messenger of Allah. When he was on his deathbed, the Messenger of Allah called him to Faith and to enter Islam, but the decree overtook him and he remained a follower of disbelief, and Allah's is the complete wisdom. Az-Zuhri said: "Sa`id bin Al-Musayyib narrated to me that his father, Al-Musayyib bin Hazan Al-Makhzumi, may Allah be pleased with him, said: "When Abu Talib was dying, the Messenger of Allah came to him and found Abu Jahl bin Hisham and `Abdullah bin Abi Umayyah bin Al-Mughirah with him. The Messenger of Allah said:

《يَا عَمِّ قُلْ: لَا إِلَهَ إِلَّا اللهُ، كَلِمَةً أُحَاجُّ لَكَ بِهَا عِنْدَ اللهِ》

(O my uncle, say La ilaha illallah, a word which I may use as evidence in your favor before Allah (in the Hereafter).) Abu Jahl bin Hisham and `Abdullah bin Abi Umayyah said: `O Abu Talib, will you leave the religion of `Abdul-Muttalib' The Messenger of Allah kept urging him to say La ilaha illallah, and they kept saying, `Will you leave the religion of `Abdul-Muttalib' -- until, at the very end, he said that he was on the religion of `Abdul-Muttalib, and he refused to say La ilaha illallah. The Messenger of Allah said:

《وَاللهِ لَأَسْتَغْفِرَنَّ لَكَ مَا لَمْ أُنْهَ عَنْك》

(By Allah, I shall certainly seek forgiveness for you unless I am told not to.) Then Allah revealed:

(It is not (proper) for the Prophet and those who believe to ask Allah's forgiveness for the idolators, even though they be of kin) (9:113). And there was revealed concerning Abu Talib the Ayah,

(Verily, you guide not whom you like, but Allah guides whom He wills.)" This was recorded (by Al-Bukhari and Muslim) from the Hadith of Az-Zuhri.

The Excuses made by the People of Makkah for not believing, and the Refutation of Their Excuses

(And they say: "If we follow the guidance with you, we would be snatched away from our land.") Allah tells us that this is the excuse which was given by some of the disbelievers for not following true guidance. They said to the Messenger of Allah:

(If we follow the guidance with you, we would be snatched away from our land.), meaning, `we are afraid that if we follow the message of guidance that you have brought, and go against the pagan Arab tribes around us, they will seek to do us harm and wage war against us, and they may snatch us away from wherever we may be.' Allah said in response to them:

(Have We not established for them a secure sanctuary,) meaning, the excuse they give is a lie and is false, because Allah has put them in a secure city and a venerated sanctuary which has been safe from the time it was built -- how could this sanctuary be safe for them when they believed in disbelief and Shirk, and how could it not be safe for them when they become Muslims and follow the truth

(to which are brought fruits of all kinds,) means, all kinds of fruits from the surrounding regions, from At-Ta'if and elsewhere. Similarly, the people of Makkah engaged in trade and other goods also came to their city.

(a provision from Ourselves, but most of them know not.) - this is why they said what they said.

Surah: 28 Ayah: 58 & Ayah: 59

وَكَمْ أَهْلَكْنَا مِن قَرْيَةٍ بَطِرَتْ مَعِيشَتَهَا فَتِلْكَ مَسَاكِنُهُمْ لَمْ تُسْكَن مِّن بَعْدِهِمْ إِلَّا قَلِيلًا وَكُنَّا نَحْنُ ٱلْوَٰرِثِينَ ۝

58. And how many a town (population) have We destroyed, which were thankless for its means of livelihood (disobeyed Allâh, and His Messengers, by doing evil deeds and crimes) ! And those are their dwellings, which have not been inhabited after them except a little. And verily! We have been the inheritors.

وَمَا كَانَ رَبُّكَ مُهْلِكَ ٱلْقُرَىٰ حَتَّىٰ يَبْعَثَ فِي أُمِّهَا رَسُولًا يَتْلُوا۟ عَلَيْهِمْ ءَايَٰتِنَا وَمَا كُنَّا مُهْلِكِى ٱلْقُرَىٰٓ إِلَّا وَأَهْلُهَا ظَٰلِمُونَ ۝

59. And never will your Lord destroy the towns (populations) until He sends to their mother town a Messenger reciting to them Our Verses. And never would We destroy the towns unless the people thereof are Zâlimûn (polytheists, wrong-doers, disbelievers in the Oneness of Allâh, oppressors and tyrants).

Transliteration

58. Wakam ahlakna min qaryatin batirat maAAeeshataha fatilka masakinuhum lam tuskan min baAAdihim illa qaleelan wakunna nahnu alwaritheena 59. Wama kana rabbuka muhlika alqura hatta yabAAatha fee ommiha rasoolan yatloo AAalayhim ayatina wama kunna muhlikee alqura illa waahluha thalimoona

Tafsir Ibn Kathir

The Destruction of Towns, which are not destroyed until Evidence is established against Them

Referring to the people of Makkah, Allah says:

(And how many a town have We destroyed, which was thankless for its means of livelihood!) They were arrogant transgressors who denied Allah's blessing of giving them ample provision. This is like the Ayah, o

(And Allah puts forward the example of a township, that dwelt secure and well-content: its provision coming to it in abundance from every place) until:

(So the torment overtook them while they were wrongdoers.) (16:112-113) Allah said:

(And those are their dwellings, which have not been inhabited after them except a little.) Their land became empty and desolate, and you can see nothing but their dwellings.

(And verily, We have been the heirs.) Their towns became ruins, with none remaining. Then Allah tells us of His justice and that He does not destroy anyone unjustly; on the contrary, He destroys those whom He destroys after establishing proof against them. So, he says:

(And never will your Lord destroy the towns until He sends to their mother town) i.e., Makkah --

(a Messenger reciting to them Our Ayat.) This indicates that the Unlettered Prophet, Muhammad was sent from the Mother of Cities as a Messenger to all cities and towns, Arab and non-Arab alike. This is like the Ayat:

(so that you may warn the Mother of Towns and all those around it) (6:92).

(Say: "O mankind! Verily, I am sent to you all as the Messenger of Allah.") (7:158),

(That I may therewith warn you and whomsoever it may reach.) (6:19)

(but those of the sects that reject it, the Fire will be their promised meeting place.) (11:17).

(And there is not a town but We shall destroy it before the Day of Resurrection, or punish it with a severe torment.) (17:58). Allah tells us that He will destroy every town before the Day of Resurrection, as He says:

(And We never punish until We have sent a Messenger.) (17:15). Allah has sent the Unlettered Prophet to all the towns (all of mankind), because he has been sent to the Mother of Cities, their source to which they all return. It was recorded in the Two Sahihs that the Prophet said:

(I have been sent to the red and the black.) Prophethood ended with him, and there is no Prophet or Messenger to come after him, but his way will remain as long as night and day remain, until the Day of Resurrection.

Surah: 28 Ayah: 60 & Ayah: 61

وَمَآ أُوتِيتُم مِّن شَىْءٍ فَمَتَـٰعُ ٱلْحَيَوٰةِ ٱلدُّنْيَا وَزِينَتُهَا ۚ وَمَا عِندَ ٱللَّهِ خَيْرٌ وَأَبْقَىٰٓ ۚ أَفَلَا تَعْقِلُونَ ۝

60. And whatever you have been given is an enjoyment of the life of (this) world and its adornment, and that (Hereafter) which is with Allâh is better and will remain forever. Have you then no sense?

$$\text{أَفَمَن وَعَدْنَـٰهُ وَعْدًا حَسَنًا فَهُوَ لَـٰقِيهِ كَمَن مَّتَّعْنَـٰهُ مَتَـٰعَ ٱلْحَيَوٰةِ ٱلدُّنْيَا ثُمَّ هُوَ يَوْمَ ٱلْقِيَـٰمَةِ مِنَ ٱلْمُحْضَرِينَ ۞}$$

61. Is he whom We have promised an excellent promise (Paradise)- which he will find true - like him whom We have made to enjoy the luxuries of the life of (this) world, then on the Day of Resurrection, he will be among those brought up (to be punished in the Hell-fire)?

Transliteration

60. Wama ooteetum min shay-in famataAAu alhayati alddunya wazeenatuha wama AAinda Allahi khayrun waabqa afala taAAqiloona 61. Afaman waAAadnahu waAAdan hasanan fahuwa laqeehi kaman mattaAAnahu mataAAa alhayati alddunya thumma huwa yawma alqiyamati mina almuhdareena

Tafsir Ibn Kathir

This World is transient and the One Whose concern is this World is not equal to the One Whose concern is the Hereafter

Allah tells us about the insignificance of this world and its contemptible adornments which are nothing in comparison to the great and lasting delights which Allah prepared for His righteous servants in the Hereafter. As Allah says:

(Whatever is with you, will be exhausted, and whatever is with Allah will remain) (16:96).

(and that which is with Allah is the best for the most righteous.) (3:198)

(whereas the life of this world as compared with the Hereafter is but a brief passing enjoyment.) (13:26)

(Nay, you prefer the life of this world. Although the Hereafter is better and more lasting.) (87:16-17). The Messenger of Allah said:

$$\text{«وَاللهِ مَا الْحَيَاةُ الدُّنْيَا فِي الْآخِرَةِ إِلَّا كَمَا يَغْمِسُ أَحَدُكُمْ إِصْبَعَهُ فِي الْيَمِّ، فَلْيَنْظُرْ مَاذَا يَرْجِعُ إِلَيْه»}$$

(By Allah, the life of this world in comparison to the Hereafter is as if one of you were to dip his finger in the sea; let him see what comes back to him.) Allah's saying:

(Have you then no sense) means, do those who prefer this world to the Hereafter have no sense

(Is he whom We have promised an excellent promise -- which he will find true -- like him whom We have made to enjoy the luxuries of the life of the world, then on the

Day of Resurrection, he will be among those brought up) Is the one who believes in the reward which Allah has promised in return for righteous deeds, which he will undoubtedly attain, like one who disbelieves in the meeting with Allah and in His promises and threats He is only enjoying a few days in this life,

(then on the Day of Resurrection, he will be among those brought up.) Mujahid and Qatadah said: "He will be among those who are punished." It was said that this was revealed concerning the Messenger of Allah and Abu Jahl, or that it was revealed concerning Hamzah and Ali, and Abu Jahl. Both views were narrated from Mujahid. The apparent meaning is that it is more general than that. This is like the Ayah where Allah describes a believer in Paradise looking out at his companion who is in Hell, and saying:

(Had it not been for the grace of my Lord, I would certainly have been among those brought forth (to Hell).) (37:57) And Allah says:

(but the Jinn know well that they have indeed to appear (before Him)) (37:158).

Surah: 28 Ayah: 62, Ayah: 63, Ayah: 64, Ayah: 65, Ayah: 66 & Ayah: 67

وَيَوْمَ يُنَادِيهِمْ فَيَقُولُ أَيْنَ شُرَكَآءِىَ ٱلَّذِينَ كُنتُمْ تَزْعُمُونَ ۝

62. And (remember) the Day when He will call to them and say: "Where are My (so-called) partners whom you used to assert?"

قَالَ ٱلَّذِينَ حَقَّ عَلَيْهِمُ ٱلْقَوْلُ رَبَّنَا هَٰٓؤُلَآءِ ٱلَّذِينَ أَغْوَيْنَآ أَغْوَيْنَٰهُمْ كَمَا غَوَيْنَا ۖ تَبَرَّأْنَآ إِلَيْكَ ۖ مَا كَانُوٓاْ إِيَّانَا يَعْبُدُونَ ۝

63. Those about whom the Word will have come true (to be punished) will say: "Our Lord! These are they whom we led astray. We led them astray, as we were astray ourselves. We declare our innocence (from them) before You. It was not us they worshipped."

وَقِيلَ ٱدْعُواْ شُرَكَآءَكُمْ فَدَعَوْهُمْ فَلَمْ يَسْتَجِيبُواْ لَهُمْ وَرَأَوُاْ ٱلْعَذَابَ ۚ لَوْ أَنَّهُمْ كَانُواْ يَهْتَدُونَ ۝

64. And it will be said (to them): "Call upon your (so-called) partners (of Allâh)", and they will call upon them, but they will give no answer to them, and they will see the torment. (They will then wish) if only they had been guided!

وَيَوْمَ يُنَادِيهِمْ فَيَقُولُ مَاذَآ أَجَبْتُمُ ٱلْمُرْسَلِينَ ۝

65. And (remember) the Day (Allâh) will call to them, and say: "What answer gave you to the Messengers?"

$$\text{فَعَمِيَتْ عَلَيْهِمُ ٱلْأَنۢبَآءُ يَوْمَئِذٍ فَهُمْ لَا يَتَسَآءَلُونَ ۝}$$

66. Then the news of a good answer will be obscured to them on that day, and they will not be able to ask one another.

$$\text{فَأَمَّا مَن تَابَ وَءَامَنَ وَعَمِلَ صَـٰلِحًا فَعَسَىٰٓ أَن يَكُونَ مِنَ ٱلْمُفْلِحِينَ ۝}$$

67. But as for him who repented (from polytheism and sins), believed (in the Oneness of Allâh, and in His Messenger Muhammad (peace be upon him)) and did righteous deeds (in the life of this world), then he will be among those who are successful.

Transliteration

62. Wayawma yunadeehim fayaqoolu ayna shuraka-iya allatheena kuntum tazAAumoona 63. Qala allatheena haqqa AAalayhimu alqawlu rabbana haola-i allatheena aghwayna aghwaynahum kama ghawayna tabarra/na ilayka ma kanoo iyyana yaAAbudoona 64. Waqeela odAAoo shurakaakum fadaAAawhum falam yastajeeboo lahum waraawoo alAAathaba law annahum kanoo yahtadoona 65. Wayawma yunadeehim fayaqoolu matha ajabtumu almursaleena 66. FaAAamiyat AAalayhimu al-anbao yawma-ithin fahum la yatasaaloona 67. Faamma man taba waamana waAAamila salihan faAAasa an yakoona mina almufliheena

Tafsir Ibn Kathir

The Idolators and Their Partners and the Emnity between Them in the Hereafter

Allah informs of how He will rebuke the idolators on the Day of Resurrection, when He will call them and say:

("Where are My (so-called) partners whom you used to assert") meaning, `where are the gods which you used to worship in the world, the idols and rivals Can they help you or save you' This is said in the nature of a rebuke and warning, as in the Ayah,

(And truly, you have come unto Us alone as We created you the first time. You have left behind you all that which We had bestowed on you. We see not with you your intercessors whom you claimed to be partners with Allah. Now all relations between you and them have been cut off, and all that you used to claim has vanished from you.) (6:94) His saying:

(Those about whom the Word will have been fulfilled) means the Shayatin and evil Jinn, and those who used to advocate disbelief.

("Our Lord! These are they whom we led astray. We led them astray, as we were astray ourselves. We declare our innocence before You. It was not us they worshipped.") They will testify against them and say that they led them astray, then they will declare their innocence of their worship. This is like the Ayat:

(And they have taken gods besides Allah, that they might give them honor, power and glory. Nay, but they will deny their worship of them, and become opponents to them.) (19:81-82)

(And who is more astray than one who calls besides Allah, who will not answer him till the Day of Resurrection, and who are (even) unaware of their calls to them And when mankind are gathered, they will become their enemies and will deny their worshipping.) (46:5-6). Ibrahim Al-Khalil, peace be upon him, said to his people:

(You have taken idols instead of Allah. The love between you is only in the life of this world, but on the Day of Resurrection, you shall disown each other, and curse each other.) (29:25)

(When those who were followed disown those who followed, and they see the torment, then all their relations will be cut off from them) until:

(And they will never get out of the Fire.) (2:166-167). Allah says:

(And it will be said (to them): "Call upon your partners,") meaning, `to save you from the predicament you are in, as you hoped that they would do in this world.'

(and they will call upon them, but they will give no answer to them, and they will see the torment.) means, they will realize for sure that they are inevitably destined for the Fire. His saying:

(If only they had been guided!) means, when they see the punishment with their own eyes, they will wish that they had been among the guided in this world. This is like the Ayah,

(And the Day He will say: "Call those partners of Mine whom you claimed." Then they will cry unto them, but they will not answer them, and We shall put a Mawbiq (a barrier) between them. And the criminals, shall see the Fire and apprehend that they have to fall in it. And they will find no way of escape from there.) (18:52-53) Their attitude towards the Messengers on the Day of Resurrection

(And the Day He will call to them, and say: "What answer gave you to the Messengers") The first call will be concerning the issue of Tawhid, which includes evidences of the prophethood -- `What was your response to the Messengers who were sent to you How did you deal with them' This is like the questions which will be asked of a person in his grave: `who is your Lord who is your Prophet and what is your religion' The believer will testify that there is no God except Allah and that Muhammad is His servant and Messenger, but the disbelievers will say, "Oh, oh, I do not know." So he will have no answer on the Day of Resurrection except to remain silent, because whoever is blind in this world (i.e., does not see Allah's signs and believes not in Him), will be blind in the Hereafter, and more astray. Allah says:

(Then the news of a good answer will be obscured to them on that Day, and they will not be able to ask one another.) Mujahid said: "The proof will be obscured from them," so they will not be able to ask one another for help by virtue of their blood ties. Allah's saying:

(But as for him who repented, believed, and did righteous deeds,) means, in this world.

(then perhaps he will be among those who are successful.) means, on the Day of Resurrection. And the word; perhaps (`Asa), when used in reference to Allah, may He be exalted, implies that the thing described will inevitably come to pass, and this will undoubtedly happen by the grace and mercy of Allah.

Surah: 28 Ayah: 68, Ayah: 69 & Ayah: 70

وَرَبُّكَ يَخْلُقُ مَا يَشَاءُ وَيَخْتَارُ مَا كَانَ لَهُمُ الْخِيَرَةُ سُبْحَانَ اللَّهِ وَتَعَالَىٰ عَمَّا يُشْرِكُونَ ۝

68. And your Lord creates whatsoever He wills and chooses: no choice have they (in any matter). Glorified is Allâh, and exalted above all that they associate (as partners with Him).

وَرَبُّكَ يَعْلَمُ مَا تُكِنُّ صُدُورُهُمْ وَمَا يُعْلِنُونَ ۝

69. And your Lord knows what their breasts conceal, and what they reveal.

وَهُوَ اللَّهُ لَا إِلَٰهَ إِلَّا هُوَ لَهُ الْحَمْدُ فِي الْأُولَىٰ وَالْآخِرَةِ وَلَهُ الْحُكْمُ وَإِلَيْهِ تُرْجَعُونَ

70. And He is Allâh; Lâ ilâha illa Huwa (none has the right to be worshipped but He). All praises and thanks are for Him (both) in the first (i.e. in this world) and in the last (i.e. in the Hereafter). And for Him is the Decision, and to Him shall you (all) be returned.

Transliteration

68. Warabbuka yakhluqu ma yashao wayakhtaru ma kana lahumu alkhiyaratu subhana Allahi wataAAala AAamma yushrikoona 69. Warabbuka yaAAlamu ma tukinnu sudooruhum wama yuAAlinoona 70. Wahuwa Allahu la ilaha illa huwa lahu alhamdu fee al-oola waal-akhirati walahu alhukmu wa-ilayhi turjaAAoona

Tafsir Ibn Kathir

Allah Alone is the One Who has the Power of Creation, Knowledge and Choice

Allah tells us that He is the only One Who has the power to create and make decisions, and there is no one who can dispute with Him in that or reverse His judgement. His saying:

(And your Lord creates whatsoever He wills and chooses,) means, whatever He wills, for what He wills, happens; and what He does not will, does not happen. All things, good and bad alike, are in His Hands and will return to Him.

Chapter 28: Al-Qasas (The story, Stories), Verses 001–088

(no choice have they.) is a negation, according to the correct view. This is like the Ayah,

(It is not for a believer, man or woman, when Allah and His Messenger have decreed a matter that they should have any option in their decision) (33:36). Then Allah says:

(And your Lord knows what their breasts conceal, and what they reveal.) He knows what is hidden in their hearts, just as He knows what they do openly.

(It is the same whether any of you conceals his speech or declares it openly, whether he be hid by night or goes forth freely by day.) (13:10).

(And He is Allah; La ilaha illa Huwa,) meaning, He is unique in His divinity, for none is to be worshipped besides Him, and there is no lord who can create what he wills and chooses besides Him.

(His is the praise, in the first and in the last,) in all that He does, He is to be praised for His justice and wisdom.

(His is the decision,) that none can put back, because of His might, power, wisdom and mercy.

(and to Him shall you be returned.) means, all of you on the Day of Resurrection, and everyone will be rewarded or punished according to his deeds, good and evil alike, and absolutely none of their deeds will be concealed from Him.

Surah: 28 Ayah: 71, Ayah: 72 & Ayah: 73

قُلْ أَرَءَيْتُمْ إِن جَعَلَ ٱللَّهُ عَلَيْكُمُ ٱلَّيْلَ سَرْمَدًا إِلَىٰ يَوْمِ ٱلْقِيَٰمَةِ مَنْ إِلَٰهٌ غَيْرُ ٱللَّهِ يَأْتِيكُم بِضِيَآءٍ أَفَلَا تَسْمَعُونَ ۝

71. Say (O Muhammad (peace be upon him)) "Tell me! If Allâh made the night continuous for you till the Day of Resurrection, which ilâh (god) besides Allâh could bring you light? Will you not then hear?"

قُلْ أَرَءَيْتُمْ إِن جَعَلَ ٱللَّهُ عَلَيْكُمُ ٱلنَّهَارَ سَرْمَدًا إِلَىٰ يَوْمِ ٱلْقِيَٰمَةِ مَنْ إِلَٰهٌ غَيْرُ ٱللَّهِ يَأْتِيكُم بِلَيْلٍ تَسْكُنُونَ فِيهِ أَفَلَا تُبْصِرُونَ ۝

72. Say (O Muhammad (peace be upon him)) "Tell me! If Allâh made the day continuous for you till the Day of Resurrection, which ilâh (god) besides Allâh who could bring you night wherein you rest? Will you not then see?"

وَمِن رَّحْمَتِهِۦ جَعَلَ لَكُمُ ٱلَّيْلَ وَٱلنَّهَارَ لِتَسْكُنُوا۟ فِيهِ وَلِتَبْتَغُوا۟ مِن فَضْلِهِۦ وَلَعَلَّكُمْ تَشْكُرُونَ ۝

73. It is out of His Mercy that He has made for you the night and the day that you may rest therein (i.e. during the night) and that you may seek of His Bounty (i.e. during the day) - and in order that you may be grateful.

Transliteration

71. Qul araaytum in jaAAala Allahu AAalaykumu allayla sarmadan ila yawmi alqiyamati man ilahun ghayru Allahi ya/teekum bidiya-in afala tasmaAAoona 72. Qul araaytum in jaAAala Allahu AAalaykumu alnnahara sarmadan ila yawmi alqiyamati man ilahun ghayru Allahi ya/teekum bilaylin taskunoona feehi afala tubsiroona 73. Wamin rahmatihi jaAAala lakumu allayla waalnnahara litaskunoo feehi walitabtaghoo min fadlihi walaAAallakum tashkuroona

Tafsir Ibn Kathir

Night and Day are among the Blessings of Allah and are Signs of Tawhid

Allah reminds His servants of His favors towards them by subjugating for them the night and day, without which they could not survive. He explains that if He made the night continuous, lasting until the Day of Resurrection, that would be harmful for them and would cause boredom and stress. So He says:

(which god besides Allah could bring you light) meaning, `with which you could see things and which would bring you relief'

(Will you not then hear) Then Allah tells us that if He had made the day continuous, lasting until the Day of Resurrection, that would also be harmful for them and their bodies would get tired from so much movement and activity. Allah says:

(which god besides Allah could bring you night wherein you rest) meaning, `to rest from your work and activity.'

(Will you not then see It is out of His mercy) towards you,

(that He has made for you the night and the day) He created both,

(that you may rest therein) during the night,

(and that you may seek of His bounty) during the day, by traveling, moving about and working.

(and in order that you may be grateful.) So that you may give thanks to Allah by performing all kinds of acts of worship at night and during the day. Whoever misses something during the night can make it up during the day, and vice versa. This is like the Ayah,

(And He it is Who has put the night and the day in succession, for such who desires to remember or desires to show his gratitude.) (25:62). And there are many similar Ayat.

Surah: 28 Ayah: 74 & Ayah: 75

وَيَوْمَ يُنَادِيهِمْ فَيَقُولُ أَيْنَ شُرَكَآءِىَ ٱلَّذِينَ كُنتُمْ تَزْعُمُونَ ﴿٧٤﴾

74. And (remember) the Day when He (your Lord - Allâh) will call to them (those who worshipped others along with Allâh), and will say: "Where are My (so-called) partners, whom you used to assert?"

وَنَزَعْنَا مِن كُلِّ أُمَّةٍ شَهِيدًا فَقُلْنَا هَاتُوا۟ بُرْهَٰنَكُمْ فَعَلِمُوٓا۟ أَنَّ ٱلْحَقَّ لِلَّهِ وَضَلَّ عَنْهُم مَّا كَانُوا۟ يَفْتَرُونَ ﴿٧٥﴾

75. And We shall take out from every nation a witness, and We shall say: "Bring your proof." Then they shall know that the truth is with Allâh (Alone), and the lies (false gods) which they invented will disappear from them.

Transliteration

74. Wayawma yunadeehim fayaqoolu ayna shuraka-iya allatheena kuntum tazAAumoona 75. WanazaAAna min kulli ommatin shaheedan faqulna hatoo burhanakum faAAalimoo anna alhaqqa lillahi wadalla AAanhum ma kanoo yaftaroona

Tafsir Ibn Kathir

Rebuking the Idolators

This is another call by way of rebuke for those who worshipped other gods besides Allah. The Lord, may He be exalted, will call to them before all the witnesses, and will say:

(Where are My (so-called) partners, whom you used to assert) meaning, in this world.

(And We shall take out from every nation a witness,) Mujahid said, "This means a Messenger."

(and We shall say: "Bring your proof.'') meaning, `of the truth of your claim that Allah had any partners.'

(Then they shall know that the truth is with Allah,) meaning, that there is no god besides Him. Then they will not speak and they will not be able to find any answer.

(and the lies which they invented will disappear from them.) they will vanish and will be of no benefit to them.

Surah: 28 Ayah: 76 & Ayah: 77

$$\bullet \text{ إِنَّ قَارُونَ كَانَ مِن قَوْمِ مُوسَىٰ فَبَغَىٰ عَلَيْهِمْ ۖ وَءَاتَيْنَاهُ مِنَ ٱلْكُنُوزِ مَا إِنَّ مَفَاتِحَهُۥ لَتَنُوٓأُ بِٱلْعُصْبَةِ أُو۟لِى ٱلْقُوَّةِ إِذْ قَالَ لَهُۥ قَوْمُهُۥ لَا تَفْرَحْ ۖ إِنَّ ٱللَّهَ لَا يُحِبُّ ٱلْفَرِحِينَ ۝}$$

76. Verily, Qârûn (Korah) was of Mûsâ's (Moses) people, but he behaved arrogantly towards them. And We gave him of the treasures, that of which the keys would have been a burden to a body of strong men. Remember when his people said to him: "Do not exult (with ungratefulness to Allâh's Favors). Verily! Allâh likes not those who are glad (with ungratefulness to Allâh's Favors).

$$\text{وَٱبْتَغِ فِيمَآ ءَاتَىٰكَ ٱللَّهُ ٱلدَّارَ ٱلْءَاخِرَةَ ۖ وَلَا تَنسَ نَصِيبَكَ مِنَ ٱلدُّنْيَا ۖ وَأَحْسِن كَمَآ أَحْسَنَ ٱللَّهُ إِلَيْكَ ۖ وَلَا تَبْغِ ٱلْفَسَادَ فِى ٱلْأَرْضِ ۖ إِنَّ ٱللَّهَ لَا يُحِبُّ ٱلْمُفْسِدِينَ ۝}$$

77. But seek, with that (wealth) which Allâh has bestowed on you, the home of the Hereafter, and forget not your portion of lawful enjoyment in this world; and do good as Allâh has been good to you, and seek not mischief in the land. Verily, Allâh likes not the Mufsidûn (those who commit great crimes and sins, oppressors, tyrants, mischief-makers, corrupts).

Transliteration

76. Inna qaroona kana min qawmi moosa fabagha AAalayhim waataynahu mina alkunoozi ma inna mafatihahu latanoo-o bialAAusbati olee alquwwati ith qala lahu qawmuhu la tafrah inna Allaha la yuhibbu alfariheena 77. Waibtaghi feema ataka Allahu alddara al-akhirata wala tansa naseebaka mina alddunya waahsin kama ahsana Allahu ilayka wala tabghi alfasada fee al-ardi inna Allaha la yuhibbu almufsideena

Tafsir Ibn Kathir

Qarun and His People's exhortation

It was recorded that Ibn `Abbas said:

(Verily, Qarun was of Musa's people,) "He was the son of his paternal uncle." This was also the view of Ibrahim An-Nakha`i, `Abdullah bin Al-Harith bin Nawfal, Sammak bin Harb, Qatadah, Malik bin Dinar, Ibn Jurayj and others; they all said that he was the cousin of Musa, peace be upon him. Ibn Jurayj said: "He was Qarun bin Yashar bin Qahith, and Musa was the son of `Imran bin Qahith.

(And We gave him of the treasures,) meaning, of wealth;

Chapter 28: Al-Qasas (The story, Stories), Verses 001–088

(that of which the keys would have been a burden to a body of strong men.) Groups of strong men would not have been able to carry them because they were so many. Al-A`mash narrated from Khaythamah, "The keys of Qarun's treasure were made of leather, each key like a finger, and each key was for a separate storeroom. When he rode anywhere, the keys would be carried on sixty mules with white blazes on their foreheads and white feet." Other views were also given, and Allah knows best.

(Remember when his people said to him: "Do not exult. Verily, Allah likes not those who exult.") means, the righteous ones among his people exhorted him. By way of sincere advice and guidance, they said: "Do not exult in what you have," meaning, `do not be arrogant and proud of your wealth.'

(Verily, Allah likes not those who exult.) Ibn `Abbas said, "This means, those who rejoice and gloat." Mujahid said, "It means those who are insolent and reckless, and do not thank Allah for what He has given them." His saying:

(But seek, with that which Allah has bestowed on you, the home of the Hereafter, and forget not your portion of lawful enjoyment in this world;) means, `use this great wealth and immense blessing Allah has given you to worship your Lord and draw closer to Him by doing a variety of good deeds which will earn you reward in this world and the Hereafter.'

(and forget not your portion of lawful enjoyment in this world;) `That which Allah has permitted of food, drink, clothing, dwelling places and women. Your Lord has rights over you, your self has rights over you, your family has rights over you, and your visitors have rights over you. So give each of them their due.'

(and be generous as Allah has been generous to you,) `Be generous to His creatures, as He has been generous to you.'

(and seek not mischief in the land.) meaning: `do not let your aim be to spread corruption on earth and do harm to Allah's creation.'

(Verily, Allah likes not the mischief-makers.)

Surah: 28 Ayah: 78

قَالَ إِنَّمَا أُوتِيتُهُۥ عَلَىٰ عِلْمٍ عِندِىٓ ۚ أَوَلَمْ يَعْلَمْ أَنَّ ٱللَّهَ قَدْ أَهْلَكَ مِن قَبْلِهِۦ مِنَ ٱلْقُرُونِ مَنْ هُوَ أَشَدُّ مِنْهُ قُوَّةً وَأَكْثَرُ جَمْعًا ۚ وَلَا يُسْـَٔلُ عَن ذُنُوبِهِمُ ٱلْمُجْرِمُونَ

78. He said: "This has been given to me only because of the knowledge I possess." Did he not know that Allâh had destroyed before him generations, men who were stronger than him in might and greater in the amount (of riches) they had collected? But the Mujrimûn (criminals, disbelievers, polytheists, sinners) will not be questioned of their sins (because Allâh knows them well, so they will be punished without being called to account).

Transliteration

78. Qala innama ooteetuhu AAala AAilmin AAindee awa lam yaAAlam anna Allaha qad ahlaka min qablihi mina alqurooni man huwa ashaddu minhu quwwatan waaktharu jamAAan wala yus-alu AAan thunoobihimu almujrimoona

Tafsir Ibn Kathir

Allah informs us how Qarun responded to the exhortations of his people when they sought to guide him to what is good.

(He said: "This has been given to me only because of the knowledge I possess.") meaning, `I have no need of your advice; Allah has only given me this wealth because He knows that I deserve it and because He loves me. ' In other words: `He has given it to me because He knows that I am fit for this.' This is like the Ayat:

(When harm touches man, he calls upon Us; then when We have changed it into a favor from Us, he says: "Only because of knowledge I obtained it.") (39:49) An alternative interpretation of this Ayah says that the meaning is: "Only because of what Allah knows about me did I obtain this favor." This is like His saying:

(And truly, if We give him a taste of mercy from Us, after some adversity has touched him, he is sure to say: "This is from me.") (41:50) meaning, "I deserved it." Imam `Abdur-Rahman bin Zayd bin Aslam explained this Ayah very well. Concerning the phrase,

(He said: "This has been given to me only because of the knowledge I possess.") He said: "Were it not for the fact that Allah is pleased with me and knows my virtue, He would not have given me this wealth." And He said:

(Did he not know that Allah had destroyed before him generations, men who were stronger than him in might and greater in the amount they had collected) This is what those who have little knowledge say when they see a person whom Allah has granted a lot of wealth; they say that if he did not deserve it, Allah would not have given it to him.

Surah: 28 Ayah: 79 & Ayah: 80

فَخَرَجَ عَلَىٰ قَوْمِهِۦ فِى زِينَتِهِۦ ۖ قَالَ ٱلَّذِينَ يُرِيدُونَ ٱلْحَيَوٰةَ ٱلدُّنْيَا يَـٰلَيْتَ لَنَا مِثْلَ مَآ أُوتِىَ قَـٰرُونُ إِنَّهُۥ لَذُو حَظٍّ عَظِيمٍ ۝

79. So he went forth before his people in his pomp. Those who were desirous of the life of the world, said: "Ah, would that we had the like of what Qârûn (Korah) has been given? Verily! He is the owner of a great fortune."

وَقَالَ ٱلَّذِينَ أُوتُوا۟ ٱلْعِلْمَ وَيْلَكُمْ ثَوَابُ ٱللَّهِ خَيْرٌ لِّمَنْ ءَامَنَ وَعَمِلَ صَـٰلِحًا وَلَا يُلَقَّىٰهَآ إِلَّا ٱلصَّـٰبِرُونَ ۝

80. But those who had been given (religious) knowledge said: "Woe to you! The Reward of Allâh (in the Hereafter) is better for those who believe and do righteous good deeds, and this none shall attain except those who are As-Sâbirûn (the patient in following the truth)."

Transliteration

79. Fakharaja AAala qawmihi fee zeenatihi qala allatheena yureedoona alhayata alddunya ya layta lana mithla ma ootiya qaroonu innahu lathoo haththin AAatheemin
80. Waqala allatheena ootoo alAAilma waylakum thawabu Allahi khayrun liman amana waAAamila salihan wala yulaqqaha illa alssabiroona

Tafsir Ibn Kathir

How Qarun went forth in His Finery, and His People's Comments

Allah tells us how Qarun went forth one day before his people with his magnificent regalia; wearing his fine clothes, accompanied by his fine horses, his servants and retinue. When those whose desires and inclinations were for the world saw his adornments and splendor, they wished that they could have the same as he had been given, and said:

(Ah, would that we had the like of what Qarun has been given! Verily, he is the owner of a great fortune.) meaning, `he is very lucky and has a great share in this world.' When the people of beneficial knowledge heard this, they said to them:

(Woe to you! The reward of Allah is better for those who believe and do righteous deeds,) `Allah's reward to His believing, righteous servants in the Hereafter is better than what you see,' as is reported in the authentic Hadith:

«يَقُولُ اللهُ تَعَالَى: أَعْدَدْتُ لِعِبَادِي الصَّالِحِينَ مَا لَا عَيْنٌ رَأَتْ وَلَا أُذُنٌ سَمِعَتْ وَلَا خَطَرَ عَلَى قَلْبِ بَشَرٍ وَاقْرَءُوا إِنْ شِئْتُمْ:

(فَلاَ تَعْلَمُ نَفْسٌ مَّآ أُخْفِىَ لَهُم مِّن قُرَّةِ أَعْيُنٍ جَزَآءً بِمَا كَانُواْ يَعْمَلُونَ)

(Allah has prepared for His righteous servants what no eye has seen, no ear has heard, and the heart of a human cannot comprehend. Recite, if you wish: (No person knows what is kept hidden for them of joy as a reward for what they used to do.)) (32:17).

(and this none shall attain except the patient.) As-Suddi said: "None shall reach Paradise except for the patient" -- as if this were the completion of the statement made by the people of knowledge. Ibn Jarir said, "This applies only to those who patiently forsake the love of this world, seeking the Hereafter. It is as if this is part of what the people of knowledge said, but it is made part of the Words of Allah, stating this fact."

Surah: 28 Ayah: 81 & Ayah: 82

$$\text{فَخَسَفْنَا بِهِ وَبِدَارِهِ ٱلْأَرْضَ فَمَا كَانَ لَهُۥ مِن فِئَةٍ يَنصُرُونَهُۥ مِن دُونِ ٱللَّهِ وَمَا كَانَ مِنَ ٱلْمُنتَصِرِينَ ۝}$$

81. So We caused the earth to swallow him and his dwelling place. Then he had no group or party to help him against Allâh, nor was he one of those who could save themselves.

$$\text{وَأَصْبَحَ ٱلَّذِينَ تَمَنَّوْا۟ مَكَانَهُۥ بِٱلْأَمْسِ يَقُولُونَ وَيْكَأَنَّ ٱللَّهَ يَبْسُطُ ٱلرِّزْقَ لِمَن يَشَآءُ مِنْ عِبَادِهِۦ وَيَقْدِرُ لَوْلَآ أَن مَّنَّ ٱللَّهُ عَلَيْنَا لَخَسَفَ بِنَا وَيْكَأَنَّهُۥ لَا يُفْلِحُ ٱلْكَٰفِرُونَ ۝}$$

82. And those who had desired (for a position like) his position the day before, began to say: "Know you not that it is Allâh Who enlarges the provision or restricts it to whomsoever He pleases of His slaves. Had it not been that Allâh was Gracious to us, He could have caused the earth to swallow us up (also)! Know you not that the disbelievers will never be successful.

Transliteration

81. Fakhasafna bihi wabidarihi al-arda fama kana lahu min fi-atin yansuroonahu min dooni Allahi wama kana mina almuntasireena 82. Waasbaha allatheena tamannaw makanahu bial-amsi yaqooloona waykaanna Allaha yabsutu alrrizqa liman yashao min AAibadihi wayaqdiru lawla an manna Allahu AAalayna lakhasafa bina waykaannahu la yuflihu alkafiroona

Tafsir Ibn Kathir

How Qarun and His Dwelling Place were swallowed up by the Earth

After telling us about Qarun's conceit and pride in his adornments, and how he was arrogant towards his people and transgressed against them, Allah then tells us how he and his dwelling place were swallowed up by the earth. This was also reported in the Sahih by Al-Bukhari from Salim, who said that his father told him that the Messenger of Allah said:

$$\text{«بَيْنَمَا رَجُلٌ يَجُرُّ إِزَارَهُ إِذْ خُسِفَ بِهِ، فَهُوَ يَتَجَلْجَلُ فِي الْأَرْضِ إِلَى يَوْمِ الْقِيَامَة»}$$

(While a man was dragging his lower garment, he was swallowed up and he will remain sinking down into the earth until the Day of Resurrection.) He also recorded

Chapter 28: Al-Qasas (The story, Stories), Verses 001–088

something similar from Salim from Abu Hurayrah from the Prophet . Imam Ahmad recorded that Abu Sa`id said, "The Messenger of Allah said:

»بَيْنَمَا رَجُلٌ فِيمَنْ كَانَ قَبْلَكُمْ خَرَجَ فِي بُرْدَيْنِ أَخْضَرَيْنِ يَخْتَالُ فِيهِمَا، أَمَرَ اللهُ الْأَرْضَ فَأَخَذَتْهُ، فَإِنَّهُ لَيَتَجَلْجَلُ فِيهَا إِلَى يَوْمِ الْقِيَامَةِ«

(When a man among the people who came before you went out wearing two green garments, walking proudly and arrogantly, Allah commanded the earth to swallow him up, and he will remain sinking down into it until the Day of Resurrection.) This version was recorded only by Ahmad, and its chain of narration is Hasan (sound).

(Then he had no group to help him against Allah, nor was he one of those who could save themselves.) means, his wealth, group, servants and retinue were of no avail to him; they could not protect him from the wrath and vengeance of Allah. Nor could he help himself or save himself. There was no one to help him, neither himself nor anybody else.

His People learned a Lesson from Him being swallowed up

Allah's saying:

(And those who had desired his position the day before,) means, those witnessed him with his finery and said:

(Those who were desirous of the life of the world, said: "Ah, would that we had the like of what Qarun has been given! Verily, he is the owner of a great fortune.") When he was swallowed up in the earth, they began to say:

(Know you not that it is Allah Who expands the provision or restricts it to whomsoever He pleases of His servants.) Wealth does not indicate that Allah is pleased with its owner, for Allah gives and withholds, allows times of difficulty and times of ease, raises and lowers, His is the most complete wisdom and most convincing proof. According to a Hadith narrated by Ibn Mas`ud,

»إِنَّ اللهَ قَسَمَ بَيْنَكُمْ أَخْلَاقَكُمْ كَمَا قَسَمَ أَرْزَاقَكُمْ، وَإِنَّ اللهَ يُعْطِي الْمَالَ مَنْ يُحِبُّ وَمَنْ لَا يُحِبُّ، وَلَا يُعْطِي الْإِيمَانَ إِلَّا مَنْ يُحِبُّ«

(Allah has alloted character among you just as He has alloted your provision. Allah gives wealth to those whom He loves and those whom He does not love, but He gives Faith only to those whom He loves.)

(Had it not been that Allah was Gracious to us, He could have caused the earth to swallow us up!) meaning, `were it not for the kindness and grace of Allah towards us, we could have been swallowed up by the earth just as he was swallowed up, because we wanted to be like him.'

(Know you not that the disbelievers will never be successful.) He was a disbeliever, and the disbelievers will never be successful before Allah in this world or in the Hereafter.

Surah: 28 Ayah: 83 & Ayah: 84

تِلْكَ ٱلدَّارُ ٱلْءَاخِرَةُ نَجْعَلُهَا لِلَّذِينَ لَا يُرِيدُونَ عُلُوًّا فِى ٱلْأَرْضِ وَلَا فَسَادًا وَٱلْعَـٰقِبَةُ لِلْمُتَّقِينَ ۝

83. That home of the Hereafter (i.e. Paradise), We shall assign to those who rebel not against the truth with pride and oppression in the land nor do mischief by committing crimes. And the good end is for the Muttaqûn (the pious and righteous persons. see V.2:2).

مَن جَآءَ بِٱلْحَسَنَةِ فَلَهُۥ خَيْرٌ مِّنْهَا وَمَن جَآءَ بِٱلسَّيِّئَةِ فَلَا يُجْزَى ٱلَّذِينَ عَمِلُوا۟ ٱلسَّيِّـَٔاتِ إِلَّا مَا كَانُوا۟ يَعْمَلُونَ ۝

84. Whosoever brings good (Islâmic Monotheism along with righteous deeds), he shall have the better thereof; and whosoever brings evil (polytheism along with evil deeds), then those who do evil deeds will only be requited for what they used to do.

Transliteration

83. Tilka alddaru al-akhiratu najAAaluha lillatheena la yureedoona AAuluwwan fee alardi wala fasadan waalAAaqibatu lilmuttaqeena   84. Man jaa bialhasanati falahu khayrun minha waman jaa bialssayyi-ati fala yujza allatheena AAamiloo alssayyi-ati illa ma kanoo yaAAmaloona

Tafsir Ibn Kathir

The Blessings of the Hereafter for the humble Believers

Allah tells us that He has made the home of the Hereafter, and its eternal delights which will never change or fade away, for His believing, humble servants who do not rebel against the truth with pride and oppression in the land. They do not exalt themselves above the creatures of Allah, arrogantly oppressing them and spreading corruption among them. `Ikrimah said that this phrase referred to haughtiness and arrogance. Ibn Jurayj said:

(those who do not want to exalt themselves in the land) "Arrogance and tyranny,

(nor cause corruption) committing sins." Ibn Jarir recorded that `Ali said, "If a man wants the straps of his sandals to be better than the straps of his companion's sandals, then he is one of those referred to in the Ayah,

(That is the home of the Hereafter, We shall assign to those who do not want to exalt themselves in the land nor cause corruption. And the good end is for those who have Taqwa.) This is understood to mean that if his intention is to show off and appear better than others, then that is to be condemned, as it was reported in the Sahih that the Prophet said:

«إِنَّهُ أُوحِيَ إِلَيَّ أَنْ تَوَاضَعُوا حَتَّى لَا يَفْخَرَ أَحَدٌ عَلَى أَحَدٍ وَلَا يَبْغِي أَحَدٌ عَلَى أَحَدٍ»

(It has been revealed to me that you should be humble to the extent that none of you boasts to others or mistreats others.) But if a person simply likes to look good, then there is nothing wrong with that. It was recorded that a man said: "O Messenger of Allah, I like to have my garment looking good and my shoes looking good -- is this a kind of arrogance" The Prophet said:

«لَا، إِنَّ اللهَ جَمِيلٌ يُحِبُّ الْجَمَالَ»

(No, for Allah is beautiful and loves beauty...) And Allah says:

(Whosoever brings good,) meaning, on the Day of Resurrection,

(he shall have the better thereof;) meaning, the reward of Allah is better than the good deeds of His servant -- how can it not be, when Allah has multiplied it many times over This is the position of generosity. Then Allah says:

(and whosoever brings evil, then those who do evil deeds will only be requited for what they used to do.) This is like the Ayah,

(And whoever brings an evil deed, they will be cast down on their faces in the Fire. (And it will be said to them) "Are you being recompensed anything except what you used to do") (27: 90). This is the postition of generosity and justice.

Surah: 28 Ayah: 85, Ayah: 86, Ayah: 87 & Ayah: 88

إِنَّ ٱلَّذِى فَرَضَ عَلَيْكَ ٱلْقُرْءَانَ لَرَادُّكَ إِلَىٰ مَعَادٍ ۚ قُل رَّبِّى أَعْلَمُ مَن جَآءَ بِٱلْهُدَىٰ وَمَنْ هُوَ فِى ضَلَٰلٍ مُّبِينٍ ۝

85. Verily, He Who has given you (O Muhammad (peace be upon him)) the Qur'an (i.e. ordered you to act on its laws and to preach it to others) will surely bring you back to the Ma'âd (place of return, either to Makkah or to Paradise after your death). Say (O Muhammad (peace be upon him)) "My Lord is Aware of him who brings guidance, and of him who is in manifest error."

$$وَمَا كُنتَ تَرْجُوٓا۟ أَن يُلْقَىٰٓ إِلَيْكَ ٱلْكِتَـٰبُ إِلَّا رَحْمَةً مِّن رَّبِّكَ ۖ فَلَا تَكُونَنَّ ظَهِيرًا لِّلْكَـٰفِرِينَ ۝٨٦$$

86. And you were not expecting that the Book (this Qur'ân) would be sent down to you, but it is a mercy from your Lord. So never be a supporter of the disbelievers.

$$وَلَا يَصُدُّنَّكَ عَنْ ءَايَـٰتِ ٱللَّهِ بَعْدَ إِذْ أُنزِلَتْ إِلَيْكَ ۖ وَٱدْعُ إِلَىٰ رَبِّكَ ۖ وَلَا تَكُونَنَّ مِنَ ٱلْمُشْرِكِينَ ۝٨٧$$

87. And let them not turn you (O Muhammad (peace be upon him)) away from (preaching) the Ayât (revelations and verses) of Allâh after they have been sent down to you: and invite (men) to (believe in) your Lord and be not of Al-Mushrikûn (those who associate partners with Allâh, e.g. polytheists, pagans, idolaters, and those who disbelieve in the Oneness of Allâh and deny the Prophethood of Messenger Muhammad (peace be upon him))

$$وَلَا تَدْعُ مَعَ ٱللَّهِ إِلَـٰهًا ءَاخَرَ ۘ لَآ إِلَـٰهَ إِلَّا هُوَ ۚ كُلُّ شَىْءٍ هَالِكٌ إِلَّا وَجْهَهُۥ ۚ لَهُ ٱلْحُكْمُ وَإِلَيْهِ تُرْجَعُونَ ۝٨٨$$

88. And invoke not any other ilâh (god) along with Allâh: Lâ ilâha illa Huwa (none has the right to be worshipped but He). Everything will perish save His Face. His is the Decision, and to Him you (all) shall be returned.

Transliteration

85. Inna allathee farada AAalayka alqur-ana laradduka ila maAAadin qul rabbee aAAlamu man jaa bialhuda waman huwa fee dalalin mubeenin   86. Wama kunta tarjoo an yulqa ilayka alkitabu illa rahmatan min rabbika fala takoonanna thaheeran lilkafireena   87. Wala yasuddunnaka AAan ayati Allahi baAAda ith onzilat ilayka waodAAu ila rabbika wala takoonanna mina almushrikeena   88. Wala tadAAu maAAa Allahi ilahan akhara la ilaha illa huwa kullu shay-in halikun illa wajhahu lahu alhukmu wa-ilayhi turjaAAoona

Tafsir Ibn Kathir

The Command to convey the Message of Tawhid

Here Allah commands His Messenger to convey the Message and recite the Qur'an to people. He tells him that he will be brought back to the return, which is the Day of Resurrection, where he will be asked about the prophethood he was entrusted with. So Allah says:

(Verily, He Who has given you the Qur'an, will surely bring you back to the return.) meaning, `the One Who has commanded you to put it into practice among mankind,'

Chapter 28: Al-Qasas (The story, Stories), Verses 001–088

(will surely bring you back to the return.) `On the Day of Resurrection, where He will question you concerning that,' as Allah said:

(Then surely, We shall question those to whom it was sent and verily, We shall question the Messengers.) (7:6) Allah said:

(On the Day when Allah will gather the Messengers together and say to them: "What was the response you received") (5:109). And He said:

(and the Prophets and the witnesses will be brought forward) (39: 69) In his Tafsir of his Sahih, Al-Bukhari recorded that Ibn `Abbas commented on the Ayah:

(will surely bring you back to the return.) "To Makkah." This was also recorded by An-Nasa'i in his Tafsir in his Sunan, and by Ibn Jarir. Al-`Awfi also reported from Ibn `Abbas that the phrase:

(will surely bring you back to the return.) means, "will surely bring you back to Makkah as He brought you out of it." Muhammad bin Ishaq recorded that Mujahid commented on:

(will surely bring you back to the return.) He said, "Back to your place of birth in Makkah." Ibn `Abbas is also reported to have interpreted it variously referring to death, to the Day of Resurrection which will come after death, and to Paradise which will be his reward and his destiny for putting the Message of Allah into practice and conveying it to the humans and Jinns, and because he is the most perfect, most eloquent and most noble of all the creation of Allah. Allah's saying:

(Say: "My Lord is Aware of him who brings guidance, and of him who is in manifest error.") means: "Say, O Muhammad, to those among your people who oppose you and disbelieve you, among the idolators and those who follow them in their disbelief, `My Lord knows best which of us, you or I, is rightly guided, and you will come to know for which of us will be the (happy) end in the Hereafter, and for which of us will be a good end and victory in this world and in the Hereafter'." Then Allah reminds His Prophet the numerous blessings He granted to him and mankind by virtue of sending him to them:

(And you were not expecting that the Book would be sent down to you,) `Before the revelation was sent down to you, you did not expect that revelation would be sent down to you.'

(but it is a mercy from your Lord.) means, `but revelation has been sent down to you from Allah as a mercy to you and to mankind because of you. Since Allah has granted you this great blessing,'

(So never be a supporter) i.e., a helper,

(of the disbelievers.) rather, separate from them, `express your hostility towards them and oppose them. '

(And let them not turn you away from the Ayat of Allah after they have been sent down to you.) meaning, `Do not let their opposition to you affect you or put people off from following your way; do not worry about that or pay any attention to it, for Allah will make your word supreme, will support your religion and will make the Message with which He has sent you prevail over all other religions.' So He says:

(and invite to your Lord) to worship your Lord Alone, with no partners or associates,

(and be not of idolators.)

(And invoke not any other god along with Allah, there is no God but Him.) means, it is not appropriate to worship anything or anybody except Him, and divinity does not befit any except His glory.

(Everything will perish save His Face.) Here Allah is telling us that He is Eternal, Ever Lasting, Ever Living, Self-Sustaining, Who, although His creation dies, He will never die, as He says:

(Whatsoever is on it will perish. And the Face of your Lord full of majesty and honor will remain forever.) (55:26-27). Allah used the word "Face" to refer to Himself, as He says here:

(Everything will perish save His Face.) meaning, everything except Him. It was reported in the Sahih via Abu Salamah that Abu Hurayrah said, "The Messenger of Allah said:

«أَصْدَقُ كَلِمَةٍ قَالَهَا الشَّاعِرُ لَبِيدُ أَلَا كُلُّ شَيْءٍ مَا خَلَا اللهَ بَاطِلُ»

(The truest word of a poet was the saying of Labid - indeed everything except Allah is false.)

(His is the decision,) means, dominion and control, and there is none who can reverse His judgement or decision.

(and to Him you shall be returned.) means, on the Day when you will be brought back, and He will reward or punish you according to your deeds: if they are good, then you will be rewarded, and if they are bad, then you will be punished. This is the end of the Tafsir of Surat Al-Qasas. To Allah be praise and blessings.

CHAPTER (SURAH) 29: AL-ANKABOOT (THE SPIDER), VERSES 001–045

(بِسْمِ اللَّهِ الرَّحْمَـنِ الرَّحِيمِ)

In the Name of Allah, the Most Gracious, the Most Merciful

Chapter 29: Al-Ankaboot (The Spider), Verses 001-045

Surah: 29 Ayah: 1, Ayah: 2, Ayah: 3 & Ayah: 4

الٓمٓ ۝

1. Alif-Lâm-Mîm. [These letters are one of the miracles of the Qur'ân, and none but Allâh (Alone) knows their meanings]

أَحَسِبَ ٱلنَّاسُ أَن يُتْرَكُوٓا۟ أَن يَقُولُوٓا۟ ءَامَنَّا وَهُمْ لَا يُفْتَنُونَ ۝

2. Do people think that they will be left alone because they say: "We believe," and will not be tested.

وَلَقَدْ فَتَنَّا ٱلَّذِينَ مِن قَبْلِهِمْ ۖ فَلَيَعْلَمَنَّ ٱللَّهُ ٱلَّذِينَ صَدَقُوا۟ وَلَيَعْلَمَنَّ ٱلْكَٰذِبِينَ ۝

3. And We indeed tested those who were before them. And Allâh will certainly make (it) known (the truth of) those who are true, and will certainly make (it) known (the falsehood of) those who are liars, (although Allâh knows all that before putting them to test).

أَمْ حَسِبَ ٱلَّذِينَ يَعْمَلُونَ ٱلسَّيِّـَٔاتِ أَن يَسْبِقُونَا ۚ سَآءَ مَا يَحْكُمُونَ ۝

4. Or think those who do evil deeds that they can outstrip Us (i.e. escape Our Punishment)? Evil is that which they judge!

Transliteration

1. Alif-lam-meem 2. Ahasiba alnnasu an yutrakoo an yaqooloo amanna wahum la yuftanoona 3. Walaqad fatanna allatheena min qablihim falayaAAlamanna Allahu allatheena sadaqoo walayaAAlamanna alkathibeena 4. Am hasiba allatheena yaAAmaloona alssayyi-ati an yasbiqoona saa ma yahkumoona

Tafsir Ibn Kathir

The Believers are tested so that it may be known Who is Sincere and Who is Lying In the beginning of the Tafsir of Surat Al-Baqarah, we discussed the letters which appear at the beginning of some Surahs.

(Do people think that they will be left alone because they say: "We believe," and will not be tested.) This is a rebuke in the form of a question, meaning that Allah will inevitably test His believing servants according to their level of faith, as it recorded in the authentic Hadith:

«أَشَدُّ النَّاسِ بَلَاءً الْأَنْبِيَاءُ، ثُمَّ الصَّالِحُونَ، ثُمَّ الْأَمْثَلُ فَالْأَمْثَلُ، يُبْتَلَى الرَّجُلُ عَلَى حَسَبِ دِينِهِ، فَإِنْ كَانَ فِي دِينِهِ صَلَابَةٌ زِيدَ لَهُ فِي الْبَلَاءِ»

(The people most severly tested are the Prophets, then the righteous, then the next best and the next best. A man will be tested in accordance with the degree of his religious commitment; the stonger his religious commitment, the stronger his test.) This Ayah is like the Ayah,

(Do you think that you will enter Paradise without Allah knowing those of you who fought (in His cause) and knowing those who are the patient) (3:142) There is a similar Ayah in Surat At-Tawbah. And Allah says:

(Or think you that you will enter Paradise without such (trials) as came to those who passed away before you They were afflicted with severe poverty and ailments and were so shaken that even the Messenger and those who believed along with him said, "When (will come) the help of Allah" Yes! Certainly, the help of Allah is near!) (2:214) Allah says here:

(And We indeed tested those who were before them so that Allah will know those who are true, and will know those who are liars.) meaning, He will make know which are sincere in their claim to be believers from those who are lying. Allah, may He be glorified and exalted, knows what has happened in the past and what is yet to come, and He knows how that which will not happen would have happened if it were to happen. All the Imams of Ahlus-Sunnah wal-Jama`ah are agreed on this. This is the view of Ibn `Abbas and others concerning phrases such as the Ayah,

(only that We know) (2:143). Meaning, only to see -- because seeing has to do with what is there, but knowledge is broader than seeing, since it includes what is not present as well as what is.

The Evildoers cannot escape from Allah

Allah said:

(Or think those who do evil deeds that they can outstrip Us Evil is that which they judge!) means, those who are not believers should not think that they will escape such trials and tests, for ahead of them lies a greater and more severe punishment. Allah says:

(Or think those who do evil deeds that they can outstrip Us) meaning, "escape" from Us.

(Evil is that which they judge!) what they think is evil.

Surah: 29 Ayah: 5, Ayah: 6 & Ayah: 7

مَن كَانَ يَرْجُواْ لِقَآءَ ٱللَّهِ فَإِنَّ أَجَلَ ٱللَّهِ لَأَتٍ وَهُوَ ٱلسَّمِيعُ ٱلْعَلِيمُ ۝

5. Whoever hopes for the Meeting with Allâh, then Allâh's Term is surely coming and He is the All-Hearer, the All-Knower.

وَمَن جَٰهَدَ فَإِنَّمَا يُجَٰهِدُ لِنَفْسِهِۦٓ إِنَّ ٱللَّهَ لَغَنِىٌّ عَنِ ٱلْعَٰلَمِينَ ۝

Chapter 29: Al-Ankaboot (The Spider), Verses 001-045

6. And whosoever strives, he strives only for himself. Verily, Allâh is free of all wants from the 'Alamîn (mankind, jinn, and all that exists).

$$\text{وَٱلَّذِينَ ءَامَنُوا۟ وَعَمِلُوا۟ ٱلصَّٰلِحَٰتِ لَنُكَفِّرَنَّ عَنْهُمْ سَيِّـَٔاتِهِمْ وَلَنَجْزِيَنَّهُمْ أَحْسَنَ ٱلَّذِى كَانُوا۟ يَعْمَلُونَ ۝}$$

7. Those who believe (in the Oneness of Allâh (Monotheism) and in Messenger Muhammad (peace be upon him) and do not give up their faith because of the harm they receive from the polytheists), and do righteous good deeds, surely, We shall expiate from them their evil deeds and shall reward them according to the best of that which they used to do.

Transliteration

5. Man kana yarjoo liqaa Allahi fa-inna ajala Allahi laatin wahuwa alssameeAAu alAAaleemu 6. Waman jahada fa-innama yujahidu linafsihi inna Allaha laghaniyyun AAani alAAalameena 7. Waallatheena amanoo waAAamiloo alssalihati lanukaffiranna AAanhum sayyi-atihim walanajziyannahum ahsana allathee kanoo yaAAmaloona

Tafsir Ibn Kathir

Allah will fulfill the Hopes of the Righteous

Allah's saying;

(Whoever hopes in meeting with Allah,) means, in the Hereafter, and does righteous deeds, and hopes for a great reward with Allah, then Allah will fulfill his hopes and reward him for his deeds in full. This will undoubtedly come to pass, for He is the One Who hears all supplications, He knows and understands the needs of all created beings. Allah says:

(Whoever hopes in meeting with Allah, then Allah's term is surely coming, and He is the All-Hearer, the All-Knower.)

(And whosoever strives, he strives only for himself.) This is like the Ayah,

(Whosoever does righteous good deed, it is for himself) (41:46). Whoever does a righteous deed, the benefit of that deed will come back to him, for Allah has no need of the deeds of His servants, and even if all of them were to be as pious as the most pious man among them, that would not add to His dominion in the slightest. Allah says:

(And whosoever strives, he strives only for himself. Verily, Allah stands not in need of any of the creatures.) Then Allah tells us that even though He has no need of His creatures, He is kind and generous to them. He will still give to those who believe and do righteous deeds the best of rewards, which is that He will expiate for them their bad deeds, and will reward them according to the best deeds that they did. He will accept the fewest good deeds and in return for one good deed will give anything between ten rewards and seven hundred, but for every bad deed, He will give only one evil merit, or even that He may overlook and forgive. This is like the Ayah,

(Surely, Allah wrongs not even the weight of a speck of dust, but if there is any good, He doubles it, and gives from Him a great reward.) (4:40). And He says here:

(Those who believe, and do righteous good deeds, surely, We shall expiate from them their evil deeds and We shall indeed reward them according to the best of that which they used to do.)

Surah: 29 Ayah: 8 & Ayah: 9

وَوَصَّيْنَا ٱلْإِنسَـٰنَ بِوَٰلِدَيْهِ حُسْنًا وَإِن جَـٰهَدَاكَ لِتُشْرِكَ بِى مَا لَيْسَ لَكَ بِهِۦ عِلْمٌ فَلَا تُطِعْهُمَآ إِلَىَّ مَرْجِعُكُمْ فَأُنَبِّئُكُم بِمَا كُنتُمْ تَعْمَلُونَ ۝

8. And We have enjoined on man to be good and dutiful to his parents; but if they strive to make you join with Me (in worship) anything (as a partner) of which you have no knowledge, then obey them not. Unto Me is your return, and I shall tell you what you used to do.

وَٱلَّذِينَ ءَامَنُوا۟ وَعَمِلُوا۟ ٱلصَّـٰلِحَـٰتِ لَنُدْخِلَنَّهُمْ فِى ٱلصَّـٰلِحِينَ ۝

9. And for those who believe (in the Oneness of Allâh and the other articles of Faith) and do righteous good deeds, surely, We shall make them enter with (in the entrance of) the righteous (in Paradise).

Transliteration

8. Wawassayna al-insana biwalidayhi husnan wa-in jahadaka litushrika bee ma laysa laka bihi AAilmun fala tutiAAhuma ilayya marjiAAukum faonabbi-okum bima kuntum taAAmaloona 9. Waallatheena amanoo waAAamiloo alssalihati lanudkhilannahum fee alssaliheena

Tafsir Ibn Kathir

The Command to be Good and Dutiful to Parents

Allah commands His servants to be dutiful to parents, after urging them to adhere to belief in His Tawhid, because a person's parents are the cause of his existence. So he must treat them with the utmost kindness and respect, his father for spending on him and his mother because of her compassion for him. Allah says:

(And your Lord has decreed that you worship none but Him. And that you be dutiful to your parents. If one of them or both of them attain old age in your life, say not to them a word of disrespect, nor shout at them, but address them in terms of honor. And lower unto them the wing of submission and humility through mercy, and say: "My Lord! Bestow on them Your mercy as they did bring me up when I was young.") (17:23-24) Although Allah orders us to show kindness, mercy and respect towards them in return for their previous kindness, He says:

(but if they strive to make associate with Me, which you have no knowledge of, then obey them not.) meaning, if they are idolators, and they try to make you follow them in their religion, then beware of them, and do not obey them in that, for you will be brought back to Me on the Day of Resurrection, and Allah will reward you for your kindness towards them and your patience in adhering to your religion. It is Allah Who will gather you with the group of the righteous, not with the group of your parents, even though you were the closest of people to them in the world. For a person will be gathered on the Day of Resurrection with those whom he loves, meaning, religious love. Allah says:

(And for those who believe and do righteous good deeds, surely, We shall make them enter with the righteous.) In his Tafsir of this Ayah, At-Tirmidhi recorded that Sa`d said: "Four Ayat were revealed concerning me -- and he told his story. He said: "Umm Sa`d said: `Did Allah not command you to honor your parents By Allah, I will not eat or drink anything until I die or you renounce Islam.' When they wanted to feed her, they would force her mouth open. Then this Ayah was revealed:

(And We have enjoined on man to be dutiful to his parents; but if they strive to make you associate with Me, of which you have no knowledge, then obey them not.)" This Hadith was also recorded by Imam Ahmad, Muslim, Abu Dawud and An-Nasa'i. At-Tirmidhi said, "Hasan Sahih.

Surah: 29 Ayah: 10 & Ayah: 11

وَمِنَ ٱلنَّاسِ مَن يَقُولُ ءَامَنَّا بِٱللَّهِ فَإِذَآ أُوذِىَ فِى ٱللَّهِ جَعَلَ فِتْنَةَ ٱلنَّاسِ كَعَذَابِ ٱللَّهِ وَلَئِن جَآءَ نَصْرٌ مِّن رَّبِّكَ لَيَقُولُنَّ إِنَّا كُنَّا مَعَكُمْ أَوَلَيْسَ ٱللَّهُ بِأَعْلَمَ بِمَا فِى صُدُورِ ٱلْعَٰلَمِينَ ۝

10. Of mankind are some who say: "We believe in Allâh," but if they are made to suffer for the sake of Allâh, they consider the trial of mankind as Allâh's punishment; and if victory comes from your Lord, (the hypocrites) will say: "Verily! We were with you (helping you)." Is not Allâh Best Aware of what is in the breast of the 'Alamîn (mankind and jinn).

وَلَيَعْلَمَنَّ ٱللَّهُ ٱلَّذِينَ ءَامَنُوا۟ وَلَيَعْلَمَنَّ ٱلْمُنَٰفِقِينَ ۝

11. Verily, Allâh knows those who believe, and verily, He knows the hypocrites (i.e. Allâh will test the people with good and hard days to discriminate the good from the wicked although Allâh knows all that before putting them to test).

Transliteration

10. Wamina alnnasi man yaqoolu amanna biAllahi fa-itha oothiya fee Allahi jaAAala fitnata alnnasi kaAAathabi Allahi wala-in jaa nasrun min rabbika layaqoolunna inna kunna maAAakum awa laysa Allahu bi-aAAlama bima fee sudoori alAAalameena 11. WalayaAAlamanna Allahu allatheena amanoo walayaAAlamanna almunafiqeena

Tafsir Ibn Kathir

The Attitudes of the Hypocrites and the Ways in which Allah tests People

Allah mentions the descriptions of the liars who falsely claim faith with their lips, while faith is not firm in their hearts. When a test or trial comes in this world, they think that this is a punishment from Allah, so they leave Islam. Allah says:

(Of mankind are some who say: "We believe in Allah." But if they are made to suffer for Allah, they consider the trial of mankind as Allah's punishment;) Ibn `Abbas said, "Meaning that their trial is leaving Islam if they are made to suffer for Allah." This was also the view of others among the Salaf. This Ayah is like the Ayah,

(And among mankind is he who worships Allah as it were upon the edge: if good befalls him, he is content therewith; but if a trial befalls him, he turns back on his face...) until:

(That is a straying far away) (22:11-12). Then Allah says:

(and if victory comes from your Lord, they will say: "Verily, we were with you.") meaning, "if victory comes from your Lord, O Muhammad, and there are spoils of war, these people will say to you, `We were with you,' i.e., we are your brothers in faith." This is like the Ayat:

(Those who wait and watch about you; if you gain a victory from Allah, they say: "Were we not with you" But if the disbelievers gain a success, they say (to them): "Did we not gain mastery over you and did we not protect you from the believers") (4:141).

(Perhaps Allah may bring a victory or a decision according to His will. Then they will become regretful for what they have been keeping as a secret in themselves) (5:52). And Allah tells us about them here:

(and if victory comes from your Lord, they will say: "Verily, we were with you.") Then Allah says:

(Is not Allah Best Aware of what is in the breasts of the creatures) meaning, `does Allah not know best what is in their hearts and what they store secretly within themselves, even though outwardly they may appear to be in agreement with you'

(And indeed Allah knows those who believe, and verily He knows the hypocrites.) Allah will test the people with calamities and with times of ease, so that He may distinguish the believers from the hypocrites, to see who will obey Allah both in times of hardship and of ease, and who will obey Him only when things are going in accordance with their desires. As Allah says:

(And surely, We shall try you till We test those who strive hard and the patient, and We shall test your facts.) (47:31) After the battle of Uhud, with its trials and tribulations for the Muslims, Allah said:

(Allah will not leave the believers in the state in which you are now, until He distinguishes the wicked from the good...) (3:179)

Surah: 29 Ayah: 12 & Ayah: 13

وَقَالَ ٱلَّذِينَ كَفَرُوا۟ لِلَّذِينَ ءَامَنُوا۟ ٱتَّبِعُوا۟ سَبِيلَنَا وَلْنَحْمِلْ خَطَـٰيَـٰكُمْ وَمَا هُم بِحَـٰمِلِينَ مِنْ خَطَـٰيَـٰهُم مِّن شَىْءٍ ۖ إِنَّهُمْ لَكَـٰذِبُونَ ۝

12. And those who disbelieve say to those who believe: "Follow our way and we will verily bear your sins." Never will they bear anything of their sins. Surely, they are liars.

وَلَيَحْمِلُنَّ أَثْقَالَهُمْ وَأَثْقَالًا مَّعَ أَثْقَالِهِمْ ۖ وَلَيُسْـَٔلُنَّ يَوْمَ ٱلْقِيَـٰمَةِ عَمَّا كَانُوا۟ يَفْتَرُونَ ۝

13. And verily, they shall bear their own loads, and other loads besides their own; and verily, they shall be questioned on the Day of Resurrection about that which they used to fabricate.

Transliteration

12. Waqala allatheena kafaroo lillatheena amanoo ittabiAAoo sabeelana walnahmil khatayakum wama hum bihamileena min khatayahum min shay-in innahum lakathiboona 13. Walayahmilunna athqalahum waathqalan maAAa athqalihim walayus-alunna yawma alqiyamati AAamma kanoo yaftaroona

Tafsir Ibn Kathir

The Arrogant Claim of the Disbelievers that They would carry the Sins of Others if They would return to Disbelief

Allah tells us that the disbelievers of Quraysh said to those who believed and followed the truth: leave your religion, come back to our religion, and follow our way;

(and let us bear your sins.) meaning, `if there is any sin on you, we will bear it and it will be our responsibility'. It is like a person saying: "Do this, and your sin will be on my shoulders." Allah says, proving this to be a lie:

(Never will they bear anything of their sins. Surely, they are liars.) in their claim that they will bear the sins of others, for no person will bear the sins of another. Allah says:

(and if one heavily laden calls another to (bear) his load, nothing of it will be lifted even though he be near of kin) (35:18).

(And no friend will ask a friend (about his condition), though they shall be made to see one another) (70:10-11).

(And verily, they shall bear their own loads, and other loads besides their own.) Here Allah tells us that those who call others to disbelief and misguidance will, on the Day of Resurrection, bear their own sins and the sins of others, because of the people they misguided. Yet that will not detract from the burden of those other people in the slightest, as Allah says:

(That they may bear their own burdens in full on the Day of Resurrection, and also of the burdens of those whom they misled without knowledge) (16:25). In the Sahih, it says:

«مَنْ دَعَا إِلَى هُدًى كَانَ لَهُ مِنَ الْأَجْرِ مِثْلُ أُجُورِ مَنِ اتَّبَعَهُ إِلَى يَوْمِ الْقِيَامَةِ مِنْ غَيْرِ أَنْ يَنْقُصَ مِنْ أُجُورِهِمْ شَيْئًا، وَمَنْ دَعَا إِلَى ضَلَالَةٍ كَانَ عَلَيْهِ مِنَ الْإِثْمِ مِثْلُ آثَامِ مَنِ اتَّبَعَهُ إِلَى يَوْمِ الْقِيَامَةِ مِنْ غَيْرِ أَنْ يَنْقُصَ مِنْ آثَامِهِمْ شَيْئًا»

(Whoever calls others to true guidance, will have a reward like that of those who follow him until the Day of Resurrection, without it detracting from their reward in the slightest. Whoever calls others to misguidance, will have a burden of sin like that of those who follow him until the Day of Resurrection, without it detracting from their burden in the slightest.) In the Sahih, it also says:

«مَا قُتِلَتْ نَفْسٌ ظُلْمًا إِلَّا كَانَ عَلَى ابْنِ آدَمَ الْأَوَّلِ كِفْلٌ مِنْ دَمِهَا، لِأَنَّهُ أَوَّلُ مَنْ سَنَّ الْقَتْلَ»

(No person is killed unlawfully, but a share of the guilt will be upon the first son of Adam, because he was the first one to initiate the idea of killing another.)

(and verily, they shall be questioned on the Day of Resurrection about that which they used to fabricate.) means, the lies they used to tell and the falsehood they used to fabricate. Ibn Abi Hatim recorded that Abu Umamah, may Allah be pleased with him, said that the Messenger of Allah conveyed the Message with which he was sent, then he said:

«إِيَّاكُمْ وَالظُّلْمَ، فَإِنَّ اللهَ يَعْزِمُ يَوْمَ الْقِيَامَةِ فَيَقُولُ: وَعِزَّتِي وَجَلَالِي لَا يَجُوزُنِي الْيَوْمَ ظُلْمٌ، ثُمَّ يُنَادِي مُنَادٍ فَيَقُولُ: أَيْنَ فُلَانُ بْنُ فُلَانٍ؟ فَيَأْتِي يَتْبَعُهُ مِنَ الْحَسَنَاتِ أَمْثَالُ الْجِبَالِ، فَيَشْخَصُ النَّاسُ إِلَيْهَا أَبْصَارَهُمْ، حَتَّى يَقُومَ بَيْنَ يَدَيِ الرَّحْمَنِ عَزَّ وَجَلَّ، ثُمَّ يَأْمُرُ الْمُنَادِيَ فَيُنَادِي: مَنْ كَانَتْ لَهُ تِبَاعَةٌ أَوْ ظَلَامَةٌ عِنْدَ

Chapter 29: Al-Ankaboot (The Spider), Verses 001-045

«فُلَانِ بْنِ فُلَانٍ فَهَلُمَّ، فَيُقْبِلُونَ حَتَّى يَجْتَمِعُوا قِيَامًا بَيْنَ يَدَيِ الرَّحْمَنِ، فَيَقُولُ الرَّحْمَنُ: اقْضُوا عَنْ عَبْدِي، فَيَقُولُونَ: كَيْفَ نَقْضِي عَنْهُ؟ فَيَقُولُ: خُذُوا لَهُمْ مِنْ حَسَنَاتِهِ، فَلَا يَزَالُونَ يَأْخُذُونَ مِنْهَا حَتَّى لَا يَبْقَى مِنْهَا حَسَنَةٌ، وَقَدْ بَقِيَ مِنْ أَصْحَابِ الظَّلَامَاتِ، فَيَقُولُ: اقْضُوا عَنْ عَبْدِي، فَيَقُولُونَ: لَمْ يَبْقَ لَهُ حَسَنَةٌ، فَيَقُولُ: خُذُوا مِنْ سَيِّئَاتِهِمْ فَاحْمِلُوهَا عَلَيْهِ»

(Beware of injustice, for Allah will swear an oath of the Day of Resurrection and will say: "By My glory and majesty, no injustice will be overlooked today." Then a voice will call out, "Where is so-and-so the son of so-and-so" He will be brought forth, followed by his good deeds which appear like mountains while the people are gazing at them in wonder, until he is standing before the Most Merciful. Then the caller will be commanded to say: "Whoever is owed anything by so-and-so the son of so-and-so, or has been wronged by him, let him come forth." So they will come forth and gather before the Most Merciful, then the Most Merciful will say: "Settle the matter for My servant." They will say, "How can we settle the matter" He will say, "Take from his good deeds and give it to them." They will keep taking from his good deeds until there is nothing left, and there will still people with scores to be settled. Allah will say, "Settle the matter for My servant." They will say, "He does not have even one good deed left." Allah will say, "Take from their evil deeds and give them to him.") Then the Prophet quoted this Ayah:

(And verily, they shall bear their own loads, and other loads besides their own; and verily, they shall be questioned on the Day of Resurrection about that which they used to fabricate.) There is a corroborating report in the Sahih with a different chain of narration:

«إِنَّ الرَّجُلَ لَيَأْتِي يَوْمَ الْقِيَامَةِ بِحَسَنَاتٍ أَمْثَالِ الْجِبَالِ وَقَدْ ظَلَمَ هَذَا، وَأَخَذَ مَالَ هَذَا، وَأَخَذَ مِنْ عِرْضِ هَذَا، فَيَأْخُذُ هَذَا مِنْ حَسَنَاتِهِ، وَهَذَا مِنْ حَسَنَاتِهِ، فَإِذَا لَمْ تَبْقَ لَهُ حَسَنَةٌ، أُخِذَ مِنْ سَيِّئَاتِهِمْ فَطُرِحَ عَلَيْهِ»

(A man will come on the Day of Resurrection with good deeds like mountains, but he had wronged this one, taken the wealth of that one and slandered the honor of another. So each of them will take from his good deeds. And if there is nothing left of his good deeds, it will be taken from their evil and placed on him.)

Surah: 29 Ayah: 14 & Ayah: 15

وَلَقَدْ أَرْسَلْنَا نُوحًا إِلَىٰ قَوْمِهِ فَلَبِثَ فِيهِمْ أَلْفَ سَنَةٍ إِلَّا خَمْسِينَ عَامًا فَأَخَذَهُمُ ٱلطُّوفَانُ وَهُمْ ظَالِمُونَ ۝

14. And indeed We sent Nûh (Noah) to his people, and he stayed among them a thousand years less fifty years (inviting them to believe in the Oneness of Allâh (Monotheism), and discard the false gods and other deities); and the Deluge overtook them while they were Zâlimûn (wrong-doers, polytheists, disbelievers).

فَأَنجَيْنَاهُ وَأَصْحَابَ ٱلسَّفِينَةِ وَجَعَلْنَاهَا ءَايَةً لِّلْعَالَمِينَ ۝

15. Then We saved him and those with him in the ship, and made it (the ship) an Ayâh (a lesson, a warning) for the 'Alamîn (mankind, jinn and all that exists).

Transliteration

14. Walaqad arsalna noohan ila qawmihi falabitha feehim alfa sanatin illa khamseena AAaman faakhathahumu alttoofanu wahum thalimoona 15. Faanjaynahu waas-haba alssafeenati wajaAAalnaha ayatan lilAAalameena

Tafsir Ibn Kathir

Nuh and His People

Here Allah consoles His servant and Messenger Muhammad by telling him that Nuh, peace be upon him, stayed among his people for this long period of time, calling them night and day, in secret and openly, but in spite of all that they still persisted in their aversion to the truth, turning away from it and disbelieving in him. Only a few of them believed with him. Allah says:

(and he stayed among them a thousand years less fifty years; and the Deluge overtook them while they were wrongdoers.) meaning, `after this long period of time, when the Message and the warning had been of no avail, so, O Muhammad, do not feel sorry because of those among your people who disbelieve in you, and do not grieve for them, for Allah guides whomsoever He wills and leaves astray whomsoever He wills. The matter rests with Him and all things will return to Him.'

(Truly, those, against whom the Word of your Lord has been justified, will not believe. Even if every sign should come to them) (10:96-97). Know that Allah will help you and support you and cause you to prevail, and He will defeat and humiliate your enemies, and make them the lowest of the low. It was recorded that Ibn `Abbas said: "Nuh received his mission when he was forty years old, and he stayed among his people for a thousand years less fifty; after the Flood he lived for sixty years until people had increased and spread."

(Then We saved him and the Companions of the Boat,) means, those who believed in Nuh, peace be upon him. We have already discussed this in detail in Surah Hud, and there is no need to repeat it here.

(and made it (the ship) an Ayah for all people.) means, `We caused that ship to remain,' whether in itself, as Qatadah said, that it remained until the beginning of Islam, on Mount Judi, or whether the concept of sailing in ships was left as a reminder to mankind of how Allah had saved them from the Flood. This is like the Ayat: s

(And an Ayah for them is that We bore their offspring in the laden ship. And We have created for them of the like thereunto, on which they ride) until:

(and as an enjoyment for a while) (36:41-44).

(Verily, when the water rose beyond its limits, We carried you in the ship. That We might make it an admonition for you and that it might be retained by the retaining ears.) (69:11-12) And Allah says here:

(Then We saved him and the Companions of the Boat, and made it an Ayah for all people.) This is a shift from referring to one specific ship to speaking about ships in general. A similar shift from specific to general is to be seen in the Ayat:

(And indeed We have adorned the nearest heaven with lamps, and We have made such lamps missiles to drive away the Shayatin (devils)) (67:5). meaning, `We have made these lamps missiles, but the lamps which are used as missiles are not the same lamps as are used to adorn the heaven.' And Allah says:

(And indeed We created man out of an extract of clay. Thereafter We made him a Nutfah in a safe lodging.) (23:12-13). There are many other similar examples.

Surah: 29 Ayah: 16, Ayah: 17 & Ayah: 18

وَإِبْرَٰهِيمَ إِذْ قَالَ لِقَوْمِهِ ٱعْبُدُواْ ٱللَّهَ وَٱتَّقُوهُ ۖ ذَٰلِكُمْ خَيْرٌ لَّكُمْ إِن كُنتُمْ تَعْلَمُونَ ۝

16. And (remember) Ibrâhîm (Abraham) when he said to his people: "Worship Allâh (Alone), and fear Him, that is better for you if you did but know.

إِنَّمَا تَعْبُدُونَ مِن دُونِ ٱللَّهِ أَوْثَٰنًا وَتَخْلُقُونَ إِفْكًا ۚ إِنَّ ٱلَّذِينَ تَعْبُدُونَ مِن دُونِ ٱللَّهِ لَا يَمْلِكُونَ لَكُمْ رِزْقًا فَٱبْتَغُواْ عِندَ ٱللَّهِ ٱلرِّزْقَ وَٱعْبُدُوهُ وَٱشْكُرُواْ لَهُۥٓ ۖ إِلَيْهِ تُرْجَعُونَ ۝

17. "You worship besides Allâh only idols, and you only invent falsehood. Verily, those whom you worship besides Allâh have no power to give you provision: so seek your provision from Allâh (Alone), and worship Him (Alone), and be grateful to Him. To Him (Alone) you will be brought back.

$$\text{وَإِن تُكَذِّبُواْ فَقَدْ كَذَّبَ أُمَمٌ مِّن قَبْلِكُمْ ۖ وَمَا عَلَى ٱلرَّسُولِ إِلَّا ٱلْبَلَـٰغُ ٱلْمُبِينُ}$$

18. "And if you deny, then nations before you have denied (their Messengers). And the duty of the Messenger is only to convey (the Message) plainly."

Transliteration

16. Wa-ibraheema ith qala liqawmihi oAAbudoo Allaha waittaqoohu thalikum khayrun lakum in kuntum taAAlamoona 17. Innama taAAbudoona min dooni Allahi awthanan watakhluqoona ifkan inna allatheena taAAbudoona min dooni Allahi la yamlikoona lakum rizqan faibtaghoo AAinda Allahi alrrizqa waoAAbudoohu waoshkuroo lahu ilayhi turjaAAoona 18. Wa-in tukaththiboo faqad kaththaba omamun min qablikum wama AAala alrrasooli illa albalaghu almubeenu

Tafsir Ibn Kathir

Ibrahim's preaching to His People

Allah tells us how His servant, Messenger and close friend Ibrahim, the Imam of the monotheists, called his people to worship Allah alone, with no partner or associate, to fear Him alone, to seek provision from Him alone, with no partner or associate, to give thanks to Him alone, for He is the One to Whom thanks should be given for the blessings which none can bestow but He. Ibrahim said to his people:

(Worship Allah, and have Taqwa of Him,) meaning worship Him and fear Him Alone, with all sincerity.

(that is better for you if you know.) if you do that you will attain good in this world and the next, and you will prevent evil from yourselves in this world and the Hereafter. Then Allah states that the idols which they worshipped were not able to do any harm or any good, and tells them, "You made up names for them and called them gods, but they are created beings just like you." This interpretation was reported by Al-`Awfi from Ibn `Abbas. It was also the view of Mujahid and As-Suddi. Al-Walibi reported from Ibn `Abbas: "You invent falsehood, means, you carve idols," which do not have the power to provide for you.

(so seek from Allah your provision,) This emphasizes the idea of asking Allah Alone. This is like the Ayat:

(You (Alone) we worship, and You (Alone) we ask for help.) (1:5) And His saying:

(My Lord! Build for me, with You, a home in Paradise) (66:11). Allah says here:

(so seek) meaning, ask for

(from Allah your provision,) meaning, do not seek it from anyone or anything other than Him, for no one else possesses the power to do anything.

(and worship Him, and be grateful to Him.) Eat from what He has provided and worship Him Alone, and give thanks to Him for the blessings He has given you.

(To Him you will be brought back.) means, on the Day of Resurrection, when He will reward or punish each person according to his deeds. His saying:

(And if you deny, then nations before you have denied.) means, `you have heard what happened to them by way of punishment for opposing the Messengers.'

(And the duty of the Messenger is only to convey plainly.) All the Messengers have to do is to convey the Message as Allah has commanded them. Allah guides whoever He wills and leaves astray whoever He wills, so strive to be among the blessed. Qatadah said concerning the Ayah:

(And if you deny, then nations before you have denied.) "These are words of consolation to His Prophet, peace be upon him." This suggestion by Qatadah implies that the narrative (about Ibrahim) is interrupted here, and resumes with the words "And nothing was the answer of (Ibrahim's) people..." in Ayah 24. This was also stated by Ibn Jarir. From the context it appears that Ibrahim, peace be upon him, said all of what is in this section. Here he establishes proof against them that the Resurrection will indeed come to pass, because at the end of this passage it says:

("And nothing was the answer of his people...")(29:24) And Allah knows best.

Surah: 29 Ayah: 19, Ayah: 20, Ayah: 21, Ayah: 22 & Ayah: 23

أَوَلَمْ يَرَوْاْ كَيْفَ يُبْدِئُ ٱللَّهُ ٱلْخَلْقَ ثُمَّ يُعِيدُهُۥٓ إِنَّ ذَٰلِكَ عَلَى ٱللَّهِ يَسِيرٌ ۝

19. See they not how Allâh originates the creation, then repeats it. Verily, that is easy for Allâh.

قُلْ سِيرُواْ فِى ٱلْأَرْضِ فَٱنظُرُواْ كَيْفَ بَدَأَ ٱلْخَلْقَ ثُمَّ ٱللَّهُ يُنشِئُ ٱلنَّشْأَةَ ٱلْأَخِرَةَ إِنَّ ٱللَّهَ عَلَىٰ كُلِّ شَىْءٍ قَدِيرٌ ۝

20. Say: "Travel in the land and see how (Allâh) originated creation, and then Allâh will bring forth the creation of the Hereafter (i.e. resurrection after death). Verily, Allâh is Able to do all things."

يُعَذِّبُ مَن يَشَآءُ وَيَرْحَمُ مَن يَشَآءُ وَإِلَيْهِ تُقْلَبُونَ ۝

21. He punishes whom He will, and shows mercy to whom He wills; and to Him you will be returned.

وَمَآ أَنتُم بِمُعْجِزِينَ فِى ٱلْأَرْضِ وَلَا فِى ٱلسَّمَآءِ وَمَا لَكُم مِّن دُونِ ٱللَّهِ مِن وَلِىٍّ وَلَا نَصِيرٍ ۝

22. And you cannot escape in the earth or in the heaven (from Allah). And besides Allâh you have neither any Walî (Protector or Guardian) nor any Helper.

وَٱلَّذِينَ كَفَرُوا۟ بِـَٔايَـٰتِ ٱللَّهِ وَلِقَآئِهِۦٓ أُو۟لَـٰٓئِكَ يَئِسُوا۟ مِن رَّحْمَتِى وَأُو۟لَـٰٓئِكَ لَهُمْ عَذَابٌ أَلِيمٌ ﴿٢٣﴾

23. And those who disbelieve in the Ayât (proofs, evidences, verses, lessons, signs, revelations, etc.) of Allâh and the Meeting with Him, it is they who have no hope of My Mercy: and it is they who will (have) a painful torment.

Transliteration

19. Awa lam yaraw kayfa yubdi-o Allahu alkhalqa thumma yuAAeeduhu inna thalika AAala Allahi yaseerun 20. Qul seeroo fee al-ardi faonthuroo kayfa badaa alkhalqa thumma Allahu yunshi-o alnnash-ata al-akhirata inna Allaha AAala kulli shay-in qadeerun 21. YuAAaththibu man yashao wayarhamu man yashao wa-ilayhi tuqlaboona 22. Wama antum bimuAAjizeena fee al-ardi wala fee alssama-i wama lakum min dooni Allahi min waliyyin wala naseerin 23. Waallatheena kafaroo bi-ayati Allahi waliqa-ihi ola-ika ya-isoo min rahmatee waolaika lahum AAathabun aleemun

Tafsir Ibn Kathir

The Evidence for Life after Death

Allah tells us that Ibrahim, peace be upon him, showed them the proof of life after death, which they denied, in their souls. For Allah created them after they had been nothing at all, then they came into existence and became people who could hear and see. The One Who originated this is able to repeat it, it is very easy for Him. Then he taught them to contemplate the visible signs on the horizons and the things that Allah has created: the heavens with their stars and planets, moving and stationary, the earth with its plains and mountains, its valleys, deserts and wildernesses, trees and rivers, fruits and oceans. All of that indicates that these are themselves created things, and that there must be a Creator Who does as He chooses, Who merely says to a thing "Be!" and it is. Allah says:

(See they not how Allah originates the creation, then repeats it. Verily, that is easy for Allah.) This is like the Ayah:

(And He it is Who originates the creation, then He will repeat it; and this is easier for Him) (30:27). Then Allah says:

(Say: "Travel in the land and see how He originated the creation, and then Allah will bring forth the creation of the Hereafter.") meaning, the Day of Resurrection.

(Verily, Allah is able to do all things.)

(He punishes whom He wills, and shows mercy to whom He wills;) He is the Ruler Who is in control, Who does as He wishes and judges as He wants, and there is none who can put back His judgement. None can question Him about what He does; rather it is they who will be questioned, for His is the power to create and to command, and whatever He decides is fair and just, for He is the sovereign who cannot be unjust in the slightest. According to a Hadith recorded by the Sunan compilers:

«إِنَّ اللهَ لَوْ عَذَّبَ أَهْلَ سَمَاوَاتِهِ وَأَهْلَ أَرْضِهِ لَعَذَّبَهُمْ وَهُوَ غَيْرُ ظَالِمٍ لَهُمْ»

(If Allah willed to punish the dwellers of His heavens and His earth, He would do so, while He would not be unjust to them.) Allah says:

(He punishes whom He wills, and shows mercy to whom He wills; and to Him you will be returned.) You will return to Him on the Day of Resurrection.

(And you cannot escape on the earth or in the heaven.) No one in heaven or on earth can flee from Him, for He is the Subduer Who is above His servants, and everything fears Him and is in need of Him, while He is the One Who is Independent of all else.

(And besides Allah you have neither any protector nor any helper. And those who disbelieve in the Ayat of Allah and the meeting with Him,) Those who disbelieved in the signs of Allah and denied the Resurrection,

(such have no hope of My mercy) they will have no share in it,

(and for such there is a painful torment.) meaning, extremely painful, in this world and the next.

Surah: 29 Ayah: 24 & Ayah: 25

فَمَا كَانَ جَوَابَ قَوْمِهِ إِلَّا أَن قَالُوا اقْتُلُوهُ أَوْ حَرِّقُوهُ فَأَنجَىٰهُ ٱللَّهُ مِنَ ٱلنَّارِ ۚ إِنَّ فِى ذَٰلِكَ لَءَايَٰتٍ لِّقَوْمٍ يُؤْمِنُونَ ﴿٢٤﴾

24. So nothing was the answer of (Ibrâhîm's (Abraham)) people except that they said: "Kill him or burn him." Then Allâh saved him from the fire. Verily, in this are indeed signs for a people who believe.

وَقَالَ إِنَّمَا ٱتَّخَذْتُم مِّن دُونِ ٱللَّهِ أَوْثَٰنًا مَّوَدَّةَ بَيْنِكُمْ فِى ٱلْحَيَوٰةِ ٱلدُّنْيَا ۖ ثُمَّ يَوْمَ ٱلْقِيَٰمَةِ يَكْفُرُ بَعْضُكُم بِبَعْضٍ وَيَلْعَنُ بَعْضُكُم بَعْضًا وَمَأْوَىٰكُمُ ٱلنَّارُ وَمَا لَكُم مِّن نَّٰصِرِينَ ﴿٢٥﴾

25. And (Ibrâhîm (Abraham)) said: "You have taken (for worship) idols instead of Allâh. The love between you is only in the life of this world, but on the Day of Resurrection, you shall disown each other, and curse each other, and your abode will be the Fire, and you shall have no helper."

Transliteration

24. Fama kana jawaba qawmihi illa an qaloo oqtuloohu aw harriqoohu faanjahu Allahu mina alnnari inna fee thalika laayatin liqawmin yu/minoona 25. Waqala innama ittakhathtum min dooni Allahi awthanan mawaddata baynikum fee alhayati alddunya thumma yawma alqiyamati yakfuru baAAdukum bibaAAdin wayalAAanu baAAdukum baAAdan wama-wakumu alnnaru wama lakum min nasireena

Tafsir Ibn Kathir

The Response of Ibrahim's People -- and how Allah controlled the Fire

Allah tells us how Ibrahim's people stubbornly and arrogantly disbelieved, and how they resisted the truth with falsehood. After Ibrahim addressed them with his words of clear guidance,

(except that they said: "Kill him or burn him.") This was because proof had clearly been established against them, so they resorted to using their power and strength.

(They said: "Build for him a building and throw him into the blazing fire!" So they plotted a plot against him, but We made them the lowest.) (37:97-98). They spent a long time gathering a huge amount of firewood, they built a fence around it, then they set it ablaze until its flames reached up to the sky. No greater fire had ever been lit. Then they went to Ibrahim, seized him and put him into a catapult, then they threw him into the fire. But Allah made it cool and safe for him, and after spending several days in it, he emerged unscathed. For this reason and others, Allah made him an Imam for mankind, for he offered himself to the Most Merciful, he offered his body to the flames, he offered his son as a sacrifice, and he gave his wealth to care for his guests. For all of these reasons he is beloved by the followers of all religions.

(Then Allah saved him from the fire.) means, He rescued him from it by making it cool and safe for him.

(Verily, in this are indeed signs for a people who believe.) Ibrahim, peace be upon him, explains to his people that idols are incapable of doing anything,

(And (Ibrahim) said: "You have taken idols instead of Allah. The love between you is only in the life of this world,) Here Ibrahim was rebuking his people for their evil deed of worshipping idols, and telling them: `You have taken these as gods and you come together to worship them so that there is friendship and love among you in this world,'

(but on the Day of Resurrection,) the situation will be the opposite, and this love and friendship will turn into hatred and enmity. Then

(you shall deny each other,) meaning, `you will denounce one another and deny whatever was between you,'

(and curse each other,) means, the followers will curse their leaders and the leaders will curse their followers.

a(Every time a new nation enters (the Fire), it curses its sister nation (that went before)) (7:37).

(Friends on that Day will be foes one to another except those who have Taqwa.) (43:67) And Allah says here:

(but on the Day of Resurrection, you shall deny each other, and curse each other, and your abode will be the Fire,) meaning, `your ultimate destiny after all accounts have been settled, will be the fire of Hell, and you will have no one to help you or save you from the punishment of Allah.' This will be the state of the disbelievers. As for the believers, it will be an entirely different matter.

Surah: 29 Ayah: 26 & Ayah: 27

﴿ فَآمَنَ لَهُۥ لُوطٌۘ وَقَالَ إِنِّى مُهَاجِرٌ إِلَىٰ رَبِّىٓ إِنَّهُۥ هُوَ ٱلۡعَزِيزُ ٱلۡحَكِيمُ ۝ ﴾

26. So Lût (Lot) believed in him (Ibrâhîm's (Abraham) Message of Islâmic Monotheism). He (Ibrâhîm (Abraham)) said: "I will emigrate for the sake of my Lord. Verily, He is the All-Mighty, the All-Wise."

﴿ وَوَهَبۡنَا لَهُۥٓ إِسۡحَٰقَ وَيَعۡقُوبَ وَجَعَلۡنَا فِى ذُرِّيَّتِهِ ٱلنُّبُوَّةَ وَٱلۡكِتَٰبَ وَءَاتَيۡنَٰهُ أَجۡرَهُۥ فِى ٱلدُّنۡيَاۖ وَإِنَّهُۥ فِى ٱلۡءَاخِرَةِ لَمِنَ ٱلصَّٰلِحِينَ ۝ ﴾

27. And We bestowed on him (Ibrâhîm (Abraham)) Ishâq (Isaac) and Ya'qûb (Jacob), and We ordained among his offspring Prophethood and the Book (i.e. the Taurât (Torah) (to Mûsâ - Moses), the Injeel (Gospel) (to 'Iesâ - Jesus), and the Qur'ân (to Muhammad (peace be upon him)) all from the offspring of Ibrâhîm (Abraham)) and We granted him his reward in this world; and verily, in the Hereafter he is indeed among the righteous.

Transliteration

26. Faamana lahu lootun waqala innee muhajirun ila rabbee innahu huwa alAAazeezu alhakeemu 27. Wawahabna lahu ishaqa wayaAAqooba wajaAAalna fee thurriyyatihi alnnubuwwata waalkitaba waataynahu ajrahu fee alddunya wa-innahu fee al-akhirati lamina alssaliheena

Tafsir Ibn Kathir

The Faith of Lut and His Emigration with Ibrahim

Allah tells us that Lut believed in Ibrahim. It was said that he was the son of Ibrahim's brother, and that his name was Lut bin Haran bin Azar. None of Ibrahim's people believed in Ibrahim besides Lut and Sarah the wife of Ibrahim. But if it is asked how we may reconcile this Ayah with the Hadith narrated in the Sahih which says that when Ibrahim passed by that tyrant and he asked about Sarah and what her relationship was to him, Ibrahim said, "My sister." Then he went to her and said, "I told him that you are my sister, so do not let him think I am lying, for there are no believers on earth except for you and I, and you are my sister in faith." It seems --

and Allah knows best -- that the meaning here is, there is no other Muslim couple on earth apart from you and I. Among his people, only Lut believed in him and migrated with him to Syria, then during Ibrahim's lifetime he was sent as a Messenger to the people of Sadum (Sodom) where he settled. We have already discussed their story and more is to come.

(He (Ibrahim) said: "I will emigrate for the sake of my Lord.") It may be that the pronoun in the verb "he said" refers to Lut, because he was the last person mentioned before this phrase; or it may refer to Ibrahim. Ibn `Abbas and Ad-Dahhak said that Ibrahim is the one who is referred in the phrase.

(So, Lut believed in him.) i.e., out of all his people. Then Allah tells us that he chose to leave them so that he might be able to follow his religion openly. So he said:

(Verily, He is the All-Mighty, the All-Wise.) Power belongs to Him and to His Messenger and to those who believe in him, and He is Wise in all that He says and does, and in all His rulings and decrees, both universal and legislative. Qatadah said, "They migrated together from Kutha, which is on the outskirts of Kufa, and went to Syria." Allah gave Ibrahim, Ishaq and Ya`qub, and ordained Prophethood in His Offspring

(And We bestowed on him, Ishaq and Ya`qub,) This is like the Ayah,

(So, when he had turned away from them and from those whom they worshipped besides Allah, We gave him Ishaq and Ya`qub, and each one of them We made a Prophet.) (19:49) That is, when he left his people, Allah gave him joy in a righteous son who was also a Prophet, to whom in turn was born, in his grandfather's lifetime, a righteous son who was also a Prophet. Allah also says:

(And We bestowed upon him Ishaq, and Ya`qub in addition) (21:72) meaning, as an additional gift. This is like the Ayah,

(But We gave her glad tidings of Ishaq, and after Ishaq, of Ya`qub.) (11:71) meaning, to this son would be born a son during their lives, who would be a delight to them.

(and We ordained among his offspring prophethood and the Book,) This is a tremendous blessing. Not only did Allah take him as a close friend and make him an Imam for mankind, but He also ordained prophethood and the Book among his offspring. After the time of Ibrahim there was no Prophet who was not from among his descendants. All of the Prophets of the Children of Israel were from among his descendants, from Ya`qub bin Ishaq bin Ibrahim to the last of them, `Isa bin Maryam, who stood in the midst of his people and announced the good news of the Hashimi Qurashi Arab Prophet, the last of all the Messengers, the leader of the sons of Adam in this world and the next, whom Allah chose from the heart of the Arab nation, from the descendants of Isma`il bin Ibrahim, may peace be upon them. There is no Prophet from the line of Isma`il besides him, may the best of blessings and peace be upon him.

Chapter 29: Al-Ankaboot (The Spider), Verses 001-045

(and We granted him his reward in this world; and verily, in the Hereafter he is indeed among the righteous.) Allah granted him happiness in this world that was connected to happiness in the Hereafter, for in this world he had plentiful provision, a splendid home, a beautiful and righteous wife, and he was and still is spoken of highly, for everyone loves him and regards him as a friend. Ibn `Abbas, Mujahid, Qatadah and others said: "He obeyed Allah in all ways." This is like the Ayah,

(And of Ibrahim who fulfilled all.) (53:37) He did all that he was commanded to do and obeyed his Lord to the utmost. Allah says:

(and We granted him his reward in this world; and verily, in the Hereafter he is indeed among the righteous.) And He says:

(Verily, Ibrahim was an Ummah, Qanit to Allah, a Hanif, and he was not one of the idolators) until:

(and in the Hereafter he shall be of the righteous) (16:120-122).

Surah: 29 Ayah: 28, Ayah: 29 & Ayah: 30

وَلُوطًا إِذْ قَالَ لِقَوْمِهِ إِنَّكُمْ لَتَأْتُونَ ٱلْفَٰحِشَةَ مَا سَبَقَكُم بِهَا مِنْ أَحَدٍ مِّنَ ٱلْعَٰلَمِينَ ۝

28. And (remember) Lût (Lot), when he said to his people: "You commit Al-Fâhishah (sodomy - the worst sin) which none has preceded you in (committing) it in the 'Alamîn (mankind and jinn)."

أَئِنَّكُمْ لَتَأْتُونَ ٱلرِّجَالَ وَتَقْطَعُونَ ٱلسَّبِيلَ وَتَأْتُونَ فِى نَادِيكُمُ ٱلْمُنكَرَ ۖ فَمَا كَانَ جَوَابَ قَوْمِهِ إِلَّآ أَن قَالُوا۟ ٱئْتِنَا بِعَذَابِ ٱللَّهِ إِن كُنتَ مِنَ ٱلصَّٰدِقِينَ ۝

29. "Verily, you practice sodomy with men, and rob the wayfarer (travelers)! And practice Al-Munkar (disbelief and polytheism and every kind of evil wicked deed) in your meetings." But his people gave no answer except that they said: "Bring Allâh's Torment upon us if you are one of the truthful."

قَالَ رَبِّ ٱنصُرْنِى عَلَى ٱلْقَوْمِ ٱلْمُفْسِدِينَ ۝

30. He said: "My Lord! Give me victory over the people who are Mufsidûn (those who commit great crimes and sins, oppressors, tyrants, mischief-makers, corrupts).

Transliteration

28. Walootan ith qala liqawmihi innakum lata/toona alfahishata ma sabaqakum biha min ahadin mina alAAalameena 29. A-innakum lata/toona alrrijala wataqtaAAoona alssabeela wata/toona fee nadeekumu almunkara fama kana jawaba qawmihi illa an

qaloo i/tina biAAathabi Allahi in kunta mina alssadiqeena 30. Qala rabbi onsurnee AAala alqawmi almufsideena

Tafsir Ibn Kathir

The preaching of Lut and what happened between Him and His People

Allah tells us that His Prophet Lut, peace be upon him, denounced his people for their evil deed and their immoral actions in having intercourse with males, a deed which none of the sons of Adam had ever committed before them. As well as doing this, they also disbelieved in Allah and rejected and opposed His Messenger, they robbed wayfarers, they would lie in wait on the road, kill people and loot their possessions.

(And practice Al-Munkar in your meetings.) This means, `in your gatherings you do and say things that are not befitting, and you do not denounce one another for doing such things.' Some said that they used to have intercourse with one another in public; this was the view of Mujahid. Some said that they used to compete in passing gas and laughing. This was the view of `A'ishah, may Allah be pleased with her, and Al-Qasim. Some of them said that they used to make rams fight one another, or organize cockfights. They used to do all of these things, and they were even eviler than that.

(But his people gave no answer except that they said: "Bring Allah's torment upon us if you are one of the truthful.") This is indicative of their disbelief, scornful attitude and stubbornness. So Allah's Prophet asked for help against them, and said:

(My Lord! Give me victory over the people who are corrupt.)

Surah: 29 Ayah: 31, Ayah: 32, Ayah: 33, Ayah: 34 & Ayah: 35

وَلَمَّا جَاءَتْ رُسُلُنَا إِبْرَاهِيمَ بِالْبُشْرَىٰ قَالُوا إِنَّا مُهْلِكُوا أَهْلِ هَـٰذِهِ ٱلْقَرْيَةِ إِنَّ أَهْلَهَا كَانُوا ظَـٰلِمِينَ ۝

31. And when Our Messengers came to Ibrâhîm (Abraham) with the glad tidings they said: "Verily, we are going to destroy the people of this (Lût's (Lot's)) town (i.e. the town of Sodom in Palestine) truly, its people have been Zâlimûn (wrong-doers, polytheists and disobedient to Allâh, and have also belied their Messenger Lût (Lot))"

قَالَ إِنَّ فِيهَا لُوطًا ۚ قَالُوا نَحْنُ أَعْلَمُ بِمَن فِيهَا ۖ لَنُنَجِّيَنَّهُ وَأَهْلَهُ إِلَّا ٱمْرَأَتَهُ كَانَتْ مِنَ ٱلْغَـٰبِرِينَ ۝

32. Ibrâhîm (Abraham) said: "But there is Lût (Lot) in it." They said: "We know better who is there. We will verily save him (Lût (Lot)) and his family except his wife: she will be of those who remain behind (i.e. she will be destroyed along with those who will be destroyed from her folk)."

Chapter 29: Al-Ankaboot (The Spider), Verses 001-045

وَلَمَّا أَن جَاءَتْ رُسُلُنَا لُوطًا سِيءَ بِهِمْ وَضَاقَ بِهِمْ ذَرْعًا وَقَالُوا لَا تَخَفْ وَلَا تَحْزَنْ إِنَّا مُنَجُّوكَ وَأَهْلَكَ إِلَّا امْرَأَتَكَ كَانَتْ مِنَ الْغَابِرِينَ ۝

33. And when Our Messengers came to Lût (Lot), he was grieved because of them, and felt straitened on their account. They said: "Have no fear, and do not grieve! Truly, we shall save you and your family, except your wife: she will be of those who remain behind (i.e. she will be destroyed along with those who will be destroyed from her folk).

إِنَّا مُنزِلُونَ عَلَىٰ أَهْلِ هَٰذِهِ الْقَرْيَةِ رِجْزًا مِّنَ السَّمَاءِ بِمَا كَانُوا يَفْسُقُونَ ۝

34. Verily, we are about to bring down on the people of this town a great torment from the sky, because they have been rebellious (against Allâh's Command)."

وَلَقَد تَّرَكْنَا مِنْهَا آيَةً بَيِّنَةً لِّقَوْمٍ يَعْقِلُونَ ۝

35. And indeed We have left thereof an evident Ayâh (a lesson and a warning and a sign - the place where the Dead Sea is now in Palestine) for a folk who understand.

Transliteration

31. Walamma jaat rusuluna ibraheema bialbushra qaloo inna muhlikoo ahli hathihi alqaryati inna ahlaha kanoo thalimeena 32. Qala inna feeha lootan qaloo nahnu aAAlamu biman feeha lanunajjiyannahu waahlahu illa imraatahu kanat mina alghabireena 33. Walamma an jaat rusuluna lootan see-a bihim wadaqa bihim tharAAan waqaloo la takhaf wala tahzan inna munajjooka waahlaka illa imraataka kanat mina alghabireena 34. Inna munziloona AAala ahli hathihi alqaryati rijzan mina alssama-i bima kanoo yafsuqoona 35. Walaqad tarakna minha ayatan bayyinatan liqawmin yaAAqiloona

Tafsir Ibn Kathir

The Angels went to Ibrahim and then to Lut, may peace be upon them both

When Lut, peace be upon him, asked Allah to help him against them, Allah sent angels to help him. They first came to Ibrahim in the form of guests, so he offered them hospitality in the appropriate manner. When he saw that they had no interest in the food, he felt some mistrust of them and was fearful of them. They started to calm him down and gave him the news of a righteous son born by his wife Sarah, who was present, and she was astonished by this, as we have already explained in our Tafsir of Surat Hud and Surat Al-Hijr. When they brought this news to Ibrahim and told him that they were sent to destroy the people of Lut, he began to speak up for them, hoping to win more time for them so that they might be guided by Allah. When they said, "We have come to destroy the people of this township,"

((Ibrahim) said: "But there is Lut in it." They said: "We know better who is there. We will verily, save him and his family except his wife, she will be of those who remain behind.") meaning, one of those who will be destroyed, because she used to support them in their disbelief and wrongdoing. Then the angels left him and visited Lut in the form of handsome young men. When he saw them like that,

(he was grieved because of them, and felt straitened on their account.) means, he was worried since if he had them as guests then he was afraid for them and what his people might do to them, but if he did not host them, he was still afraid of what might happen to them. At that point he did not know who they were.

(They said: "Have no fear, and do not grieve! Truly, we shall save you and your family except your wife: she will be of those who remain behind. Verily, we are about to bring down on the people of this town a great torment from the sky, because they have been rebellious.") Jibril, peace be upon him, uprooted their town from the depths of the earth, lifted it up to the sky, then threw it upside down upon them. Allah rained upon them:

(stones of Sijjil, in a well-arranged manner one after another. Marked from your Lord; and they are not ever far from the evil doers.) (11:82-83) Allah turned the place where they had lived into a putrid, stinking lake, which will remain as a lesson to mankind until the Day of Resurrection, and they will be among those who are most severely punished on the Day of Resurrection. Allah says:

(And indeed We have left thereof an evident Ayah) i. e., a clear sign, n

(for a folk who understand.) This is like the Ayah,

(Verily, you pass by them in the morning And at night; will you not then reflect) (37:137-138)

Surah: 29 Ayah: 36 & Ayah: 37

وَإِلَىٰ مَدْيَنَ أَخَاهُمْ شُعَيْبًا فَقَالَ يَـٰقَوْمِ ٱعْبُدُواْ ٱللَّهَ وَٱرْجُواْ ٱلْيَوْمَ ٱلْأَخِرَ وَلَا تَعْثَوْاْ فِى ٱلْأَرْضِ مُفْسِدِينَ ۝

36. And to (the people of) Madyan (Midian), We sent their brother Shu'aib (Shuaib). He said: "O my people! Worship Allâh, and hope for (the reward of good deeds by worshipping Allâh Alone, on) the last Day, and commit no mischief on the earth as Mufsidûn (those who commit great crimes, oppressors, tyrants, mischief-makers, corrupts).

فَكَذَّبُوهُ فَأَخَذَتْهُمُ ٱلرَّجْفَةُ فَأَصْبَحُواْ فِى دَارِهِمْ جَـٰثِمِينَ ۝

37. And they belied him (Shu'aib): so the earthquake seized them, and they lay (dead), prostrate in their dwellings.

Transliteration

36. Wa-ila madyana akhahum shuAAayban faqala ya qawmi oAAbudoo Allaha waorjoo alyawma al-akhira wala taAAthaw fee al-ardi mufsideena 37. Fakaththaboohu faakhathat-humu alrrajfatu faasbahoo fee darihim jathimeena

Tafsir Ibn Kathir

Shu`ayb and His People

Allah tells us that His servant and Messenger Shu`ayb, peace be upon him, warned his people, the people of Madyan, and commanded them to worship Allah Alone with no partner or associate, and to fear the wrath and punishment of Allah on the Day of Resurrection. He said:

(O my people! Worship Allah and hope for the last Day,) Ibn Jarir said: "Some of them said that this meant: Fear the Last Day." This is like the Ayah,

(for those who look forward to (meeting with) Allah and the Last Day) (60:6).

(and commit no mischief on the earth as mischief-makers.) This is forbidding them to make mischief on earth by spreading corruption, which means going around doing evil to people. They used to cheat in weights and measures, and ambush people on the road; this is in addition to their disbelief in Allah and His Messenger. So Allah destroyed them with a mighty earthquake that convulsed their land, and the Sayhah (shout) which tore their hearts from their bodies, and the torment of the Day of Shade, when their souls were taken. This was the torment of a great day. We have already examined their story in detail in Surat Al-A`raf, Surat Hud and Surat Ash-Shu`ara'.

(and they lay, prostrate in their dwellings.) Qatadah said, "They were dead." Others said that they were thrown on top of one another.

Surah: 29 Ayah: 38, Ayah: 39 & Ayah: 40

وَعَادًا وَثَمُودَا۟ وَقَد تَّبَيَّنَ لَكُم مِّن مَّسَـٰكِنِهِمْ ۖ وَزَيَّنَ لَهُمُ ٱلشَّيْطَـٰنُ أَعْمَـٰلَهُمْ فَصَدَّهُمْ عَنِ ٱلسَّبِيلِ وَكَانُوا۟ مُسْتَبْصِرِينَ ۝

38. And 'Ad and Thamûd (people)! And indeed (their destruction) is clearly apparent to you from their (ruined) dwellings. Shaitân (Satan) made their deeds fair-seeming to them, and turned them away from the (Right) Path, though they were intelligent.

وَقَـٰرُونَ وَفِرْعَوْنَ وَهَـٰمَـٰنَ ۖ وَلَقَدْ جَآءَهُم مُّوسَىٰ بِٱلْبَيِّنَـٰتِ فَٱسْتَكْبَرُوا۟ فِى ٱلْأَرْضِ وَمَا كَانُوا۟ سَـٰبِقِينَ ۝

39. And (We destroyed also) Qârûn (Korah), Fir'aun (Pharaoh), and Hâmân. And indeed Mûsâ (Moses) came to them with clear Ayât (proofs, evidences, verses,

lessons, signs, revelations, etc.), but they were arrogant in the land, yet they could not outstrip Us (escape Our punishment).

فَكُلاًّ أَخَذْنَا بِذَنبِهِ ۖ فَمِنْهُم مَّنْ أَرْسَلْنَا عَلَيْهِ حَاصِبًا وَمِنْهُم مَّنْ أَخَذَتْهُ ٱلصَّيْحَةُ وَمِنْهُم مَّنْ خَسَفْنَا بِهِ ٱلْأَرْضَ وَمِنْهُم مَّنْ أَغْرَقْنَا وَمَا كَانَ ٱللَّهُ لِيَظْلِمَهُمْ وَلَٰكِن كَانُوٓا۟ أَنفُسَهُمْ يَظْلِمُونَ ۝

40. So We punished each (of them) for his sins; of them were some on whom We sent Hâsib (a violent wind with shower of stones) (as the people of Lût (Lot)) and of them were some who were overtaken by As-Saihah (torment - awful cry. (as Thamûd or Shu'aib's people)) and of them were some whom We caused the earth to swallow (as Qârûn (Korah)) and of them were some whom We drowned (as the people of Nûh (Noah), or Fir'aun (Pharaoh) and his people). It was not Allâh Who wronged them, but they wronged themselves.

Transliteration

38. WaAAadan wathamooda waqad tabayyana lakum min masakinihim wazayyana lahumu alshshaytanu aAAmalahum fasaddahum AAani alssabeeli wakanoo mustabsireena 39. Waqaroona wafirAAawna wahamana walaqad jaahum moosa bialbayyinati faistakbaroo fee al-ardi wama kanoo sabiqeena 40. Fakullan akhathna bithanbihi faminhum man arsalna AAalayhi hasiban waminhum man akhathat-hu alssayhatu waminhum man khasafna bihi al-arda waminhum man aghraqna wama kana Allahu liyathlimahum walakin kanoo anfusahum yathlimoona

Tafsir Ibn Kathir

The Destruction of Nations Who rejected Their Messengers

Allah tells us about these nations who disbelieved in their Messengers, and how He destroyed them and sent various kinds of punishments and vengeance upon them. `Ad, the people of Hud, peace be upon him, used to live in the Ahqaf (curved sand-hills), near Hadramawt, in the Yemen. Thamud, the people of Salih, lived in Al-Hijr, near Wadi Al-Qura. The Arabs used to know their dwelling place very well, and they often used to pass by it. Qarun was the owner of great wealth and had the keys to immense treasures. Fir`awn, the king of Egypt at the time of Musa, and his minister Haman were two Coptics who disbelieved in Allah and His Messenger, peace be upon him.

(So, We punished each for his sins,) their punishments fit their crimes. (of them were some on whom We sent a Hasib,) This was the case with `Ad, and this happened because they said: "Who is stronger than us" So, there came upon them a violent, intensely cold wind, which was very strong and carried pebbles which it threw upon them. It carried them through the air, lifting a man up to the sky and then hurling him headlong to the ground, so that his head split and he was left as a body without a head, like uprooted stems of date palms.

(and of them were some who were overtaken by As-Sayhah,) This is what happened to Thamud, against whom evidence was established because of the she-camel who came forth when the rock was split, exactly as they had asked for. Yet despite that they did not believe, rather they persisted in their evil behavior and disbelief, and threatening to expel Allah's Prophet Salih and the believers with him, or to stone them. So the Sayhah struck them, taking away their powers of speech and movement.

(and of them were some whom We caused the earth to swallow,) This refers to Qarun who transgressed, he was evil and arrogant. He disobeyed his Lord, the Most High, and paraded through the land in a boastful manner, filled with self-admiration, thinking that he was better than others. He showed off as he walked, so Allah caused the earth to swallow him and his house, and he will continue sinking into it until the Day of Resurrection.

(and of them were some whom We drowned.) This refers to Fir`awn, his minister Haman and their troops, all of whom were drowned in a single morning, not one of them escaped.

(It was not Allah Who wronged them,) in what He did to them,

(but they wronged themselves.) that happened to them as a punishment for what they did with their own hands.

Surah: 29 Ayah: 41, Ayah: 42 & Ayah: 43

مَثَلُ ٱلَّذِينَ ٱتَّخَذُوا۟ مِن دُونِ ٱللَّهِ أَوْلِيَآءَ كَمَثَلِ ٱلْعَنكَبُوتِ ٱتَّخَذَتْ بَيْتًا ۖ وَإِنَّ أَوْهَنَ ٱلْبُيُوتِ لَبَيْتُ ٱلْعَنكَبُوتِ ۚ لَوْ كَانُوا۟ يَعْلَمُونَ ۝

41. The likeness of those who take (false deities as) Auliyâ' (protectors, helpers) other than Allâh is as the likeness of a spider who builds (for itself) a house; but verily, the frailest (weakest) of houses is the spider's house - if they but knew.

إِنَّ ٱللَّهَ يَعْلَمُ مَا يَدْعُونَ مِن دُونِهِۦ مِن شَىْءٍ ۚ وَهُوَ ٱلْعَزِيزُ ٱلْحَكِيمُ ۝

42. Verily, Allâh knows what things they invoke instead of Him. He is the All-Mighty, the All-Wise.

وَتِلْكَ ٱلْأَمْثَٰلُ نَضْرِبُهَا لِلنَّاسِ ۖ وَمَا يَعْقِلُهَآ إِلَّا ٱلْعَٰلِمُونَ ۝

43. And these similitudes We put forward for mankind; but none will understand them except those who have knowledge (of Allâh and His Signs).

Transliteration

41. Mathalu allatheena ittakhathoo min dooni Allahi awliyaa kamathali alAAankabooti ittakhathat baytan wa-inna awhana albuyooti labaytu alAAankabooti law kanoo yaAAlamoona   42. Inna Allaha yaAAlamu ma yadAAoona min doonihi min shay-in

wahuwa alAAazeezu alhakeemu 43. Watilka al-amthalu nadribuha lilnnasi wama yaAAqiluha illa alAAalimoona

Tafsir Ibn Kathir

Likening the gods of the Idolators to the House of a Spider

This is how Allah described the idolators in their reverence of gods besides Him, hoping that they would help them and provide for them, and turning to them in times of difficulties. In this regard, they were like the house of a spider, which is so weak and frail, because by clinging to these gods they were like a person who holds on to a spider's web, who does not gain any benefit from that. If they knew this, they would not take any protectors besides Allah. This is unlike the Muslim believer, whose heart is devoted to Allah, yet he still does righteous deeds and follows the Laws of Allah, for he has grasped the most trustworthy handle that will never break because it is so strong and firm. Then Allah warns those who worship others besides Him and associate others with Him that He knows what they do and the rivals they associate with Him. He will punish them for their attribution, for He is All-Wise and All-Knowing. Then He says: (And these are the examples We give for mankind; but none will understand them except those who have knowledge.) meaning, no one understands them or ponders them except those who are possessed of deep knowledge. Ibn Abi Hatim recorded that `Amr bin Murrah said, "I never came across an Ayah of the Book of Allah that I did not know, but it grieved me, because I heard that Allah says: (And these are the examples We give for mankind; but none will understand them except those who have knowledge.)"

Surah: 29 Ayah: 44 & Ayah: 45

خَلَقَ ٱللَّهُ ٱلسَّمَٰوَٰتِ وَٱلْأَرْضَ بِٱلْحَقِّ إِنَّ فِى ذَٰلِكَ لَءَايَةً لِّلْمُؤْمِنِينَ ۝

44. (Allâh says to His Prophet Muhammad (peace be upon him)) "Allâh (Alone) created the heavens and the earth with truth (and none shared Him in their creation)." Verily! Therein is surely a sign for those who believe.

ٱتْلُ مَآ أُوحِىَ إِلَيْكَ مِنَ ٱلْكِتَٰبِ وَأَقِمِ ٱلصَّلَوٰةَ إِنَّ ٱلصَّلَوٰةَ تَنْهَىٰ عَنِ ٱلْفَحْشَآءِ وَٱلْمُنكَرِ وَلَذِكْرُ ٱللَّهِ أَكْبَرُ وَٱللَّهُ يَعْلَمُ مَا تَصْنَعُونَ ۝

45. Recite (O Muhammad (peace be upon him)) what has been revealed to you of the Book (the Qur'ân), and perform As-Salât (Iqamât-as-Salât). Verily, As-Salât (the prayer) prevents from Al-Fahshâ' (i.e. great sins of every kind, unlawful sexual intercourse) and Al-Munkar (i.e. disbelief, polytheism, and every kind of evil wicked deed) and the remembering (praising) of (you by) Allâh (in front of the angels) is greater indeed (than your remembering (praising) of Allâh in prayers. And Allâh knows what you do.

Transliteration

44. Khalaqa Allahu alssamawati waal-arda bialhaqqi inna fee thalika laayatan lilmumineena 45. Otlu ma oohiya ilayka mina alkitabi waaqimi alssalata inna alssalata

tanha AAani alfahsha-i waalmunkari walathikru Allahi akbaru waAllahu yaAAlamu ma tasnaAAoona

Tafsir Ibn Kathir

Allah tells us of His immense power, that He created the heavens and the earth with truth, meaning for a higher purpose than mere play, (that every person may be rewarded for that which he strives) (20:15). (that He may requite those who do evil with that which they have done, and reward those who do good, with what is best) (53:31). (Verily, therein is surely a sign for those who believe.) meaning, there is clear evidence that Allah is alone in creating, controlling, and in His divinity

The Command to convey the Message, to recite the Qur'an and to pray

Then Allah commands His Messenger and the believers to recite the Qur'an, which means both reciting it and conveying it to people. (and perform the Salah. Verily, the Salah prevents from Al-Fahsha' and Al-Munkar and the remembrance of Allah is greater indeed.) Prayer includes two things: the first of which is giving up immoral behavior and evil deeds, i.e., praying regularly enables a person to give up these things. Imam Ahmad recorded that Abu Hurayrah said: "A man came to the Prophet and said, `So-and-so prays at night, but when morning comes, he steals.' The Prophet said:

«إِنَّهُ سَيَنْهَاهُ مَا تَقُول»

(What you are saying (i.e., the Salah) will stop him from doing that.)" Prayer also includes the remembering of Allah, which is the higher objective, Allah says: (and the remembrance of Allah is greater indeed.) more important than the former. (And Allah knows what you do.) means, He knows all that you do and say. Abu Al-`Aliyah commented on the Ayah: (Verily, the Salah prevents from immoral sins and evil wicked deeds) "Prayer has three attributes, and any prayer that contains none of these attributes is not truly prayer: Being done purely and sincerely for Allah alone (Ikhlas), fear of Allah, and remembrance of Allah. Ikhlas makes a person do good deeds, fear prevents him from doing evil deeds, and the remembrance of Allah is the Qur'an which contains commands and prohibitions." Ibn `Awn Al-Ansari said: "When you are praying, you are doing good, it is keeping you away from immoral sins and evil wicked deeds and what you are doing is part of the remembrance of Allah which is greater."

www.ingramcontent.com/pod-product-compliance
Lightning Source LLC
Chambersburg PA
CBHW081114080526
44587CB00021B/3589